SUCCESSFUL GARDENING
A-Z of DECIDUOUS TREES & SHRUBS

Published by The Reader's Digest Association Limited.

First Edition Copyright © 1994
The Reader's Digest Association Limited,
Berkeley Square House, Berkeley Square, London W1X 6AB

Copyright © 1994
The Reader's Digest Association Far East Limited
Philippines Copyright 1994
The Reader's Digest Association Far East Limited

Originally published as a partwork.
Successful Gardening
Copyright © 1990
Eaglemoss Publications Ltd.

Consultant editor: Lizzie Boyd

Typeset in Century Schoolbook

PRINTED IN SPAIN

ISBN 0 276 42094 2

Opposite: A paperbark maple (*Acer griseum*) is the stunning
focal point in a mixed border of shrubs and perennials.

Overleaf: The hybrid tea rose 'Fragrant Dream' bears elegant
well-shaped, golden-apricot blooms throughout summer.

Pages 6-7: The bare branches of dormant trees and shrubs
are etched with frost in this attractive winter scene.

Reader's
Digest

PUBLISHED BY THE READER'S DIGEST ASSOCIATION LIMITED
LONDON NEW YORK MONTREAL SYDNEY CAPE TOWN

Originally published in partwork form
by Eaglemoss Publications Limited

SUCCESSFUL GARDENING

A-Z of DECIDUOUS
TREES & SHRUBS

CONTENTS

SPECIAL FEATURES

Garden trees	10-13
Versatile shrubs	66-69

A-Z OF DECIDUOUS TREES

Acer – Alnus	14-17
Betula – Crataegus	18-25
Davidia – Gleditsia	26-30
Halesia – Koelreuteria	30-32
Laburnum – Liriodendron	32-36
Magnolia – Morus	37-41
Nothofagus – Ostrya	42-44
Parrotia – Pyrus	45-50
Quercus – Robinia	51-54
Salix – Styrax	55-59
Taxodium – Ulmus	60-63

A-Z OF DECIDUOUS SHRUBS

Abelia – Buddleia	70-76
Callicarpa – Cytisus	77-92
Daphne – Exochorda	93-97
Forsythia – Genista	98-100
Hamamelis – Kolkwitzia	101-107
Lavatera – Menziesia	108-112
Paeonia – Punica	113-124
Rhamnus – Rubus	124-130
Salix – Tamarix	131-138
Vaccinium – Vitis	139-142
Weigela – Wisteria	142-144

A-Z of Roses

Climbing roses	148-152
Floribunda roses	153-155
Hybrid tea roses	156-159
Miniature and patio roses	160-161
Modern shrub roses	162-165
Old garden roses	166-170
Polyantha & ground cover roses	171
Rambler roses	172-173
Species roses	174-175

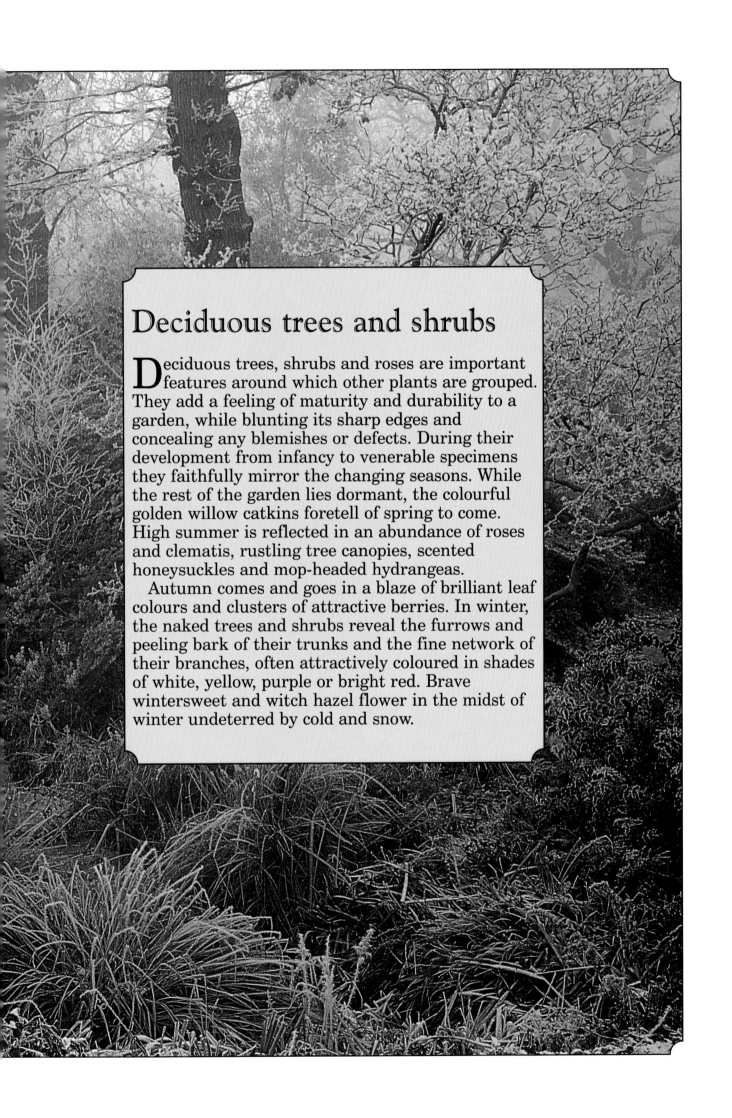

Deciduous trees and shrubs

Deciduous trees, shrubs and roses are important features around which other plants are grouped. They add a feeling of maturity and durability to a garden, while blunting its sharp edges and concealing any blemishes or defects. During their development from infancy to venerable specimens they faithfully mirror the changing seasons. While the rest of the garden lies dormant, the colourful golden willow catkins foretell of spring to come. High summer is reflected in an abundance of roses and clematis, rustling tree canopies, scented honeysuckles and mop-headed hydrangeas.

Autumn comes and goes in a blaze of brilliant leaf colours and clusters of attractive berries. In winter, the naked trees and shrubs reveal the furrows and peeling bark of their trunks and the fine network of their branches, often attractively coloured in shades of white, yellow, purple or bright red. Brave wintersweet and witch hazel flower in the midst of winter undeterred by cold and snow.

Scarlet oak True to its name, the scarlet oak (*Quercus coccinea*) is a dazzling sight in autumn.

A-Z of deciduous trees

Trees play an essential part in the earth's ecological balance as they transform carbon dioxide into vital oxygen, temper the effects of the sun and wind and prevent soil erosion. On a domestic scale, trees frame and define the style of a house and its garden, adding depth and scale, and colour and textural interest. Deciduous trees in particular mirror the annual growth cycle – swelling buds bursting into fresh, young leaves in spring, cool, dappling shade in summer, before dying off in rich autumn colours, leaving in their wake a tracery of bare branches against winter skies.

The great deciduous oaks, chestnuts and sycamores commonly found in forests and parklands are too large for the average garden, but there are plenty of dwarf varieties and other small, decorative deciduous trees to choose from. Popular choices include maples with their striking autumn colours, elegant birches, summer-flowering dogwoods, ornamental thorns and magnificent magnolias. Crab apples combine some of the best features of all ornamental trees – manageable size, spectacular blooms, striking autumn leaf colours and attractive fruits.

Before choosing a tree, take into account its height and spread when fully grown, its growth rate and the density of shade it casts. Consider how it will look with surrounding plants, and the type of soil and conditions it needs in order to thrive for decades to come. A site can radically affect a tree's eventual shape – in a windswept position a tree will seem to lean with the prevailing wind, and so support with strong stakes is essential during the formative years. A tree denied adequate space and light will grow excessively tall, with a sparse crown of branches. It is tempting to plant trees close together for quick effect, but they need ample space in which to spread and develop their true beauty.

GARDEN TREES

**Deciduous trees respond to each new season
with a display of blossom, foliage, fruits or bark
to delight the eye and bring life to the garden.**

The impact of trees on a garden exceeds that of any other plant group. Trees set the scene and add variety with the changes they bring as the seasons pass; they stand as focal points and define garden boundaries.

Spring arrives in a burst of joyful colour from bulbs and early flowering plants, but it is the explosion of bloom from ornamental cherries, crab apples and magnolias that announces the true arrival of spring. Later come the golden laburnums and the pink and white blossom of redbuds (*Cercis*) and dogwoods.

An infinite variety of foliage is displayed throughout summer – the shimmering silver of ornamental pears, the elegant leaf fronds of honey locusts, the coppery tones of weeping beeches, and the gold of false acacias. The leaf canopy of such trees as catalpas and mulberries offer shade from hot sun, while stewartias stand draped with white flowers.

Autumn brings forth a blaze of colours, ranging from those of the maples and sweet gums, nyssas and oaks, parrotias and hornbeams to the huge bunches of colourful fruits on crab apples, rowans, whitebeams and wingnuts.

In winter, even deciduous trees divert attention from the bleakness of the rest of the garden. They display a graceful tracery or contorted spirals of naked branches draped with dormant catkins, as well as the gleaming white trunks of birches, the glowing red bark of ornamental cherries and the violet-black willow stems.

▲ **Japanese pagoda tree**
The stiff, weeping branches of the Japanese pagoda tree (*Sophora japonica* 'Pendula') are etched with frost in this still winter garden. Apparently lifeless, this fine mature specimen tree will awaken from its slumber draped with long sprays of creamy pea-like flowers.

▼ **Chinese witch hazel** From early winter on, braving snow and frost, the naked branches of the Chinese witch hazel (*Hamamelis mollis*) are clothed with sweetly scented, golden-yellow and red-flushed spidery flower clusters.

◄ **Scarlet willow** Radiant in winter sunshine, the scarlet willow (*Salix alba* 'Britzensis') glows against the frost-covered ground. Related to the native white willow that inhabits wetlands, ornamental varieties of this graceful tree need severe pruning every other year in early spring in order to retain the brilliant colours of their young shoots. Site them well away from house foundations and drainage systems as their roots run deep and wide in search of water.

▲ **Silver pear** By late spring, the ornamental pear (*Pyrus salicifolia* 'Pendula') has unfolded its silver-grey foliage, that ripples like a waterfall from the weeping branches, over an underplanting of white tulips. The clusters of small, cream-white flowers, as yet in bud, develop into tiny inedible pears by early autumn. This sturdy, ultra-hardy tree thrives in all types of good soil and in all kinds of positions.

◄ **Pink blossom** A shrub border is enhanced by the bright colour of a mature prunus tree in a neighbouring garden. Smothered in pale pink blossom in mid spring, the ornamental cherry tree will later shield the purple and variegated shrubby acers from the effects of the hot summer sun.

▲ **Golden summer** The Indian bean tree (*Catalpa bignonioides*) is a magnificent shade tree with huge heart-shaped leaves. It is particularly striking in the golden form 'Aurea', seen here in a pleasing association with a soft yellow *Juniperus chinensis* clipped into a pyramid shape. Mature catalpas bear large clusters of white and yellow, foxglove-like flowers in late summer.

▶ **Distant vista** A mixed border brimming with roses, flowering shrubs, tall foxgloves and billowing lady's mantle is eclipsed by a purple-leaved cherry plum (*Prunus cerasifera* 'Nigra'). Flowering profusely with pink blossom in early spring, the tree retains its purple-black colour until leaf fall.

▲ **Autumn harvest** The native hawthorn (*Crataegus monogyna*) is an accommodating garden tree. It is a delight in late spring with its sweetly scented pink and white blossom, and in autumn the foliage echoes the colour of the long-lasting, orange-red berries.

◀ **Acer group** The maples (*Acer*) display enormous differences in growth habit, leaf shape and colour. Highly ornamental, acers range from wide-spreading trees to slender columns and low shrubs; they are all magnificently coloured in autumn.

▼ **Colour contrast** Among the numerous birches, the Himalayan species, *Betula jacquemontii*, is particularly striking. Its white trunk and branches look dazzling against crimson-scarlet Japanese maples (*Acer palmatum* 'Atropurpureum').

Acer

maple

Acer pseudoplatanus 'Brilliantissimum', spring

Acer platanoides 'Columnare', autumn

Acer circinatum, autumn

- ☐ Height at 25 years 2.5-10.5m (8-35ft)
- ☐ Spread 2.5-9m (8-30ft)
- ☐ Moist, cool soil
- ☐ Hardy broadleaf
- ☐ Features – bright summer and autumn foliage; attractive bark

Beautiful in summer with its full, usually rounded top, maple is even more outstanding in autumn when its handsome, palmate foliage develops striking orange, red and yellow tints. Some species also have attractive striped or peeling bark. The fruits (keys) consist of a pair of winged nuts.

The leaves may have three, five, seven, nine or more lobes and are pale, mid or bright green in summer, and may be tinted red when young. The genus includes the tall, spreading sycamore, but there are numerous medium and small species and varieties suitable for smaller gardens. For shrubby maples, see pages 70-71.

Popular species

Acer capillipes, about 7.5m (25ft) high and wide, is an upright tree with greenish, white-striped bark. The narrow, three-lobed leaves are tinted red when they open, later turning mid green and then crimson in autumn. The winged seeds hang in long clusters.

Acer cappadocicum, a fast-growing, spreading tree 9m (30ft) high and 4.5m (15ft) across, has glossy dark green, five- or seven-lobed leaves which turn a rich yellow colour during autumn. Varieties include: 'Aureum' (young leaves red, turning yellow then green and finally yellow in autumn) and 'Rubrum' (young leaves deep red).

Acer circinatum (vine maple) grows to 4.5m (15ft) high and across as a small tree or 2.5m (8ft) high and across as a shrub. The branches twist and spread to form a rounded head and the seven- or nine-lobed, almost circular, mid green leaves are red and orange in autumn. Clusters of white and red-purple flowers appear in mid spring. The species tolerates dry soil and a shady site.

Acer davidii, a variable tree up to 6m (20ft) high and 3m (10ft) wide, has greenish grey, white-striped bark, particularly if it is grown in partial shade. The dark green undivided, red-stalked leaves are tinged red-bronze when young, and yellow, red and purple in autumn. 'George Forrest' has a more wide-spreading habit.

Acer griseum (paperbark maple), 4.5m (15ft) high and 2.5m (8ft) wide, is a slow-growing tree. The toothed, three-lobed, mid green leaves turn red and orange in autumn. The bark peels off to reveal orange-brown patches.

Acer negundo (box-elder) grows rapidly up to 7.5m (25ft) high and 6m (20ft) wide. The pale to mid green leaves are divided into three or five-toothed leaflets. Varieties include: 'Elegans' (bright yellow leaf margins); and 'Variegatum' (white margins).

Acer griseum, bark

Acer pensylvanicum (snake-bark maple) grows rapidly to 6m (20ft) high and 3m (10ft) wide. It is an upright tree, with the young green bark striped white. The pale to mid green leaves, with three-pointed lobes, are tinged pink when young, and turn yellow in autumn. The tree dislikes chalk. 'Erythrocladum' has young pink shoots but is less robust.

Acer platanoides (Norway maple), up to 11m (36ft) high and 6m (20ft) wide, is a useful town tree with a dense, rounded head and bright green, five-lobed leaves which turn yellow in autumn. Varieties include: 'Columnare' (columnar shape); 'Crimson King' (deep purple-crimson leaves); 'Drummondii' (broad white leaf margins); 'Globosum' (to 6m/20ft high, dense mop-head shape); 'Laciniatum' (eagle's-claw maple, small five-lobed leaves pointed like claws); 'Reitenbachii' (leaves red, then green, deep red in autumn); and 'Schwedleri' (young leaves crimson, turning green).

Acer pseudoplatanus (sycamore), up to 10.5m (35ft) high and 4.5m (15ft) wide, is suitable as a windbreak, and tolerates pollution. It self-seeds freely. The deep green, toothed leaves have five lobes. Varieties include: 'Atropurpureum' (leaves purple underneath); 'Brilliantissimum' (to 4.5m/15ft high, leaves pink, turning yellow, then green); 'Erectum' ('Fastigiatum', narrow, upright); 'Leopoldii' (leaves yellow-pink, then green marked with yellow and pink); and 'Worleei' (golden sycamore, leaves yellow, then green).

Acer rubrum (red maple), up to 7.5m (25ft) high and 3m (10ft)

Acer negundo 'Variegatum', fruits

wide, is an ultra-hardy tree with a dense, round head. It has three- or five-lobed dark green leaves which are blue-white underneath and turn red and yellow in autumn. Best on acid soils. Varieties include: 'Columnare' (columnar shape); 'Scanlon' (columnar shape, rich autumn colour); and 'Schlesingeri' (outstanding rich scarlet autumn colour).

Acer saccharinum (silver maple), syn. *A. dasycarpum*, grows rapidly to 12m (40ft) high and 9m (30ft) wide. The attractive drooping branches bear deeply lobed leaves, bright green above and silvery white beneath, with yellow autumn tints. Varieties include 'Laciniatum' (deeply cut, toothed leaves) and 'Pyramidale' ('Fastigiatum', narrow, upright form).

Cultivation

Plant from mid autumn to early spring in any good, well-drained but moist and cool soil in sun or partial shade. Plant species grown for their autumn foliage in sites protected from autumn winds and frosts.

Pruning Prune out reverted all-green shoots from *A. negundo* 'Variegatum' and *A. platanoides* 'Drummondii' to maintain variegations. Prune *A. platanoides* 'Schwedleri' every other autumn for the best leaf colour. Other species and varieties require no pruning.

Pests and diseases

Aphids cause sticky and sooty foliage, especially on sycamores.
Coral spot can cause die-back.
Gall mites cause galls on the leaves of sycamores.
Honey fungus kills trees.
Scorching may turn leaf margins brown. They then shrivel.
Tar spot shows as large black spots with yellow edges.
Verticillium wilt causes sudden wilting of leaves and die-back of shoots. Internally affected shoots have brown or green-brown streaks.

15

Ailanthus
tree of heaven

Ailanthus altissima, summer fruits

Ailanthus altissima

☐ Height at 25 years 9-12m (30-45ft)
☐ Mature height 20m (65ft) or more
☐ Spread 4.5-9m (15-30ft)
☐ Any garden soil
☐ Hardy broadleaf
☐ Features – fruits (female tree only)

An excellent tree for urban areas, the fast-growing tree of heaven (*Ailanthus altissima* syn. *A. glandulosa* and *A. peregrina*) tolerates a high degree of pollution, thrives in any kind of soil, including acid types, and resists attacks by most pests and diseases.

The huge compound leaves of this wide-spreading tree are ash-like, up to 90cm (3ft) long and divided into numerous leaflets. They are bronzy-red when they unfurl in the spring, but quickly turn a rich dark green. The leaves are borne in heavy bunches at the end of short twigs and create a changing pattern of filtered sun and shade. The variety 'Pendulifolia' has particularly large pendulous leaves.

Tree of heaven, originally from northern China, is unisexual, being either male or female. Both types bear insignificant yellow-green flowers in summer, which on female trees are followed by large drooping clusters of attractive reddish-brown winged seeds known as keys. These are scattered over a wide area but will only develop into seedlings if they have been pollinated by a male tree. Male flowers have an unpleasant scent.

The only drawback to this easily-grown and handsome shade tree is its tendency to produce underground suckering shoots which often appear above ground over quite a distance.

Cultivation
Plant, weather permitting, at any time from mid autumn to mid spring, in any kind of garden soil and in sun or light shade. Avoid sites that are exposed to strong winds. Stake young trees until established.

Pruning Cut hard back in spring to control growth; young trees can be stooled annually and grown as multi-stemmed shrubs. Dig up and remove suckers where they sprout from the roots; destroy the suckers or use them for propagation purposes.

Pests and diseases Generally trouble free.

ALDER – see *Alnus*
ALMOND, ORNAMENTAL – see *Prunus*

Alnus
alder

Alnus glutinosa, catkins

☐ Height 9-12m (30-40ft)
☐ Mature height 18m (60ft) or more
☐ Spread 4.5-5.5m (15-18ft)
☐ Moist to wet, acid soil
☐ Hardy broadleaf
☐ Features – catkins; cones

Alder, a conical or pyramid-shaped tree, bears outstanding yellow to orange catkins on leafless branches in early spring. The shorter, female catkins, which appear alongside the male catkins, later develop into striking dark brown or blackish woody cones, resembling the seed cases of a conifer. After the winged seeds disperse – by air or by water – the spent cones may remain on the branches for up to a year.

Happiest in wet soils, alder is ideal for a riverside garden or for a boggy corner.

Popular species
Alnus cordata (Italian alder), up to 12m (40ft) high and 5.5m (18ft) across, is a fast-growing, conical-shaped species from Corsica and southern Italy. The glossy mid green leaves are heart-shaped and the catkins are up to 3cm (1¼ in) long. This species tolerates shallow chalky and dryish soil.
Alnus glutinosa (black or common

Alnus cordata

alder) is a conical tree, native to Britain. Up to 9m (30ft) high and 4.5m (15ft) across, it has deep green leaves and sticky young growth. Yellow catkins appear in early spring. Varieties include 'Aurea' (yellow leaves) and 'Imperialis' (feathery foliage).
Alnus incana (grey or white alder) is an ultra-hardy tree or large shrub up to 12m (40ft) high and 5.5m (18ft) across. It has pale green oval leaves which are grey beneath, soft grey young growth and bears profuse catkins. Varieties include 'Aurea' (young yellow leaves and shoots, red-tinted catkins) and 'Pendula' (weeping habit).
Alnus rubra (red or Oregon alder) is a fast-growing species from western North America. Up to 12m (40ft) high and 4.5m (15ft)

across, it has drooping branches forming a pyramid shape. The leaves and male catkins are up to 15cm (6in) long.
Alnus x spaethii, up to 12m (40ft) high and 4.5m (15ft) across, has larger leaves than other species. The catkins are outstanding.

Cultivation
Plant in moist to wet soil from mid autumn to early spring in sun or partial shade. Most alders dislike chalky or dry soils, though *A. cordata* is more tolerant of these conditions.
Pruning None required.
Pests and diseases Trouble free.

ASH – see *Fraxinus*
ASPEN – see *Populus*
BEECH – see *Fagus*
BENTHAMIA – see *Cercis*

Betula

birch

Betula 'Grayswood Ghost'

Betula albo-sinensis septentrionalis, bark

☐ Height at 25 years 7.5-11m (25-36ft)
☐ Spread 3-4.5m (10-15ft)
☐ Loamy soil
☐ Hardy broadleaf
☐ Features – bark; catkins; graceful habit

The airy, small-leaved birch, with its slender trunk and narrow branches, is one of the most graceful garden trees, well deserving the title 'Lady of the Woods'.

A favourite specimen tree, birch is renowned for its peeling silvery white bark, though some species have grey or orange-brown bark. The mid green, toothed leaves, which cast little shade, unfurl in mid spring and are broadly ovate, though they are sometimes oval or diamond-shaped. They turn yellow in autumn.

The upright, greenish female catkins appear with the leaves, later developing into club-shaped cones which scatter their seeds in autumn. The pendent 5cm (2in) long male catkins are reddish brown, though they look yellow when covered with pollen, and appear in mid to late spring.

Birch is a shallow-rooted, short-lived tree, rarely lasting for more than 80 years. It can be grown on most soils, but rarely attains maximum size on shallow chalk soil.

Popular species
Betula albo-sinensis septentrionalis, up to 7.5m (25ft) high and 3m (10ft) across, is from western China. It has orange-brown to orange-red bark with a greyish bloom. The oval mid green leaves are covered in short silky hairs.
Betula ermanii, from north-east Asia, is up to 9m (30ft) high and 4.5m (15ft) across. It has cream-pink peeling bark and orange-brown branches. The ovate mid green leaves are up to 7.5cm (3in) long. This species starts growth early in the year and may suffer frost damage in exposed sites and northern gardens.
Betula 'Grayswood Ghost', up to 6m (20ft) high and 4.5m (15ft) across, has attractive white bark and a conical form.
Betula nigra (river, black or red birch), from the central and eastern United States, is up to 7.5m (25ft) high and 4.5m (15ft) across. The diamond-shaped soft green leaves are white underneath, and the peeling bark is pinkish-orange. This species thrives in damp ground.
Betula papyrifera (paper, canoe or white birch), a North American tree up to 9m (30ft) high and 4.5m (15ft) across, has peeling white bark and triangular mid green

Betula ermanii

Betula pendula 'Gracilis', autumn

leaves which turn yellow in autumn.

Betula pendula (silver birch), up to 9m (30ft) high and 3.5m (12ft) across, is a graceful British and European tree with weeping branch tips. The silvery bark becomes rough and blackened at the base of older trees; the diamond-shaped leaves are mid green. Varieties include: 'Dalecarlica' (Swedish birch with drooping branches, deeply cut leaves);

'Golden Cloud' (golden yellow leaves); 'Gracilis' (finely cut leaves); 'Tristis' (narrow, symmetrical form, slender, weeping branches); and 'Youngii' (Young's Weeping Birch, dome-shaped, weeping).

Betula utilis (Himalayan birch), up to 7.5m (25ft) high and 4.5m (15ft) across, has peeling reddish-brown bark and is a native of the Himalayas. The oval leaves are 5-9cm (2-3½in) long. *B.u.* var.

jacquemontii has dazzling white branches and peeling white bark.

Cultivation

Plant from mid autumn to early spring in good loamy soil. Species which come into growth early should be planted in sites sheltered from wind and frost. Do not plant birch close to borders or fences, as it has wide spreading surface roots.

Pruning None required.

Pests and diseases

Aphids, caterpillars, sawfly larvae and weevils attack foliage.

Bracket fungi may enter dead wood, rotting heart wood.

Honey fungus may kill trees.

A physiological disorder due to unsuitable soil conditions shows as brown blotches or yellowing of the leaves followed by premature leaf-fall.

Rust shows on the leaves as bright red-yellow spots.

Witches' brooms show as dense clumps of branching twigs on the trunk and/or main branches.

Betula pendula 'Youngii'

BIRCH – see *Betula*
BIRD CHERRY – see *Prunus*
BLACK GUM – see *Nyssa*
BOX ELDER – see *Acer*

Carpinus
hornbeam

Carpinus betulus, autumn foliage

☐ Height at 25 years 3-9m (10-30ft)
☐ Mature height 18m (60ft)
☐ Spread 3.5-4.5m (12-15ft)
☐ Any soil
☐ Hardy broadleaf
☐ Features – fluted trunk; attractive fruits and winter leaves

An imposing specimen tree, hornbeam has a distinctive grey fluted trunk bearing a round, densely branched head. Thickly clothed with rough, toothed mid green leaves which turn yellow or russet in autumn, it also makes an excellent hedging plant which retains its brown leaves in winter.

The yellow-green male and the shorter green female catkins appear together from mid to late spring. The female catkins resemble leafy shoots, and are later replaced by attractive pendent clusters of winged nutlets.

Popular species
Carpinus betulus (common hornbeam), a native of Britain and Europe, grows up to 7.5m (25ft) high and 4.5m (15ft) across. A good specimen or hedging tree, it is pyramid-shaped when young and rounded when mature. The oval leaves are prominently veined and sharply toothed. They develop yellow tints in autumn. Varieties include 'Columnaris' (to 3m/10ft, slow-growing, dense, columnar) and 'Fastigiata' ('Pyramidalis', slenderly conical when young, rounded when mature).
Carpinus japonica, a slow-growing, spreading tree from Japan, is up to 5.5m (18ft) high and 3.5m (12ft) across. It has corrugated, oblong mid green leaves, tinted red in autumn.

Cultivation
Plant from mid autumn to early spring in any soil. For hedging, plant *C. betulus* at 38-50cm (15-20in) wide intervals. Fork in a general fertilizer prior to planting at the rate of 100g per sq m (4oz per sq yd). Keep the young plants moist and mulch annually.
Pruning In mid summer, clip young hedges lightly to the required shape, and established hedges fairly hard.
Pests and diseases Honey fungus may cause the rapid death of trees.

Carpinus betulus 'Fastigiata'

Castanea
chestnut

Castanea sativa 'Variegata'

☐ Height at 25 years 7.5-15m (25-50ft)
☐ Mature height 15-30m (50-100ft)
☐ Spread 6-12m (20-40ft)
☐ Any good, deep soil
☐ Hardy broadleaf
☐ Features – ornamental catkins; edible nuts

The chestnut tree is at its most ornamental in mid summer when clusters of long, fluffy catkins appear, looking from a distance rather like huge starry yellowish flowers. The large oval or lance-shaped leaves are mid green and prominently veined and toothed. In autumn they turn a rich brown-yellow, forming a crisp carpet underfoot when they fall.

On older trees, the bark becomes a distinctive feature, developing a grey tint and deep fissures which twist up the bole in spirals.

In mid autumn the fruits of *C. sativa* open to reveal the edible sweet chestnut, a glossy brown nut which can be roasted, boiled or glazed.

This useful tree is drought resistant, very hardy and long-lived, with some specimens in Britain well over 100 years old.

Popular species
Castanea mollissima, from China and Korea, is up to 7.5m (25ft) high and 6m (20ft) across. It has downy young shoots opening into oval or oblong leaves which are toothed and sometimes felted underneath.

Catalpa

Indian bean tree

Castanea sativa, fruit

Catalpa bignonioides, fruit

Catalpa bignonioides

Castanea sativa (sweet or Spanish chestnut) is a fast-growing tree up to 15m (50ft) high and 12m (40ft) across and originates from southern Europe, North Africa and Asia Minor. The highly ornamental upright, fluffy yellowish green male catkins are 7.5-15cm (3-6in) long and appear with female catkins in clusters in mid summer. They are followed later by clusters of spiny burrs containing edible nuts which are about 2.5cm (1in) across. The oblong to lance-shaped leaves are toothed and prominently veined. Varieties include: 'Albomarginata' (leaves edged yellow); 'Marron de Lyon' ('Macrocarpa', profuse fruits produced at an early age); and 'Variegata' (leaves variegated yellow).

Cultivation

Plant in any open site from mid autumn to early spring. Chestnut thrives in most well-drained soils, including clay, but dislikes shallow chalky soil.
Pruning None required.
Pests and diseases Trouble free.

□ Height at 25 years 6-7.5m (20-25ft)
□ Mature height 12m (40ft)
□ Spread 6-7.5m (20-25ft)
□ Any good well-drained soil
□ Hardy broadleaf
□ Features – handsome foliage; foxglove-like flowers; bean-like seed pods

Even before its showy flowers appear in mid summer, the Indian bean tree is a fine garden feature with its low, wide-spreading canopy of branches, densely clothed with large green leaves.

The white foxglove-like flowers, marked yellow and purple inside, are held in large upright clusters on established trees, and are followed by clusters of pendent seed pods resembling green beans. They remain on the branches for many months to provide winter interest.

When mature, the Indian bean tree tends to be broader than it is high. It does best in sheltered southern gardens.

Popular species

Catalpa bignonioides, from the eastern United States, is up to 6m (20ft) high and 7.5m (25ft) across. It has bright green heart-shaped leaves with an unpleasant aroma when crushed. The flowers are white with purple and yellow markings. The variety 'Aurea' has large, velvety yellow leaves.
Catalpa x *erubescens*, syn. *C.* x

hybrida, is up to 6m (20ft) high and 7.5m (25ft) across. The leaves, some of which are entire and some of which are divided into three lobes, are purple when they open and can measure up to 30cm (1ft) long. The flowers are similar to those of *C. bignonioides*, but smaller and more profuse. The variety 'Purpurea' has dark purple, almost black, young leaves and shoots, later turning dark green.
Catalpa speciosa, from the central United States, is up to 7.5m (25ft) high and 6m (20ft) across. It is more upright than *C. bignonioides* with leathery, heart-shaped leaves up to 30cm (1ft) long. The white, purple-marked flowers are larger than those of *C. bignonioides*, but there are fewer blooms in each cluster.

Cultivation

Plant Indian bean tree during suitable weather from mid autumn to early spring in any good, well-drained garden soil. The trees prefer a sunny, sheltered position.
Pruning None required.
Pests and diseases A physiological disease due to unsuitable soil conditions causes brown blotching or yellowing of the leaves.

CAUCASIAN WINGNUT – see *Pterocarya*

Cercis

redbud

Cercis siliquastrum

☐ Height at 25 years 4.5-6m (15-20ft)
☐ Mature height up to 9m (30ft)
☐ Spread 3-6m (10-20ft)
☐ Any good garden soil
☐ Hardy broadleaf
☐ Features – profuse flowers; seed pods; distinctive foliage

Redbud's spreading, rounded top is a spectacular mass of colour in late spring when hundreds of pink pea-like blooms crowd in clusters along the naked branches and even on the trunk. The flowers often appear before the distinctive foliage, and are followed later by conspicuous green seed pods. They are tinted red when ripe and remain on the tree until winter.

The heart-shaped or rounded leaves are generally bright green or grey-green.

Redbud may be grown as a single-stemmed tree or as a multi-stemmed shrub and can be trained against a wall as an espalier.

Popular species

Cercis canadensis is a North American species up to 6m (20ft) high and wide. It has a broad rounded head with bright green heart-shaped leaves and pale rose-pink flowers in late spring to early summer. The foliage takes on golden tints in autumn. It flowers most freely in sunny, sheltered climates. Varieties include: 'Forest Pansy' (pink flowers, reddish purple foliage); 'Oklahoma' (deep red flowers); and 'Plena' (double pink flowers).
C. canadensis var. *texensis*, Texas redbud, is of shrubby habit, with glossy green, blunt-tipped leaves.

Cercis canadensis 'Forest Pansy'

Cercis occidentalis is a small tree or large shrub up to 4.5m (15ft) high and 3m (10ft) across from the western United States. The heart-shaped, leathery leaves are bright green and rounded and the short-stalked rose-coloured flowers are borne in clusters. This species tolerates drought and needs warm summers and cold winters to produce the best show of flowers.
Cercis racemosa, from China, grows 6m (20ft) or more in height and spread, with ovate leaves that are bright green above and downy underneath. Drooping, 10cm (4in) long clusters of rose-pink, pea-shaped flowers are borne in profusion in late spring on trees that are more than eight years old. They are followed by attractive seed pods up to 12.5cm (5in) long.
Cercis siliquastrum (Judas tree), from the eastern Mediterranean, is up to 7.5m (25ft) high and 6m (20ft) across. This wide-spreading, flat-topped tree or shrub has rounded grey-green leaves. Clusters of rich rose-purple flowers appear on the leafless branches in groups of four to six in late spring. They are followed by flat green seed pods up to 10cm (4in) long. These are tinted red when ripe in late summer. This species, according to legend, was the tree on which Judas hanged himself – hence its common name. Varieties include: 'Alba' (white flowers and pale green foliage) and 'Bodnant' (deep purple flowers).

Cercis occidentalis

Cultivation

Redbud thrives in any good garden soil in full sun. Large trees resent root disturbance, so plant only young pot-grown specimens, ideally in mid autumn or mid to late spring. The flowers of *C. siliquastrum* may be damaged by late spring frosts; to avoid this grow this species in a sheltered position. In northern gardens plant by a south wall for protection. It is suitable for training as an espalier. Redbud is not recommended for gardens with heavy clay soil.

Pruning None required, but wall-trained specimens can be cut back to shape after flowering.

Pests and diseases Coral spot causes die-back of shoots; pink to red cushion-like pustules appear at the base of the dead wood. Large branches may be killed.

CHERRY, ORNAMENTAL – see *Prunus*
CHESTNUT – see *Castanea*
CORNELIAN CHERRY – see *Cornus*

Cornus
dogwood

Cornus kousa chinensis

Cornus nuttallii, flowers

Cornus kousa, fruit

☐ Height at 25 years 3-6m (10-20ft)
☐ Mature height up to 7.5m (25ft)
☐ Spread 4.5-5.5m (15-18ft)
☐ Any good garden soil
☐ Hardy broadleaf
☐ Features – profuse flowers and berries; autumn foliage

The dogwoods range from prostrate creepers to wide-spreading medium-sized shrubs and small single-stemmed trees.

The ornamental flowers consist of striking bracts surrounding insignificant true flowers. They appear in clusters at the end of winter before the foliage, or in late spring to early summer. The oval leaves are mid to dark green, often with rich autumn tints in shades of red, yellow and bronze. The fruits, which appear as the leaves turn, may be black or red berries or resemble strawberries.

Some species are now included in different genera but are still commonly listed under *Cornus.*

For shrubby dogwoods see pages 86-88.

Popular species
Cornus (Swida) controversa, up to 6m (20ft) high and 5.5m (18ft) wide, is from the Far East. It has tiered, sweeping horizontal branches and oval mid green leaves with purple-red autumn tints, and bears broad, flat clusters of white flowers in early to mid summer, followed by black berries. 'Variegata' is smaller with silver variegated leaves.

Cornus (Benthamia) kousa, from the Far East, develops into a bush or small bushy tree with a height and spread of 3m (10ft). The oval mid to dark green leaves have wavy margins and turn bronze and crimson in autumn. Purple-green flowers surrounded by large pointed white bracts appear in early summer followed by strawberry-like fruits. The variety *chinensis* is taller and more open with larger leaves and bracts.

Cornus mas (Cornelian cherry) from central and southern Europe, develops into a small tree, about 3.5m (12ft) high and 3m (10ft) wide, with dense branches and dark green oval leaves. Round clusters of golden yellow flowers appear from late winter to mid spring before the leaves, followed by red, semi-translucent, edible berries. The variety 'Variegata' has white-edged leaves.

Cornus (Benthamia) nuttallii (Pacific dogwood), from northwest America, forms a tree up to 7.5m (25ft) high and 4.5m (15ft) across. It has dull green leaves with yellow or red autumn tints. Round white flowers, surrounded by large creamy white bracts which later turn pink, open in late spring. The strawberry-like fruits are orange-red.

Cultivation
Plant dogwood in autumn in any good garden soil and in a sunny or partially shady site. Not recommended for shallow chalk.
Pruning None required.
Pests and diseases Trouble free.

Cotoneaster

cotoneaster

Cotoneaster 'Hybridus Pendulus'

☐ Height at 25 years 1.8-4.5m (6-15ft)
☐ Mature height rarely more than 6m (20ft)
☐ Spread 1.8-4.5m (6-15ft)
☐ Hardy broadleaf
☐ Ordinary garden soil
☐ Features – berries; flowers; decorative foliage

Though cotoneaster is better known for its shrubs (see page 91), this large genus includes several small trees grown for their neat foliage, creamy white flower clusters and dazzling show of red berries, carried in heavy bunches in autumn and winter.

Popular species

Cotoneaster frigidus, from the Himalayas, is a fast-growing deciduous or semi-evergreen small tree or large shrub up to 4.5m (15ft) high and across with mid to dark green oblong leaves and white to pink flowers in early summer. The red berries last well into winter. The variety 'Fructu-luteo' has cream-yellow berries.
Cotoneaster 'Hybridus Pendulus' is a semi-evergreen carpeting shrub. Grafted on to *C. frigidus* it makes an outstanding weeping dwarf tree up to 1.8m (6ft) high, with glossy green leaves and a profusion of brilliant red berries.

Cotoneaster frigidus

Cultivation

Plant from mid autumn to late winter in ordinary garden soil.
Pruning None required.
Pests and diseases Birds may eat the berries. Fireblight and honey fungus can kill trees.

CRAB APPLE – see *Malus*

Crataegus

hawthorn

Crataegus laevigata 'Paul's Scarlet'

☐ Height at 25 years 5.5-7.5m (18-25ft)
☐ Mature height rarely more than 7.5m (25ft)
☐ Spread 2.5-6m (8-20ft)
☐ Ordinary garden soil
☐ Hardy broadleaf
☐ Features – flowers; fruit; attractive foliage

The hawthorn is a familiar sight in the British countryside, with its dense, thorny branches heavily laden with clusters of scented flowers in late spring and rich foliage tints and clusters of colourful berries (haws) in autumn.

The genus provides a good choice of useful and decorative garden trees. Those described are ultra hardy, with a height and spread of 6m (20ft) after 25 years, unless otherwise stated.

Popular species

Crataegus crus-galli (cockspur thorn), from eastern and central North America, has viciously thorny branches and glossy green leaves turning scarlet in autumn. The white flowers appear in early summer, followed by red haws lasting until mid winter.
Crataegus laciniata, syn. *C. orientalis*, from the Far East, is almost thornless. The branch tips sometimes droop and the deeply lobed,

Crataegus monogyna, haws

Crataegus laevigata 'Rosea Flore Pleno'

Crataegus laevigata 'Plena', flowers

downy dark green leaves are grey beneath. The haws are yellow-red.

Crataegus laevigata (Midland hawthorn), syn. *C. oxyacantha*, has white, fragrant flowers in late spring followed later by crimson oval haws. The dark green leaves have three or five lobes. Varieties and hybrids include: 'Aurea' (yellow fruits); 'Gireoudii' (young leaves mottled pink and white); 'Paul's Scarlet' ('Coccinea Plena', double scarlet flowers); 'Plena' (double white flowers, ageing pink); and 'Rosea Flore Pleno' (double pink flowers).

Crataegus x *lavallei*, syn. *C.* x *carrierei*, is a dense leafy tree with glossy dark green foliage which can persist until mid winter. The haws are orange-red.

Crataegus mollis, from central North America, is up to 3m (10ft) high and 3.5m (12ft) wide with red haws as large as cherries.

Crataegus monogyna (common English hawthorn or May) is a densely branched thorny tree up to 7.5m (25ft) high and 6m (20ft) wide. Suitable as a specimen tree and for hedging and screening, it has glossy dark green lobed and toothed leaves. Clusters of strongly sweet-smelling white flowers cover the branches in late spring, followed in autumn by small crimson haws in large clusters. The variety 'Stricta' or 'Fastigiata' is a narrow tree up to 5.5m (18ft) high and 2.5m (8ft) across.

Crataegus phaenopyrum (Washington thorn), from the southeastern United States, has glossy, maple-like leaves with rich autumn tints and crimson haws.

Crataegus x *prunifolia* has shiny oval leaves turning rich red in autumn, and large crimson haws.

Crataegus tanacetifolia, from Asia Minor, is thornless with downy grey, deeply lobed leaves and orange haws like small apples.

Cultivation

Plant from late autumn to early spring in any ordinary garden soil. Hawthorn tolerates partial shade but prefers sun. It withstands exposure and pollution, and periods of drought and waterlogging.

When planting *C. monogyna* as a hedge, use plants 30-45cm (1-1½ft) high at intervals of 30-38cm (12-15in). For screening, use 90cm-1.2m (3-4ft) high trees at intervals of 60-90cm (2-3ft).

Pruning Trim hedges or screens of *C. monogyna* from mid summer to early spring. Tall neglected hedges can be heavily pruned from mid to late summer.

Pests and diseases

Fireblight causes blackening and shrivelling of flowers and a progressive die-back of branches bearing brown and withered leaves.

Honey fungus kills trees rapidly.

Leaf spot shows as small brown or black spots.

Powdery mildew is a white powdery coating on the leaves.

Rust shows as yellow or orange swellings on young shoots, leaves and fruits in early summer.

Davidia

handkerchief or dove tree

Davidia involucrata

☐ Height at 25 years 5.5-7.5m (18-25ft)
☐ Mature height 10-15m (30-50ft)
☐ Spread 4.5m (15ft)
☐ Hardy broadleaf
☐ Any good moist garden soil
☐ Features – flower bracts

Handkerchief tree (*Davidia involucrata*) is a spectacular sight when it blooms in late spring. The true flowers form dense round heads, concealed by two large, glistening whitish flower bracts of uneven sizes. The bracts resemble dove wings or loosely folded handkerchiefs dangling among the bright green, heart-shaped, toothed and veined leaves. These are up to 15cm (6in) long and covered with grey down underneath.

The young tree is fairly narrow but later develops a rounded top.

Handkerchief tree is an excellent specimen tree.

The variety *vilmoriniana* has smoother, paler leaves.

Cultivation

Plant in any good moist garden soil from mid autumn to early spring in sun or partial shade.
Pruning None required.
Pests and diseases Trouble free.

DAWN REDWOOD – see *Metasequoia*
DOGWOOD – see *Cornus*
DOVE TREE – see *Davidia*
ELM – see *Ulmus*

Fagus

beech

Fagus sylvatica 'Zlatia'

☐ Height at 25 years 3-9m (10-30ft)
☐ Mature height 15-30m (50-100ft)
☐ Spread 1.5-9m (5-30ft)
☐ Any good, well-drained soil
☐ Hardy broadleaf
☐ Features – foliage colour

The stately long-living beech tree brings an air of nobility to many British parks with its dense, broad top, massive, smooth grey trunk, pale green young foliage and yellow and russet autumn tints. It can be clipped for hedging, and several smaller forms, with narrow or weeping growth habits and foliage in shades of green and gold, make excellent specimen trees for gardens, including the famous 'copper beeches' with their outstanding purple foliage.

The pointed oval, sometimes toothed leaves, generally about 10cm (4in) long, cast deep shade. The insignificant flowers are followed in some years by a profuse crop of woody, prickly fruits which open to reveal two triangular brown nuts (mast).

Popular species

Fagus engleriana, from central China, grows up to 7.5m (25ft) high and 6m (20ft) wide. This rare, handsome tree often has several trunks. The branches are slender and the leaves are greyish green.
Fagus sylvatica (common beech), a very hardy native of Europe, forms a tree 9m (30ft) high and wide with a rounded head and a thick grey trunk. The wavy-edged

Fagus sylvatica, fruit

Fagus sylvatica 'Purpurea Pendula'

Fagus sylvatica 'Dawyck'

Fagus sylvatica 'Pendula', autumn

leaves are bright green when young, maturing to mid or deep green and developing rich yellow and russet tints in autumn. This species makes an excellent tall hedge which retains its russet leaves throughout winter if trimmed in late summer.

The many varieties include: 'Albovariegata' (leaves edged and streaked white); 'Asplenifolia' (fern-leaved beech, narrow, deep-cut leaves); 'Aurea Pendula' (tall, narrow tree, to 4.5/15ft high and 1.5m/5ft across, pendent branches, golden yellow leaves, best in light shade); 'Dawyck' ('Fastigiata', Dawyck beech, columnar tree to 9m/30ft high and 2m/7ft wide, broadening with age); 'Dawyck Purple' (purple-leaved form of 'Dawyck'); 'Hetero-phylla' ('Laciniata', similar to 'Asplenifolia'); 'Pendula' (weeping beech, pendent branches or horizontal branches with pendent branchlets); 'Purpurea' (purple-red leaves); 'Purpurea Pendula' (weeping, round-headed tree, to 3m/10ft high and 1.8m/6ft wide, purple foliage); 'Riversii' ('Rivers' Purple', deep purple leaves); and 'Zlatia' (young golden yellow leaves turning green).

Cultivation

Beech grows well on all soils except heavy wet ones. Plant from mid autumn to early spring in an open sunny position.

For hedging, plant trees 45cm (1½ft) high at intervals of 45-60cm (1½-2ft). Remove the upper quarter of all shoots after planting to encourage branching; repeat this tipping again the following year.

Pruning Trim hedges in late summer. Specimen trees require no pruning once established.

Pests and diseases

Aphids produce tufts of white wax on the undersides of leaves and excrete sticky honeydew.

Beech scale insects produce tufts of white wax. Severe infestations cause yellowing of the foliage and loss of vigour.

Bracket fungi may enter dead wood and cause rotting of the heartwood; later, large bracket-shaped fruiting bodies develop on the trunk of neglected trees.

Coral spot may develop on dead shoots and cause die-back; pink to red cushion-like spore pustules appear at the base of dead wood.

Frost damage shows as browning of foliage and die-back of young shoots.

Honey fungus causes rapid death.

Scorching of the foliage occurs on beeches with purple leaves, particularly in spring. The leaves turn brown, especially round the margins; they curl and shrivel, giving a scorched appearance.

Sunken cankers on branches and stems of young trees may be caused by apple canker or other closely related fungi; shoots girdled by cankers die back.

Weevil larvae may tunnel into, and damage, leaf tissues.

FALSE ACACIA – see *Robinia*
FOXGLOVE TREE – see
Paulownia

Fraxinus

ash

Fraxinus excelsior, fruit

☐ Height at 25 years 6-9m (20-30ft)
☐ Mature height 9-30m (30-100ft)
☐ Spread 3-5.5m (10-18ft) or more
☐ Any ordinary garden soil
☐ Hardy broadleaf
☐ Features – elegant appearance

Fraxinus excelsior 'Jaspidea'

With its extensive root system and wide-spreading branches clothed with leaves divided into many lance-shaped leaflets, the ash tree stands solid against the strongest winds, even sea gales. Many of the species of this fast-growing genus are too large for most gardens but smaller forms are available and many have fine autumn tints in shades of yellow and purple.

Fraxinus ornus, flowers

Popular species

Fraxinus americana (white ash), from eastern North America, is 9m (30ft) or more high and 7.5m (25ft) wide and has furrowed bark. The mid green leaves are divided into seven pointed oval leaflets, paler beneath. The foliage may develop amber, yellow and purple autumn tints. Female trees bear narrow winged fruits. Excellent shade tree.

Fraxinus excelsior (common ash), from Britain and Europe, is up to 9m (30ft) high and 4.5m (15ft) wide; it may eventually reach 30m (100ft) high. The dark green leaves are up to 30cm (1ft) long and divided into 9 to 13 narrow oblong leaflets which turn yellow in autumn. The roots are invasive. Varieties include: 'Diversifolia' ('Monophylla', one-leaved ash, single, undivided leaves); 'Jaspidea' (golden ash, young leaves yellow, yellow autumn tints); 'Pendula' (weeping ash, pendent branches); and 'Westhof's Glorie' (upright, later rounded habit, dark glossy leaves).

Fraxinus ornus (manna ash) is a handsome tree from southern Europe and Asia Minor. Up to 6m

(20ft) high and wide, it is more suitable for small gardens than other species. It has a bushy round head with greyish green leaves divided into seven oval leaflets. Dense and showy clusters, up to 10cm (4in) wide, of cream-white flowers appear in late spring.

Fraxinus velutina (velvet ash), from the south-west United States and northern Mexico, is up to 9m (30ft) high and 6m (20ft) wide with thick velvety leaves.

Cultivation

Plant ash from mid autumn to early spring in any ordinary garden soil in sun or partial shade. Do not plant *F. excelsior* close to buildings as the spreading roots may undermine foundations.
Pruning None required.

Pests and diseases

Ash canker causes damage ranging from small warts on the bark to large black cankers.
Bracket fungi may enter dead wood and cause rotting of the heartwood. Later, large bracket-shaped fruiting bodies may develop on the trunks and branches.
Honey fungus may kill trees.

Ginkgo
maidenhair tree

Ginkgo biloba 'Fastigiata', autumn

☐ Height at 25 years 7.5-10m (25-30ft)
☐ Mature height 25m (82ft)
☐ Spread 3-6m (10-20ft)
☐ Any good garden soil
☐ Hardy deciduous conifer
☐ Features – unique leaves; autumn
   tints; tolerates pollution

The maidenhair tree (*Ginkgo biloba*) is an ancient primitive tree

Ginkgo biloba, foliage

related to conifers. It grew in many parts of the world, including Britain, 160 million years ago. Its beautiful fan-shaped, leathery leaves are fresh green in spring, gradually darkening throughout the summer and tinted golden yellow in autumn.

This slow-growing tree is usually conical when young and may broaden as it matures. Only suitable for large gardens.

Varieties include 'Fastigiata' (columnar) and 'Pendula' (weeping branches).

Cultivation
Plant in mid spring in fertile, well-drained soil.
Pruning Maidenhair tree resents pruning. Shortened shoots die back.
Pests and diseases Trouble free.

Gleditsia
honey locust, sweet locust

Gleditsia triacanthos

☐ Height at 25 years 5.5-10m (18-33ft)
☐ Mature height 18m (60ft) or more
☐ Spread 2.5-9m (8-30ft)
☐ Hardy broadleaf
☐ Any good garden soil
☐ Features – ornamental foliage and
   seed pods; tolerates pollution

Grown for its handsome foliage, honey locust (*Gleditsia triacanthos*) is a large elegant tree from the central and eastern United States. It is highly resistant to town and industrial pollution.

The species is up to 10m (33ft) high and 9m (30ft) wide. It has light green, frond-like leaves, divided into 20 to 32 oblong to lance-shaped leaflets, with clear yellow autumn tints. The shiny brown twisted seed pods remain on the tree throughout winter.

The branches are armed with viciously sharp thorns which may measure up to 30cm (1ft) long. These can inflict unpleasant wounds, so it is advisable to plant a thornless variety such as *inermis* or 'Sunburst' as garden specimen trees.

Honey locust is fast-growing and excellent as a shade tree in a large lawn; its near-black trunk and branches look dramatic in winter.

Popular varieties
'**Bujoti**' is a shrub or small tree

Halesia

snowdrop tree

Gleditsia triacanthos, foliage

Halesia monticola, flowers

up to 6m (20ft) high and 2.5m (8ft) wide. It has narrower leaflets than the species and slender, pendulous branches.

G.t. inermis is similar to the species but is thornless.

'Ruby Lace' has purplish young leaves becoming bronze-green as they mature.

'Shademaster' is an upright, thornless form with dark green foliage.

'Sunburst', also known as 'Inermis Aurea', is thornless with bright yellow young foliage.

Cultivation

Honey locust thrives in any good garden soil; plant during suitable weather from mid autumn to early spring in a sunny position.

Pruning None required except to remove any dead wood in early spring.

Pests and diseases Trouble free.

☐ Height at 25 years 4.5-10m (15-33ft)
☐ Spread 4.5-9m (15-30ft)
☐ Moist, lime-free soil
☐ Hardy broadleaf
☐ Features – flowers

A beautiful specimen tree for gardens with lime-free soil, snowdrop tree bears profuse clusters of drooping silver-white bell-shaped flowers in late spring, while the branches are still leafless.

This wide-spreading tree bears light green oval, pointed leaves which turn clear yellow in autumn. The flowers are later followed by cigar-shaped four-winged fruits up to 5cm (2in) long.

Popular species

Halesia carolina, syn. *H. tetraptera,* from the United States, is up to 7.5m (25ft) high and wide, often with a multi-stemmed trunk.

Halesia monticola, from the mountains of the south-eastern United States, is up to 7.5m (25ft)

high and wide with larger flowers and fruits than *H. carolina.* Varieties include: 'Rosea' (pale pink flowers) and *H. m. vestita* (larger white flowers, tinged pink).

Cultivation

Snowdrop tree requires moist, lime-free soil and a sunny, slightly sheltered position. It thrives in woodland conditions, in association with rhododendrons. Plant in mid autumn to early spring.

Pruning Long shoots may be shortened after flowering.

Pests and diseases Trouble free.

GOLDEN CHAIN – see *Laburnum*
GOLDEN RAIN TREE – see *Koelreuteria, Laburnum*

HANDKERCHIEF TREE – see *Davidia*
HAWTHORN – see *Crataegus*
HONEY LOCUST – see *Gleditsia*
HOP HORNBEAM – see *Ostrya*
HORNBEAM – see *Carpinus*
INDIAN BEAN TREE – see *Catalpa*
JUDAS TREE – see *Cercis*

Juglans
walnut

Juglans regia

Juglans nigra, foliage and fruit

Juglans regia, fruits

- ☐ Height at 25 years 7.5-12m (25-40ft)
- ☐ Mature height 25-30m (80-100ft)
- ☐ Spread 6-9m (20-30ft)
- ☐ Any fertile, well-drained soil
- ☐ Hardy broadleaf
- ☐ Features – handsome specimen tree; attractive foliage; nuts

The fast-growing walnut tree makes a handsome specimen for larger gardens with its broad, dense top and attractive foliage.

The large mid to light green leaves can be as much as 90cm (3ft) long and are divided into many oval leaflets which are aromatic when bruised. The tree bears catkins in spring followed later, when pollinated, by green fruits which open in autumn to reveal edible, wrinkled nuts.

Popular species
Juglans ailantifolia, syn. *J. sieboldiana* (Japanese walnut), is up to 7.5m (25ft) high and wide. The leaves are up to 90cm (3ft) long. It rarely fruits in Britain.

Juglans cinerea (butternut), from eastern North America, is up to 7.5m (25ft) high and wide. The hairy leaves are up to 50cm (20in) long. This tree bears larger nuts than other species.

Juglans nigra (black walnut), from the eastern United States, is up to 12m (40ft) high and 9m (30ft) wide with furrowed bark. The glossy leaves are up to 60cm (2ft) long; nuts have rough black shells.

Juglans regia (common walnut), from south-eastern Europe, the Himalayas and China, is up to 7.5m (25ft) high and 6m (20ft) wide. The glossy, leathery leaves are 20-45cm (8-18in) long and the nuts have brown, wrinkled shells. 'Laciniata', commonly known as cut-leaved walnut, has drooping branchlets and deeply cut leaflets.

Cultivation
Buy walnut trees when they are young as they do not transplant well. Plant in mid autumn to early spring in any fertile well-drained soil in an open site protected from late spring frosts.

Mulch annually in spring with well-rotted manure for the first few years until the tree is established. Trees do not fruit until they are at least eight years old; for regular crops, several trees should be planted to ensure cross-pollination.

Pruning Remove dead branches in late summer. Otherwise, no regular pruning is needed; walnuts 'bleed' profusely if cut in spring.

Pests and diseases
Squirrels and birds eat the nuts.
Gall mites cause blister-like pouches on the leaves.
Fungi may enter frost-damaged shoots, causing die-back.
Honey fungus rapidly kills trees.

Koelreuteria

golden rain tree

Koelreuteria paniculata

☐ Height at 25 years 6m (20ft)
☐ Mature height 12m (40ft) or more
☐ Spread 4.5m (15ft)
☐ Good loamy soil
☐ Hardy broadleaf
☐ Features – flowers; foliage; inflated
   seed pods

Golden rain tree (*Koelreuteria paniculata*), from China, is a beautiful and easy-to-care-for centrepiece for a sunny garden. Also known as pride of India and varnish tree, it is quite spectacular in mid to late summer when hundreds of yellow star-shaped flowers, held in panicles up to 30cm (1ft) long, appear at the tips of the shoots, turning the dense, round head into a mass of colour.

The fan-like mid green leaves are up to 45cm (1½ft) long and divided into many deeply toothed oval leaflets which are tinted yellow in autumn.

The flowers are followed by bladder-like green fruits which become flushed red as they ripen.

Golden rain tree is sparsely branched when young but becomes compact and broad-headed with age. The variety 'Fastigiata' is a rare, slow-growing, columnar tree.

Cultivation

Plant golden rain tree from mid autumn to early spring in good loamy soil and in full sun. Tolerant of town pollution and drought.

Pruning None required.

Pests and diseases Coral spot fungus enters through cuts and wounds, appearing as pink spots.

Koelreuteria paniculata, seed pods

Koelreuteria paniculata, flowers

Laburnum

golden rain, golden chain

Laburnum x *watereri* 'Vossii', flowers

☐ Height at 25 years 1.8-6m (6-20ft)
☐ Mature height 6-7.5m (20-25ft)
☐ Spread 1-4.5m (3-15ft)
☐ Any well-drained soil
☐ Hardy broadleaf
☐ Features – flowers

The light and airy laburnum, from central and southern Europe, is an elegant feature in late spring with its long drooping racemes of yellow pea-like flowers.

The tree is usually up to 6m (20ft) high and 4.5m (15ft) wide at maturity, and has small oval mid to light green leaves. All parts, especially the seeds, are poisonous. Laburnum is often short-lived – whole branches or trunks may suddenly die.

Popular species

Laburnum alpinum bears flower racemes 30cm (1ft) long or more. 'Pendulum', up to 1.8m (6ft) high and 1m (3ft) across, is slow-growing with a domed head and pendent branches.

Laburnum anagyroides (common laburnum) produces flower racemes 10-25cm (4-10in) long. 'Aureum' has soft yellow leaves and 'Pendulum' has slender drooping branches.

Laburnum x *watereri* has glossy leaves and slender flower racemes 25cm (10in) long or more. The variety 'Vossii' bears flower sprays up to 60cm (2ft) long and produces fewer seed pods.

Cultivation

Plant from mid autumn to early spring in any deep, well-drained soil. Stake young trees.

Pruning None required, but cut out weak branches and seed pods after flowering.

Pests and diseases Honey fungus and silver leaf may kill laburnum.

Laburnum anagyroides

Larix

larch

Larix decidua 'Pendula'

Larix kaempferi 'Nana'

☐ Height at 25 years 9-18m (30-60ft)
☐ Mature height 20-30m (65-100ft) or
   more
☐ Spread 5.5-9m (18-30ft)
☐ Any well-drained soil
☐ Hardy deciduous conifer
☐ Features – foliage; flowers; cones

Fast-growing larch – the only common deciduous conifer – is an elegant and graceful tree with wide-spreading, upward curving branches. The light twiggy outline makes it an attractive feature, even in winter. The needle-like leaves, which are softer than the foliage of other conifers, are pale green in spring, then turning bright green and finally golden or russet in autumn before they fall. They are borne in spirals on young shoots and in rosettes on spurs on older wood.

Male and female flowers occur in early spring on even young trees; the females are the most conspicuous, red, pale green or yellow. They are followed by attractive, small brown rounded cones that remain on the tree until the following winter. They are popular in flower arrangements.

Popular species
Larix decidua (European larch), from the European Alps, is up to 18m (60ft) high and 7.5m (25ft) wide. It is conical when young,

Larix decidua, young cones

broadening with maturity. 'Pendula' has downward-arching branches.

Larix kaempferi (Japanese larch), syn. *L. leptolepis*, up to 18m (60ft) high and 7.5m (25ft) wide, has young red shoots with sea-green foliage, broader than in the other species. The variety 'Blue Haze' has blue-green leaves; 'Nana' is compact and slow-growing, and 'Pendula' has long weeping branches.

Larix occidentalis (western larch), from North America, is the tallest of the larches, growing 18m (60ft) high with a spread of 6m (20ft). The yellow or pale orange shoots are clothed with glossy, grey-green foliage; the purple-brown cones are oblong, with pointed bracts protruding from between the scales.

Larix x *pendula* (weeping larch) grows 16m (52ft) tall, its pendulous branches sweeping down to the ground. The young pink shoots mature to purple by late summer.

Cultivation
Plant larch in any good soil that is deep and well-drained, in an open sunny position in late autumn or early spring. Buy young trees under 60cm (2ft) tall. Larch grows well in windy and exposed sites.

Pruning Prune out competing leading shoots, to leave the strongest. On mature specimen trees, the lowest branches can be cut off flush with the bole for a neat appearance.

Pests and diseases Adelgids eat leaves and stems, producing tufts of white waxy wool. Growth may be checked. Sawfly larvae feed on shoots. Harmless rust shows on the foliage as yellow bladder-like pustules.

LIME – see *Tilia*
LINDEN – see *Tilia*

Liquidambar

sweet gum

Liquidambar styraciflua

☐ Height at 25 years 7.5m (25ft)
☐ Mature height 15m (50ft) or more
☐ Spread 5m (17ft)
☐ Deep moist soil
☐ Hardy broadleaf
☐ Features – foliage; autumn colours

Few trees equal the fiery orange and red autumn tints of the magnificent sweet gum tree. It grows in a column or pyramid shape when young, but gradually spreads and broadens as it matures. The leaves are maple-like, glossy dark green and with three, five or seven lobes. Mature trees have rough grey furrowed bark and the twigs sometimes develop corky outgrowths. They make outstanding specimen trees in large gardens.

Popular species

Liquidambar formosana, a native of southern China and Taiwan, is up to 10m (33ft) high and 5m (17ft) wide. The three- or five-lobed leaves are red-tinted in spring, and have red or crimson autumn tints. The variety *L.f. monticola* has larger three-lobed leaves.

Liquidambar styraciflua, from the eastern United States, is up to 10m (33ft) high and 5m (17ft) across. The shiny dark green leaves have five or seven lobes and turn brilliant orange or scarlet in autumn. Varieties include: 'Golden Treasure' (slow-growing; deep yellow leaf edges); 'Lane Roberts' (rich dark crimson-red autumn tints); 'Moonbeam' (buttery cream variegations); and 'Variegata' (striped and mottled with yellow).

Cultivation

Plant sweet gum in deep moist but well-drained soil in a sheltered site from late autumn to early spring. Not suitable for shallow chalk.

Pruning Remove unwanted and crossed branches in late autumn.

For a round-headed tree with a straight trunk, grow to the desired height, then cut off the tip of the leading shoot to encourage branch development. The following year, reduce all new growths by one-third and remove all feathers and side-growths.

Pests and diseases Trouble free.

Liriodendron
tulip tree

Liriodendron tulipifera 'Fastigiatum'

☐ Height at 25 years 7.5m (25ft)
☐ Mature height 18m (60ft)
☐ Spread 4.5m (15ft) or more
☐ Any good well-drained soil
☐ Hardy broadleaf
☐ Features – attractive foliage; flowers

Grown for its handsome foliage and flowers, the tulip tree (*Liriodendron tulipifera*), from North America, is a stately and imposing specimen tree for larger gardens.

The light to mid green leaves, tinted butter-yellow in autumn, have four pointed lobes with a broad, squared-off tip. Mature trees, 15 to 20 years old, bear beautiful tulip-shaped flowers with prominent stamens in early and mid summer; they are yellowish-green marked with orange.

Varieties include 'Aureomarginatum' (leaves edged yellow or greenish yellow) and 'Fastigiatum' (broadly columnar).

Liriodendron tulipifera, flower

Cultivation
Plant from mid autumn to early spring in moist but well-drained garden soil in sun or light shade.
Pruning None required.
Pests and diseases Trouble free.

LOCUST – see *Robinia*

Magnolia
magnolia

Magnolia x *soulangiana*, flowers

☐ Height at 25 years 3-10m (10-33ft)
☐ Mature height 4.5-10m (15-33ft)
☐ Spread 3-6m (10-20ft) or more
☐ Well-drained loamy soil
☐ Generally hardy broadleaf
☐ Features – flowers; attractive leaves

Despite their exotic appearance, magnolia trees will grow in most British gardens in a protected site, providing a spectacular display both in leaf and in flower.

The exquisitely formed, chalice- or goblet-shaped flowers in shades of pink, purple and white often open out flat to a width of 25cm (10in). The leaves are generally broadly lance-shaped.

Most tree magnolias do not begin to flower until they are 15 to 20 years old. The shrubby magnolias (see pages 110-112) flower when they are still young.

Some species require lime-free soil, and early-flowering types should be protected from spring frosts and cold winds.

Popular species
Magnolia acuminata (cucumber tree), from the eastern United States, is a fast-growing, spreading, lime-tolerant tree up to 7.5m (25ft) high and 3.5m (12ft) across. The greenish-yellow flowers, about 7.5cm (3in) high, appear in early summer among the leaves and are followed later by cucumber-like purplish red fruits.
Magnolia campbellii (pink tulip tree), from the Himalayas, is up to

Magnolia denudata

Magnolia campbellii 'Charles Raffill'

10m (33ft) high and 5.5m (18ft) wide. The pink flowers appear before the leaves from late winter to early spring, opening out to reveal paler insides. Varieties include: *alba* (white); 'Charles Raffill' (pink-purple, white-stained within); 'Darjeeling' (deep rose); *mollicomata* (mauve-pink); and 'Wakehurst' (rose-purple, white-stained within). All dislike lime.

Magnolia cordata, sometimes listed as *Magnolia acuminata* var. *cordata*, is a fast-growing small tree eventually 7.5-9m (25-30ft) tall with a spread of 4.5-6m (15-20ft). A good shade tree from the south-eastern United States, it carries canary-yellow flowers among the foliage in mid summer and again in early autumn. It flowers while still quite young.

Magnolia denudata, syn *M. conspicua* (Yulan or lily tree), is a slow-growing tree from China that takes many years to reach 3m (10ft) high and wide. The fragrant, cup-shaped, pure white flowers open in profusion from early to late spring before the leaves unfurl. These are ovate, 15cm (6in) long, mid green above and white and downy beneath. The variety 'Purple Eye' has exceptionally large flowers, stained purple at the base.

Magnolia liliiflora, from China, is a small tree or large shrub up to 3m (10ft) high and wide. The narrow upright flowers are flushed purple on the outside, opening out flat to reveal a creamy inside. They appear in late spring and early summer. 'Nigra' has larger, darker flowers than the species. All but chalky soils are suitable.

Magnolia x *loebneri* is a lime-tolerant small tree or large shrub up to 7.5m (25ft) high and wide. The profuse, fragrant flowers have white, strap-shaped petals and appear in early spring before the leaves. The variety 'Leonard Messel' has lilac-pink flowers opening from darker buds.

Magnolia macrophylla is a spectacular tree of open habit from the south-eastern United States. Up to 6m (20ft) high and 5.5m (18ft) wide, it has light green leaves up to 90cm (3ft) long. The fragrant, purple-marked ivory flowers are up to 30cm (1ft) across and appear from early summer. This species needs shelter and lime-free soil.

Magnolia salicifolia (anise or willow-leaf magnolia), from Japan, is a broadly conical tree or large shrub up to 7.5m (25ft) high and 4m (13ft) across. It has narrow willow-like leaves and bears creamy flowers in spring before the foliage; it flowers while still young. When bruised, the leaves, bark and wood smell of lemons. Lime-free soil.

Magnolia x *soulangiana* is a

Magnolia x *loebneri* 'Leonard Messel'

Malus
crab apple

Malus x robusta

☐ Height at 25 years 4.5-6m (15-20ft)
☐ Mature height rarely more than 7.5m (25ft)
☐ Spread 1.2-6m (4-20ft)
☐ Ordinary, well-drained soil
☐ Hardy broadleaf
☐ Features – flowers; fruit; autumn tints

Magnolia x soulangiana

shrub or small tree with fragrant, purple-flushed, white tulip-shaped flowers appearing before the leaves in mid spring. Varieties which flower when young include: 'Alba Superba' (white); 'Brozzonii' (late-flowering, large white flowers, purple at base); 'Lennei' (large leaves, rose-purple flowers, creamy white, stained soft purple inside; sometimes flowers again in autumn); 'Picture' (purple, white inside); and 'Rustica Rubra' (cup-shaped, rosy red). All are best in lime-free soil.

Magnolia x *veitchii* is a vigorous tree, 12m (40ft) or more high at maturity, with a spread of 7.5m (25ft). It flowers from the age of 10 years, bearing blush pink, 25cm (10in) wide goblet flowers in mid spring before the leaves appear, opening purple and maturing to dark green, 25cm (10in) long. The variety 'Isca' is creamy-white.

Magnolia virginiana, syn. *M. glauca,* is a shrub or small tree from the eastern United States. Up to 6m (20ft) high and 3m (10ft) across, it retains its leaves in mild winters in warm areas and

tolerates lime. The waxy cream-white flowers are fragrant and measure about 7.5cm (3in) across. They appear throughout summer and are followed by red fruits.

Magnolia wilsonii, from western China, is a large shrub or a small tree up to 6m (20ft) high and wide. The scented, white flowers are saucer-shaped with red stamens and appear in summer. This species prefers partial shade.

Cultivation
Plant in early to mid spring in well-drained but moisture-retentive loamy soil in a site sheltered from north and east winds. For the first few years, stake the trees and top-dress annually in mid spring with organic matter. The majority dislikes lime.
Pruning None required.
Pests and diseases Grey mould may appear on frost-damaged shoots, causing die-back. Honey fungus kills trees.

MAIDENHAIR TREE – see *Ginkgo*

Flowering crab apple is one of the most beautiful of garden trees, in full bloom rivalling – and sometimes mistaken for – the outstanding, but less robust ornamental cherry (*Prunus*).

The clusters of bowl-shaped, single, semi-double or fully double flowers have golden anthers and cover the branches in white or in shades of pink and purple from late spring to early summer. The round or oval bright red or yellow fruits (crab apples) may be the size of plump cherries or as big as golf balls. They provide a magnificent display in autumn, and sometimes remain on the branches long after the leaves have fallen. Many are excellent for making into preserves.

The trees may be round-headed, weeping, narrow or spreading with long arching branches; most of those offered by nurseries are grafted standards, with the head of branches beginning at 0.9-1.2m (3-4ft) or more above a clear trunk. The slightly pointed oval leaves are generally mid green and finely toothed.

Malus x purpurea

Malus tschonoskii, autumn

Popular species

Malus baccata (Siberian crab), from Asia, is an ultra-hardy rounded tree up to 5.5m (18ft) high and 6m (20ft) wide with fragrant white flowers and red or yellow fruits. The variety *mandshurica* flowers earlier and has slightly larger fruits than the species.

Malus floribunda (Japanese crab) is a beautiful rounded tree with long arching branches. Up to 4.5m (15ft) high and wide, it has mid green, narrowly oval, coarsely toothed leaves and profuse blush-pink flowers opening from crimson buds. The fruits are yellow.

Malus hupehensis, from China and Japan, is up to 6m (20ft) high and wide, with stiff ascending branches and deep green, oval, sharply serrated leaves. Profuse scented white flowers open from pink buds in late spring to early summer, followed by red-tinted yellow fruits.

Malus x purpurea is up to 6m (20ft) high and 3m (10ft) wide. It has purple-flushed, mid green oval leaves and profuse, single rosy red flowers in mid spring. The small fruits are dull purple.

Malus x robusta (cherry crab, sometimes wrongly called Siberian crab), up to 5.5m (18ft) high and 6m (20ft) wide, has white or pink flowers and profuse cherry-like red or yellow fruits about 2.5cm (1in) across that remain on the tree into winter. Varieties include: 'Red Siberian' (red fruits) and 'Yellow Siberian'.

Malus spectabilis, originally cultivated in China, is a small tree up to 4.5m (15ft) high and wide. It has glossy leaves and double blush-pink flowers up to 5cm (2in) across, opening from deep rose-red buds. Varieties include 'Riversii' with upright branches and semi-double rosy pink flowers.

Malus tschonoskii, from Japan, is a conical tree up to 6m (20ft) high and 1.8m (6ft) across. It has white, pink-tinged flowers and coarsely toothed leaves with fine orange, scarlet and purple autumn tints. The brownish fruits are rather insignificant.

Hybrids are generally round-headed, 4.5-6m (15-20ft) high and 3-5.5m (10-18ft) across. They include: 'Golden Hornet' (white flowers, yellow fruits up to 2.5cm/1in across); 'John Downie' (white flowers, conical orange and red fruits 3cm/1¼in across); 'Katherine' (semi-double pink fading to white flowers up to 5cm/2in wide, tiny bright red yellow-flushed fruits); 'Lemoinei' (purple foliage, crimson-purple flowers, bronze autumn colours);

Malus floribunda

Mespilus
medlar

Malus x robusta, flowers

Malus 'Golden Hornet', fruits

Mespilus germanica, fruits

☐ Height at 25 years 4.5m (15ft)
☐ Mature height 6m (20ft)
☐ Spread 5.5m (18ft)
☐ Ordinary well-drained soil
☐ Hardy broadleaf
☐ Features – picturesque form; flowers; fruit

'Prince George' (late flowering, double, scented pale pink flowers); 'Profusion' (spreading, young leaves purplish, profuse wine-red flowers, dark red fruits); 'Red Jade' (weeping, pink and white flowers, small but profuse, long-lasting red fruits); 'Red Sentinel' (white flowers, profuse, very long-lasting, large dark red fruits); and 'Van Eseltine' (narrow tree, up to 5.5m/18ft high, 1.2m/4ft wide, semi-double shell-pink flowers, yellow fruits).

Cultivation
Crab apple thrives in any ordinary well-drained soil enriched with organic matter. Plant in sun or partial shade from mid autumn to early spring. To obtain the best crops, plant several varieties close together.

Stake until established. Mulch young trees annually in mid spring with well-rotted manure. Specimen trees grown on lawns need a grass-free root run of 90cm-1.2m (3-4ft) for several years until well established.

Pruning Remove dead or straggly shoots in late winter.

To train a standard tree, cut the main stem back to 15cm (6in) above the desired trunk height in early spring. The following early spring cut back the resulting three or four shoots to 30cm (1ft). Any shoots on the trunk below the top branches should be pinched back to three or four leaves. Any further feathering shoots should be pinched back in summer. Do not remove these spurs for at least two years as they help to thicken the trunk.

Pests and diseases
Aphids infest shoots, leaves and fruit. Woolly aphids cover branches and twigs with tufts of white waxy wool, and often encourage the growth of disfiguring galls.

Apple mildew shows as a white powdery deposit on new growth. Severely diseased foliage may wither and fall.

Apple scab produces black or brown scabs on the fruits and olive green blotches on foliage, which may fall prematurely. Small blister-like pimples develop on the shoots; they later crack the bark leaving ring-like scabs.

Capsid bugs cause distorted and tattered leaves; some buds may fail to develop.

Caterpillars feed on leaves and buds.

Fruit tree red spider mites attack the underside of leaves. With severe infestations, leaves turn bronze, wither and fall.

Honey fungus may kill trees.

MAPLE – see *Acer*
MAY – see *Crataegus*
MEDLAR – see *Mespilus*

The medlar tree (*Mespilus germanica*) is picturesque even in winter with its wide-spreading, rather crooked and thorny branches. It makes an ornamental specimen tree for a lawn.

The finely toothed, dull green leaves develop rich russet and yellow tints in autumn. Large saucer-shaped white flowers appear singly in late spring to early summer, followed by round brown fruits with five stiff leafy structures (calyces). They are edible when half-rotten and soft. Medlar originates from south-eastern Europe and Turkey.

Cultivation
Plant medlar from mid autumn to early spring in an open sunny position in ordinary, well-drained but moisture-retentive soil enriched with decayed manure. Stake until established and mulch annually in spring.

Pruning Most trees are offered as grafted standards and require no pruning. On untrained trees, cut back all lateral shoots to two or three leaf buds in mid autumn or early spring. When the tree has reached the desired height, pinch out the leading shoots to encourage bushy growth.

Pests and diseases Trouble free.

Metasequoia

dawn redwood

Metasequoia glyptostroboides

- ☐ Height at 25 years 12m (40ft)
- ☐ Mature height 15m (50ft)
- ☐ Spread 4.5m (15ft)
- ☐ Any fertile moist soil
- ☐ Hardy deciduous conifer
- ☐ Features – attractive form and foliage tints; shaggy bark

The first living specimen of the vigorous dawn redwood (*Metasequoia glyptostroboides*), previously only known as a fossil, was discovered in China in 1941.

This decorative conifer forms a slim cone with shaggy cinnamon-brown bark. The feathery, needle-like leaves are light green in spring, darkening to mid green in summer and turning pink and deep red and finally golden brown in autumn.

Cultivation

Dawn redwood likes any good, moist but well-drained soil; light woodland or the edge of a pool are ideal. Plant trees 30-90cm (1-3ft) tall from late autumn to early winter. Keep the soil round the base free from grass for several years and scatter nitro-chalk over the root run three times annually during the growing season.

Pruning If necessary, prune to maintain a single leader.

Pests and diseases Honey fungus can kill trees.

Morus

mulberry

Morus nigra

- ☐ Height at 25 years 4.5m (15ft)
- ☐ Mature height 4.5-7.5m (15-25ft)
- ☐ Spread 4.5m (15ft)
- ☐ Deep, rich moist soil
- ☐ Hardy broadleaf
- ☐ Features – ornamental foliage; fruits; gnarled form

The delightful mulberry tree makes a picturesque feature for gardens where space is limited and it thrives in seaside locations, if sheltered from gales. In summer it casts dense shade with its wide-spreading canopy of rough heart-shaped leaves on branches which become increasingly gnarled and rugged.

The insignificant green catkins are followed by fruits resembling blackberries – particularly delicious in the black mulberry.

Popular species

Morus alba (white mulberry), a rugged looking tree from China, was originally cultivated for its foliage, which is used to feed silkworms. About 4.5m (15ft) high and wide, it has heart-shaped or oval to lance-shaped leaves up to 15cm (6in) long. The white fruits, which are sweet but rather insipid, ripen to red-pink. The variety 'Pendula' has dense, pendulous branches.

Morus nigra (black or common mulberry), from western Asia, is a long-lived tree up to 4.5m (15ft) high and wide. It develops a gnarled and picturesque appearance as it matures and has rough,

Morus nigra, foliage and fruits

coarsely toothed, heart-shaped leaves up to 20cm (8in) long. The tasty dark red fruits are up to 2.5cm (1in) long and stain paths where they fall.

Cultivation

Plant mulberry trees in deep, rich loamy soil, well-drained but moisture-retentive. Plant in autumn.

Pruning Remove dead wood and crossing branches from established trees in winter. Avoid unnecessary pruning as the trees bleed.

Pests and diseases Canker and die-back are due to a fungus which can girdle a tree.

MOUNTAIN ASH – see *Sorbus*
MULBERRY – see *Morus*

Nothofagus

southern beech

Nothofagus obliqua

Nothofagus obliqua, flowers

Nothofagus obliqua, bark

☐ Height at 25 years 9-15m (30-50ft)
☐ Mature height 9-18m (30-60ft) or more
☐ Spread 4.5-9m (15-30ft)
☐ Deep, well-drained, lime-free soil
☐ Hardy broadleaf
☐ Features – glossy foliage; autumn tints

Closely related to the beech tree (*Fagus*), but with smaller leaves, southern beech is an ideal tree for large, sheltered gardens and for town planting.

Deciduous southern beeches are rapid growers of upright columnar or broad-headed habit, and make excellent specimen trees. The branches are densely covered with ovate or heart-shaped, toothed, glossy green leaves that assume handsome autumn colours of yellow and red. Insignificant greenish flowers are followed by bristly fruit cases (mast) with three small nuts.

The species described are all native to Chile.

Popular species

Nothofagus antarctica (Antarctic beech) forms an elegant, open tree up to 12m (40ft) high and 6m (20ft) across. The heart-shaped leaves turn yellow in autumn. Trunk and main branches are often twisted.

Nothofagus obliqua (roble beech) is a fast-growing tree up to 15m (50ft) high and 9m (30ft) across. It has arching branches and larger leaves than the other species.

Nothofagus procera grows rapidly to 18m (60ft) high and 4.5m (15ft) or more wide. The oval, 10cm (4in) long leaves are prominently veined and finely toothed; they take on golden-yellow and scarlet autumn colours.

Cultivation

Plant from late autumn to early spring in a site sheltered from strong winds. The trees grow well in any good well-drained soil but will not tolerate chalk.

Pruning None required.

Pests and diseases Trouble free.

Nyssa

tupelo

Nyssa sylvatica, autumn

- ☐ Height at 25 years 7.5-9m (25-30ft)
- ☐ Mature height up to 15m (50ft)
- ☐ Spread 4.5-5.5m (15-18ft)
- ☐ Moist, lime-free soil
- ☐ Hardy broadleaf
- ☐ Features – autumn foliage; pyramidal shape

Throughout much of the year, tupelo is a handsome if unremarkable tree, but it is truly spectacular in autumn with its foliage in shades of scarlet , orange and yellow. It is especially effective when grown near water, where the autumn colouring can be reflected.

Also known as black gum, this moisture-loving tree has glossy mid green, pointed oval leaves, which often develop their autumn colour earlier than other trees.

The insignificant flowers are followed by small, blue-black fruits.

Popular species

Nyssa sinensis, a rare species from China, is a large shrub or small tree up to 7.5m (25ft) high and 4.5m (15ft) across, with narrow oval leaves up to 15cm (6in) long and 5cm (2in) across. The leaves are tinted red or purple when young, and turn many shades of red and orange in autumn.

Nyssa sylvatica grows wild in the eastern United States. Up to 9m (30ft) high and 5.5m (18ft) across, it eventually reaches 15m (50ft) high or more. It has gleaming mid green, pointed oval leaves which develop brilliant scarlet, red and

orange shades in autumn. Varieties include 'Jermyns Flame' (vivid orange and flame-coloured autumn tints) and 'Sheffield Park' (rich autumn tints two or three weeks earlier than the species.)

Cultivation

Plant young trees from mid autumn to early spring in moist, lime-free soil in sun or partial shade. They resent disturbance.
Pruning None required.
Pests and diseases Trouble free.

OAK – see *Quercus*
ORNAMENTAL ALMOND/
CHERRY/PLUM – see *Prunus*

Ostrya

hop hornbeam

Ostrya carpinifolia, fruit

☐ Height at 25 years 6-7.5m (20-25ft)
☐ Mature height 9-18m (30-60ft)
☐ Spread 5.5-6m (18-20ft)
☐ Any well-drained soil
☐ Hardy broadleaf
☐ Features – catkins; fruits; bark

Closely resembling true hornbeam (*Carpinus*), hop hornbeams are handsome ornamental trees, which are easy to grow and are outstanding for their catkins in spring and for their hop-like fruits and fine foliage in autumn.

Ostrya virginiana

Popular species

Ostrya carpinifolia grows about 7.5m (25ft) high and 6m (20ft) wide. The short trunk has rough bark beneath a dense round head. The oval, toothed leaves are mid green and about 10cm (4in) long; they take on clear yellow autumn tints. In early spring, the tree is decked with a profusion of drooping yellow-green male catkins; the pendent hop-like fruit clusters add to the tree's attraction in autumn.

Ostrya japonica, Japanese hop hornbeam, is similar to *O. carpinifolia,* but smaller and with leaves that are velvety underneath. It is outstanding in autumn, with green seed husks up to 12.5cm (5in) long.

Ostrya virginiana, ironwood, from the eastern United States, is slow-growing, but eventually reaches a height of 9m (30ft), with a similar spread when fully grown. It is a graceful conical-shaped tree with spreading branches which, in spite of their slenderness, are extremely tough and wind-resistant, hence the common name. It has hairy shoots and mid green leaves which turn warm golden-yellow in autumn. In early spring, the tree is adorned with clusters of green catkins. In autumn the seed husks resemble the fruits of the hop (*Humulus lupulus*).

Cultivation

Plant ostryas during suitable weather from mid autumn until early spring. They grow in any type of good soil that is well-drained but moisture-retentive, and in full sun or light shade. They are not suitable for shallow chalky soils.

Pruning Mature trees require no pruning; on young trees, crossing and weak branches can be removed in late winter or early spring in order to control shape.

Pests and diseases Generally trouble free.

PAGODA TREE – see *Sophora*

Parrotia

parrotia

Parrotia persica, autumn

☐ Height at 25 years 4.5m (15ft)
☐ Mature height 4.5-6m (15-20ft)
☐ Spread 7.5m (25ft)
☐ Well-drained loamy soil
☐ Hardy broadleaf
☐ Features – autumn foliage; bark; winter flowers

The lovely parrotia tree (*Parrotia persica*), from northern Iran to the Caucasus Mountains, provides interest all year with its leafy, spreading top, fine autumn tints, winter flowers and flaking bark.

This attractive tree is slow-growing, naturally developing a single short trunk or several stems growing from the base. It can be pruned to a single trunk or left to develop into a spreading shrub. With age, the grey bark flakes off to reveal large patches of silver-white or golden new bark underneath.

The rounded oval leaves, up to 10cm (4in) long, are mid green, and develop beautiful amber, crimson and golden tints before they fall. In winter curious flowers, consisting mainly of prominent red stamens, appear on the leafless branches.

Parrotia persica, flowers

The variety 'Pendula' has pendent branches and forms a small dome-shaped tree.

Cultivation

Plant in well-drained soil from mid autumn to early spring. The tree thrives in neutral to slightly acid soil but is also tolerant of lime and shallow chalk. Although it will flourish in light shade, the finest autumn colours occur in a sunny position.

Pruning None required.

Pests and diseases Trouble free.

Parrotia persica, bark

Paulownia

foxglove tree, princess tree

Paulownia tomentosa

Paulownia tomentosa, flowers

☐ Height at 25 years 9-10m (30-33ft)
☐ Mature height 9-18m (30-60ft) or more
☐ Spread 7-9m (23-30ft)
☐ Deep, well-drained, loamy soil
☐ Hardy broadleaf
☐ Features – foxglove-like flowers; foliage

One of the grandest of ornamental flowering trees, foxglove tree is quite spectacular in full bloom, with upright sprays of foxglove-like flowers held above heart-shaped leaves up to 30cm (1ft) across.

The flower buds of these dense, round-topped trees are fully formed in autumn and may be killed by prolonged frosts before they open the following late spring or early summer on well-established trees.

The trees are sometimes pruned hard back to the ground (stooled) each year and grown as spot or accent plants. With this treatment, the vigorous shoots will grow up to 3m (10ft) high in a season, bearing leaves up to 60cm (2ft) across, but no flowers.

Popular species

Paulownia fargesii, from western China, is up to 10m (33ft) high and 7m (23ft) wide after 25 years and may eventually reach a height of over 18m (60ft). It has mid green heart-shaped leaves which end in slender points. The fragrant pale lilac flowers with purple-speckled throats are up to 6cm (2¼in) long and appear in early summer. This tree flowers at an earlier age than the better-known *P. tomentosa*.

Paulownia tomentosa, syn. *P. imperialis*, from China, is up to 9m (30ft) high and wide. The fragrant flowers, slightly darker and smaller than those of *P. fargesii*, appear in late spring. The mid green leaves are heart-shaped.

Cultivation

Plant in a sunny sheltered position from mid autumn to early spring in deep, well-drained loamy soil. Tolerant of pollution, the trees cast dense shade and litter the ground in autumn with leaf pods and huge fallen leaves.

Pruning Normally no pruning is required. However, if grown as a stooled plant, the foxglove tree should be cut down to ground level every year in early spring.

Pests and diseases Honey fungus may cause the rapid death of trees. Leaf spot shows as irregular yellow-brown lesions, which later turn grey, or as spots with dark margins.

PEAR, ORNAMENTAL – see *Pyrus*
PLUM, ORNAMENTAL – see *Prunus*

Populus

poplar

Populus trichocarpa

☐ Height at 25 years 7.5-18m (25-60ft)
☐ Mature height 15-30m (50-100ft)
☐ Spread 2.5-9m (8-30ft)
☐ Ordinary garden soil
☐ Hardy broadleaf
☐ Features – foliage; fast-growing

Poplars are fast-growing trees which are highly ornamental, tolerant of pollution and provide useful windbreaks for exposed sites.

Popular species

Populus alba (white poplar, abele), up to 12m (40ft) high and 9m (30ft) wide, has grey-green lobed leaves with white woolly undersides; they take on yellow autumn tints. Pyramidalis ('Bolleana') is conical, with erect branches.
Populus balsamifera (balsam poplar), syn. *P. tacamahacca*, up to 12m (40ft) high and 6m (20ft) wide, has oval leaves which are white on the underside and smell of balsam when unfurling.
Populus x *canadensis* describes a large group of trees known as the black poplar hybrids. Usually up to 18m (60ft) high and columnar in shape, they include: 'Eugenei' (young leaves coppery); 'Robusta'

Populus x *candicans* 'Aurora'

(young leaves coppery); 'Serotina' (open habit, young leaves bronze); and 'Serotina Aurea' (young golden leaves mature through yellowish-green to golden in autumn).
Populus x *candicans* is similar to *P. balsamifera* but broader. 'Aurora', one of the best poplars for smaller gardens, has creamy white, pink-tinged leaves.
Populus lasiocarpa (Chinese poplar), up to 12m (40ft) high and 5m (17ft) wide, has bright green, heart-shaped leathery leaves with red veins and stalks.
Populus nigra betulifolia (Manchester poplar), up to 15m (50ft) high and 9m (30ft) wide, is a bushy-headed tree with downy young shoots. *P. n.* 'Italica' (Lombardy poplar) is a dense, narrowly columnar tree up to 15m (50ft) high and 2.5m (8ft) wide.
Populus tremula (aspen), similar to *P. alba* but smaller, has toothed leaves. 'Pendula' (weeping aspen) has drooping branches, attractive in winter when they are draped with purple-grey catkins.
Populus trichocarpa (black cottonwood) is similar to *P. balsamifera*, but grows rapidly to 18m (60ft) high and 6m (20ft) wide.

Cultivation

Plant in any type of garden soil in a sunny open position from late autumn to early spring. Position the tallest types at least 30m (100ft) from buildings and drains, which can be damaged by the roots.
Pruning None required.
Pests and diseases Bacterial canker, bracket fungus, rust and silver leaf may cause problems.

PRINCESS TREE – see *Paulownia*

Prunus

cherry, almond, plum

Prunus padus, flowers

☐ Height at 25 years 3.5-12m (12-40ft)
☐ Mature height up to 12m (40ft)
☐ Spread 1.5-9m (5-30ft)
☐ Any ordinary soil
☐ Hardy broadleaf
☐ Features – flowers; autumn foliage

The large *Prunus* genus includes some of our most beautiful flowering trees – ornamental almonds, cherries and plums. They bloom from late winter onwards, before or at the same time as the leaves unfold, and many have outstanding autumn colours.

Prunus species and varieties make spectacular specimen trees, with types to suit the smallest gardens. For shrubby kinds, see pages 122-124.

Popular species

Ornamental almonds flower in early spring before the toothed lance-shaped leaves appear. The green fruits rarely ripen.
Prunus x *amygdalo-persica* 'Pollardii', up to 4.5m (15ft) high and 3m (10ft) wide, has large rich pink flowers.
Prunus dulcis (common almond), syn. *P. amygdalus*, is up to 7.5m (25ft) high and wide with soft pink flowers. 'Roseoplena' has double pink flowers, and 'Alba' is white.
Ornamental cherries have toothed, pointed oval leaves and dense clusters or sprays of flowers from early to late spring.
Prunus avium (wild or mazzard cherry), up to 12m (40ft) high and 9m (30ft) wide, has crimson autumn tints. Pendent clusters of white flowers appear in mid-spring followed by dark red fruits. 'Plena' has profuse double flowers.

47

Prunus serrula, bark

Prunus sargentii, autumn

Prunus avium 'Plena'

Prunus 'Kanzan'

Prunus padus (bird cherry), up to 11m (36ft) high and 6m (20ft) wide, has drooping sprays of small white, almond-scented flowers in late spring, and black fruits. Varieties include: 'Albertii' (erect, profuse flowers); 'Colorata' (coppery young foliage, pale pink flowers); 'Plena' (double flowers); and 'Watereri' (flower sprays up to 20cm/8in long).

Prunus sargentii, a round-headed tree up to 9m (30ft) high and wide, has rich brown bark. The foliage is bronze-red in spring and orange and crimson in early autumn. The large, clear pink flowers appear from early spring. This tree dislikes pollution.

Prunus serotina (black or rum cherry), up to 11m (36ft) high and 9m (30ft) across, has glossy, deep green leaves with yellow autumn tints. Sprays up to 15cm (6in) long of white flowers appear in late spring to early summer.

Prunus serrula is up to 4.5m (15ft) high and wide. It has glistening, mahogany-brown flaking bark, narrow leaves and small white flowers in mid spring.

Prunus subhirtella (spring cherry), up to 6m (20ft) high and wide, bears profuse pale pink flowers in early spring before the leaves appear. The tree has black fruits and handsome autumn coloured foliage. Varieties include: 'Autum-

nalis' (autumn cherry, semi-double white or pale pink flowers in mild spells from late autumn to early spring); 'Autumnalis Rosea' (semi-double, pink flowers from late autumn); 'Fukubana' (semi-double, deep pink); 'Pendula Rosea' (drooping branches, blush pink); and 'Pendula Rubra' (drooping branches, rose-pink flowers).

Japanese cherries, usually up to 6m (20ft) high and wide, with bronze young leaves and flowers in mid to late spring, include: 'Amanogawa' (erect and narrow, to 6m/20ft high, 1.5/5ft across, semi-double, pale pink); 'Asano' (broad-headed, large double mauve-pink flowers); 'Cheal's

Prunus 'Amanogawa'

Prunus subhirtella 'Fukubana'

Prunus cerasifera 'Pissardii'

Weeping' (often sold as 'Kiku Shidare Sakura', weeping, deep pink, double); 'Fudanzakura' (pink buds, white flowers, late autumn to mid spring); 'Fugenzo' (dense, flat-topped tree, large double rose-pink flowers); 'Jo-nioi' (white); 'Kanzan' (popular, vase-shaped tree, purple-pink double flowers); 'Mount Fuji' (wide-spreading, often weeping at branch tips; long drooping clusters of fragrant, pure white flowers in mid spring); 'Ojochin' (pink flowers); 'Pink Perfection' (vase-shaped tree, clear pink); 'Shirofugen' (drooping branches, orange autumn tints, large double white flowers, turning purple-pink, late spring); 'Tai Haku' (robust tree, large single, glistening white flowers with young copper-red leaves); and 'Ukon' (red, copper and purple autumn tints, large, semi-double greenish yellow flowers).

Ornamental plums have oval, narrow and purple leaves.

Prunus x blireana is a small tree or large shrub up to 3.5m (12ft) high and 4.5m (15ft) wide. Double rose-pink flowers appear in early to mid spring just before the bronze young leaves which eventually turn green.

Prunus cerasifera (cherry plum), a bushy tree up to 5.5m (18ft) high and wide, is useful for hedging. It bears profuse white flowers in late winter before the mid green leaves appear. Mature trees bear red or yellow small fruits. Varieties include: 'Nigra' (black-purple leaves and pink flowers); 'Pissardii' ('Atropurpurea', dark red young leaves turning deep purple, white flowers opening from pink buds).

Cultivation
Plant in autumn in any well-drained soil. The trees thrive on alkaline soil.

Pruning Remove crossing and damaged shoots in late summer.

Pests and diseases Birds may eat young winter buds. Aphids may infest leaves and shoots and caterpillars sometimes eat the leaves. Troublesome diseases include canker, chlorosis, honey fungus, silver leaf and witches' brooms.

Pterocarya
Caucasian wingnut

Pterocarya fraxinifolia, fruits

☐ Height at 25 years 10m (33ft)
☐ Mature height up to 24m (80ft)
☐ Spread 9m (30ft)
☐ Any moist, fertile soil
☐ Hardy broadleaf
☐ Features – foliage; catkins; fruits

Caucasian wingnut (*Pterocarya fraxinifolia*, syn. *P. caucasica*) is as handsome as its better-known relative the walnut (*Juglans*). It is a fast-growing tree with a broad, spreading top and is decorated in autumn with long, dangling strings of winged fruits.

The leaves are up to 60cm (2ft) long and are divided into numerous finely toothed leaflets, each up to 20cm (8in) long. The greenish catkins, which appear in summer, are up to 50cm (20in) long. The tree usually has a short thick trunk with deeply furrowed bark. Occasionally, however, it forms a thicket of several stems.

The hybrid *P. x rehderiana* has long-lasting catkins and fruits.

Cultivation
Plant young Caucasian wingnuts in mid autumn to early spring in any fertile and deep, moist soil in an open site. These trees do well by water.
Pruning None required, but competing stems can be pruned out in summer.
Pests and diseases Gall mites cause blister-like pouches on the leaves. Fungi may enter frost-damaged shoots, causing die-back. Honey fungus kills trees.

Pyrus
ornamental pear

Pyrus salicifolia 'Pendula'

☐ Height at 25 years 3-7.5m (10-25ft)
☐ Mature height up to 9m (30ft)
☐ Spread 1.8-5.5m (6-18ft)
☐ Any well-drained soil
☐ Hardy broadleaf
☐ Features – foliage; flowers; autumn tints

An ornamental pear is a fine sight in the middle of a lawn, flourishing even in cold areas and tolerant of sea winds and both wet and dry soils. The genus *Pyrus*, which includes the common fruiting pear, provides a fine range of beautiful specimen trees for large and small gardens, with their profuse clusters of snowy flowers and pale foliage.

The toothed leaves, generally up to 10cm (4in) long, are green or grey-green, and sometimes glossy. Some species develop rich autumn tints in shades of bronze, crimson, orange or yellow. The five-petalled flowers are white or creamy white and appear in clusters in mid spring, though *P. ussuriensis* flowers in early spring. They are followed later by small rounded or pear-shaped fruits which are generally rather inconspicuous and largely inedible.

Popular species
Pyrus calleryana, a Chinese tree up to 6m (20ft) high and 3.5m (12ft) across, has thorny branches and oval, glossy green, finely toothed leaves. The small fruits are brownish. The variety 'Chanticleer' is a conical and narrow free-flowering tree without thorns and grows up to 5.5m (18ft) high and 3m (10ft) wide.
Pyrus communis 'Beech Hill', a narrow form of the common pear, is up to 6m (20ft) high and 1.8m (6ft) wide. The rounded to oval glossy leaves have fine yellow and orange autumn tints. Profuse white flowers appear in mid spring, followed later by brown, sweet, edible fruits.
Pyrus nivalis (snow pear), from southern Europe, is up to 5m (16ft) high and wide. The profuse white flowers appear with the silvery grey young leaves. The small rounded fruits are yellowish green and sweet-tasting.
Pyrus salicifolia (willow-leaved pear), a graceful tree from the Caucasus, is up to 5.5m (18ft) high and 4.5m (15ft) wide, and often weeping. The narrow wil-

Quercus

oak

Pyrus ussuriensis 'Hondoensis', flowers

Quercus rubra 'Aurea'

low-like leaves are silvery at first, later becoming grey-green. The creamy white flowers are followed by small brownish fruits. The variety 'Pendula' has weeping branches, often right to the ground, and more silvery foliage.
Pyrus ussuriensis (Chinese pear) is up to 7.5m (25ft) high and 5.5m (18ft) wide. The oval or rounded leaves have bristly teeth and turn bronze-crimson in autumn. Profuse white flowers appear in early spring, followed later by rounded yellowish fruits.

Cultivation

Plant ornamental pear trees in any well-drained soil in a sunny position during suitable weather from late autumn to early spring. They are exceptionally frost-hardy and resistant to pollution.
Pruning None required, except to maintain shape, which should be done in winter or early spring.

Pests and diseases

Aphids may infest young growths. Black sooty mould grows on their sticky deposits, and young leaves are distorted.
Apple canker causes egg-shaped cankers on the bark.
Fireblight blackens and shrivels the flowers and kills young shoots and branches. Leaves turn brown and shrivel, but do not fall. Cankers appear in autumn.
Honey fungus can kill trees rapidly.

- ☐ Height at 25 years 4.5-12m (15-40ft)
- ☐ Mature height up to 30m (100ft)
- ☐ Spread 3-9m (10-30ft)
- ☐ Any ordinary garden soil
- ☐ Hardy broadleaf
- ☐ Features – foliage; fruits; attractive form

The noble English oak (*Q. robur*) belongs to a group of distinctive trees from as far afield as America, Europe and Africa. Though many oaks are slow to establish, they are long-lived, usually with the characteristic broad, spreading head of branches, attractively lobed leaves and rich autumn tints. They have curious fruits (acorns), consisting of an oval nut in a saucer-like husk.

Oaks make fine specimen trees for larger gardens.

Popular species

Quercus alba (white oak) is an American species, 10-12m (33-40ft) tall with an equal spread. The horizontal branches bear oval, irregularly lobed leaves which, in spite of their name, open pinkish-red, mature to soft green and turn purple-crimson in autumn.
Quercis cerris (Turkey oak) is up to 10m (33ft) high and 6m (20ft) wide. It is the fastest-growing of all oaks and does well on deep chalk and by the sea. It has deeply lobed, green, hairy leaves and the acorns have mossy cups. The cultivar 'Variegata' has wide creamy-white margins to the leaves.
Quercus coccinea (scarlet oak) is up to 12m (40ft) high and 9m (30ft) wide and hates lime. It has toothed, lobed, glossy green leaves, scarlet in autumn, and persisting well into winter. 'Splendens' has especially rich scarlet autumn tints.
Quercus robur (English oak), syn. *Q. pedunculata*, is a native, slow-growing, spreading and long-lived species up to 20m (65ft) high and 15m (50ft) wide after 50 years, but eventually reaching a height of 30m (100ft). The mid to deep green leaves have rounded lobes and very short stalks, while the acorns are set on long stalks. Varieties include: 'Concordia' (golden oak, slow-growing, rounded tree up to 4.5m/15ft high and wide, golden yellow leaves); 'Fastigiata' (columnar); 'Fastigiata Purpurea' (columnar, smaller than 'Fastigiata', young leaves purple); and 'Pendula' (a small, weeping tree).
Quercus rubra is a rounded tree up to 9m (30ft) high and wide. The leaves have deep, pointed lobes and develop red, yellow and brown autumn tints. It grows fairly fast and is resistant to air pollution. The variety 'Aurea' has

Quercus robur 'Concordia'

Quercus cerris 'Variegata', foliage

bright yellow young leaves; it does best in light shade.

Cultivation

Grow oak trees in any rich, deep and well-drained garden soil, preferably in an open site in full sun, though they tolerate partial shade. Apart from *Q. alba* and *Q. rubra*, all are lime-tolerant and will flourish on deep chalky soil; shallow chalk is unsuitable. Plant from mid autumn to early spring. During the first few years apply an annual mulch of well-rotted organic matter.

Pruning Remove lateral branches in late winter when the trees are two to three years old to maintain a clean trunk.

Pests and diseases

Bracket fungi may enter dead wood and cause rotting of the heartwood.

Caterpillars and chafer beetles eat the leaves.

Honey fungus can kill trees.

Oak phylloxera insects form colonies on the undersides of leaves and may cause extensive discoloration and leaf fall.

Powdery mildew shows as a white powdery deposit.

REDBUD – see *Cercis*
REDWOOD – see *Metasequoia*

Rhus

sumach

Rhus typhina, autumn

Rhus typhina, fruits

Rhus typhina

☐ Height at 25 years 4.5-6m (15-20ft)
☐ Mature height up to 7.5m (25ft)
☐ Spread 4.5-6m (15-20ft)
☐ Any ordinary garden soil
☐ Hardy broadleaf
☐ Features – interesting foliage and
  bark; flowers; autumn tints

Sumachs are outstanding small garden trees, with attractive foliage developing dramatic autumn tints in shades of red, orange, yellow and purple. In summer they produce dense and fluffy upright sprays of creamy or greenish flowers, followed later on female trees by showy clusters of red fruits.

The leaves, which are 15-60cm (6-24in) long, are divided into many coarsely toothed leaflets.

For shrubby sumach, see page 128.

Popular species

Rhus chinensis (Chinese sumach) is a round-headed tree or large shrub from Japan, China and Korea to Malaysia. Up to 6m (20ft) high and 4.5m (15ft) across, it has leaves up to 15cm (6in) long with rich autumn tints. The creamy-white flower sprays are up to 25cm (10in)

high and appear in late summer. This species does best in mild, sheltered gardens; late growths may be cut back by frost.

Rhus typhina (stag's-horn sumach), from eastern North America, is a small tree or large shrub eventually up to 7.5m (25ft) high and wide. It is flat-topped with sparse, spreading branches, giving a gaunt appearance in winter. The young shoots, leaves and fruits are covered with soft velvety hairs. The mid green leaves are up to 60cm (2ft) long and divided into numerous toothed leaflets. From early autumn they develop rich tints in shades of orange, red, yellow and purple. The upright flower clusters are greenish and measure up to 20cm (8in) high. On female trees they are followed by long-lasting red fruits. This species can be pruned back to the ground annually, so that it forms a coppice of lush foliage. It tolerates atmospheric pollution, making it a good tree for town gardens. 'Laciniata' is a female tree with deeply cut, fern-like leaflets, turning orange and yellow from mid autumn.

Cultivation

Sumach thrives in any ordinary garden soil. Plant from mid autumn to mid-spring, preferably in a sunny position.

Pruning None is essential. However, to obtain abundant foliage, prune *R. typhina* to the ground each year from late winter to mid spring. Suckering stems can be removed at the same time.

Pests and diseases Die-back may be caused by a physiological disorder due to unsuitable conditions, or by verticillium wilt. Coral spot fungus enters through cuts and wounds and appears on the branches as raised coral pink spots.

Robinia

locust

Robinia pseudoacacia

Robinia pseudoacacia, flowers

Robinia pseudoacacia, bark

☐ Height at 25 years up to 10m (33ft)
☐ Mature height 12-18m (40-60ft)
☐ Spread 4.5-6m (15-20ft)
☐ Any ordinary soil
☐ Hardy broadleaf
☐ Features – flowers; attractive foliage

Locusts are popular ornamental trees, fast-growing and flourishing in even the polluted air and poor soil of town gardens. In summer they bear drooping clusters of fragrant pink or white pea-like flowers.

The fern-like leaves are divided into numerous oval leaflets and cast light shade; the branches are often thorny. For shrubby *Robinia* see page 129.

Popular species

Robinia x *ambigua*, up to 10m (33ft) high and 6m (20ft) wide, is a hybrid of *R. pseudoacacia* and *R. viscosa*. It has slightly sticky young growths and clusters of fragrant pink flowers in early sum-

mer. Varieties include: 'Bellarosea' (stickier shoots, larger flowers); and 'Decaisneana' (large sprays of pale pink flowers).

Robinia pseudoacacia (common acacia, false acacia, black locust), from the eastern United States, is up to 12m (40ft) high and 6m (20ft) across. This species has rugged, blackish bark which is deeply furrowed. The leaves are divided into many light green, oval leaflets and turn golden or rich orange in autumn. The white flowers, which appear in early summer, are held in drooping sprays up to 20cm (8in) long and attract bees. They are followed later by poisonous brown fruits. Varieties include: 'Frisia' (red thorns and young growths, golden yellow leaves); 'Inermis' ('Umbraculifera', mop-head acacia, thornless, compact growth, rarely flowers); 'Pyramidalis' (narrow columnar tree); and 'Rozyn-

skyana' (spreading branches, drooping at tips, drooping leaves).

Cultivation

Plant from mid autumn to early spring in any ordinary, well-drained soil in a reasonably sheltered, sunny position. Robinias generally thrive in areas of low rainfall.

Pruning None required; suckering stems should be removed as soon as seen.

Pests and diseases Scale insects may infest the trees.

ROWAN – see *Sorbus*

Salix
willow

Salix babylonica

Salix alba 'Chermesina', winter

Salix matsudana 'Tortuosa'

☐ Height at 25 years 5.5-12m (18-40ft)
☐ Mature height 9-18m (30-60ft) or more
☐ Spread 2.5-12m (8-40ft)
☐ Moist soil
☐ Hardy broadleaf
☐ Features – graceful form; catkins; winter shoots

Willows range from creeping alpines to lofty trees that make outstanding specimen trees for large gardens. They are admired for their graceful form, fluffy, early-spring catkins and coloured winter shoots which can be encouraged by regular pruning. See also pages 131-132.

Popular species
Salix alba (white willow) is up to 12m (40ft) high and 7.5m (25ft) wide, with drooping branch tips and tapering, narrow, downy grey-green leaves. Varieties include: 'Chermesina' (orange-red winter shoots); 'Sericea' (slower growing, silvery leaves); and *S.a. vitellina* (bright yellow shoots).
Salix babylonica (weeping willow) is up to 11m (36ft) high and 12m (40ft) wide, with narrow leaves on pendulous branches. 'Annularis'

or 'Crispa' has twisted leaves.
Salix x *chrysocoma* (golden weeping willow), sometimes sold as *S. alba* 'Vitellina Pendula', is a beautiful weeping tree up to 12m (40ft) high and 9m (30ft) wide. It has arching branches and slender yellow branchlets.
Salix daphnoides (violet willow) is up to 9m (30ft) high and 4.5m (15ft) wide. The arching purple shoots have a white bloom particularly noticeable in winter. Yellow male catkins appear in early spring before the glossy green leaves.
Salix matsudana (Peking willow) is up to 9m (30ft) high and 4.5m (15ft) across. Usually conical, it has yellow young shoots and pointed leaves which are grey beneath. This species tolerates drought. Varieties include 'Pendula' (weeping) and 'Tortuosa' (corkscrew willow, twisted leaves and branches).
Salix pentandra (bay willow) is a handsome upright tree up to 5.5m (18ft) high and 2.5m (8ft) across. The twigs and aromatic bay-like leaves are glossy.

Cultivation
Plant from mid autumn to late

winter in deep moist soil. They should be sited well away from buildings and drains.
Pruning Remove dead wood between late autumn and late winter. Willows grown for their coloured stems should be cut hard back annually or every other year in early spring.
Pests and diseases Aphids and sawfly larvae may infest leaves. Caterpillars and various beetle larvae eat leaves. Honey fungus, die-back and rust may strike.

SERVICE TREE – see *Sorbus*
SNOWBELL – see *Styrax*
SNOWDROP TREE – see *Halesia*

Sophora
sophora

Sophora japonica 'Pendula'

Sorbus
mountain ash, rowan, whitebeam

Sorbus aucuparia, flowers

☐ Height at 25 years 6-7.5m (20-25ft)
☐ Mature height 12m (30-40ft)
☐ Spread up to 6m (20ft)
☐ Any well-drained soil
☐ Hardy broadleaf
☐ Features – foliage; flowers

Also known as Japanese pagoda tree, *Sophora japonica*, from China, Korea and Japan, is an elegant and ornamental tree whose graceful foliage casts light shade. It is rather slow-growing, but eventually becomes a round-headed tree with a height of 9-12m (30-40ft) at maturity, with a spread of 6m (20ft).

The attractive mid green leaves, up to 30cm (12in) long, are divided into rounded to oval leaflets arranged in pairs. Established trees, 15-20 years old, bear a profusion of creamy-white, pea-like flowers in pendent clusters up to 25cm (10in) long in late summer and early autumn. Flowering is most profuse after hot summers and may be followed by long yellow seed pods that persist well into winter.

The variety 'Pendula', with its stiffly drooping branches and graceful outline in winter, makes a fine lawn specimen. 'Regent' is more vigorous and flowers at an earlier age than the species, while 'Variegata' has glossy green leaves edged with creamy-white.

Cultivation
Plant in early or mid spring when the ground has warmed up, in any good and well-drained but

Sophora japonica, flowers

moisture-retentive soil. Sophoras do best in full sun, sheltered from cold north and east winds; they are tolerant of air pollution but are not recommended for cold northern gardens.

Pruning None required, but lower branches can be pruned away in autumn to give headroom and leave a clear section of trunk.

Pests and diseases Generally trouble free.

☐ Height at 25 years 3.5-7.5m (12-25ft)
☐ Mature height up to 15m (50ft)
☐ Spread 3-5.5m (10-18ft)
☐ Any well-drained soil
☐ Hardy broadleaf
☐ Features – foliage; autumn tints; fruit

Sorbus is an important group of tough, hardy trees. Most have attractive foliage and produce a brief show of white flowers in late spring to early summer. But they come into their full glory in late summer to early autumn when the branches are hung with bunches of berries in shades of red, yellow, orange, pink and white. These brilliant colours are soon afterwards complemented by fine autumn foliage tints.

Garden varieties of the genus generally belong to either the Aria (whitebeam) group with simple toothed leaves, or the Aucuparia (mountain ash) group with leaves divided into many sharply toothed leaflets.

Popular species
Sorbus aria (whitebeam), from Europe, up to 6m (20ft) high and 4.5m (15ft) wide, has oval toothed leaves. Silvery white when young, they later become glossy dark green with grey-white, hairy undersides and turn russet and gold in autumn. The cream-white flowers form flattened clusters up to 13cm (5in) across. The red berry clusters, up to 4cm (1¾in) wide, appear in early autumn. Varieties include: 'Chrysophylla'

Sorbus aria

Sorbus aucuparia, autumn

(yellow leaves); 'Decaisneana' ('Majestica', larger leaves and fruits); and 'Lutescens' (cream-white young leaves, later grey-green).

Sorbus aucuparia (mountain ash, rowan), from Europe, is up to 5.5m (18ft) high and 4.5m (15ft) wide. It has mid green leaves which are grey beneath and divided into many sharply toothed leaflets. They turn yellow and red from mid autumn onwards. White flower heads, up to 15cm (6in) wide, in late spring are followed by large bunches of edible orange-red fruits which begin to ripen in late summer. The tree is short-lived in shallow chalky soils. Varieties include: 'Asplenifolia' (ferny leaves); 'Beissneri' (compact, upright, red young shoots, bark amber/orange, yellow-green leaves); 'Edulis' (larger leaves and fruits); and 'Fastigiata' (columnar, slow-growing).

Sorbus cashmiriana, from Kashmir, is an elegant, open tree up to 4.5m (15ft) high and 3m (10ft) wide. It has leaves similar to *S. aucuparia*. In late spring pale pink flowers appear in 10cm (4in) wide clusters, followed by glisten-

ing white, long-lasting fruits.

Sorbus 'Golden Wonder', up to 4.5m (15ft) high and 3.5m (12ft) wide, belongs to the Aucuparia group. It has fine crimson-purple autumn tints and large bunches of yellow fruits.

Sorbus hupehensis, from western China, is up to 6m (20ft) high and 3.5m (12ft) across with ascending branches. It has blue-green leaves similar to *S. aucuparia*, and red or orange autumn tints. White flowers in clusters up to 7.5cm (3in) wide appear in summer followed by long-lasting, loose bunches of white or pink-tinged fruits.

Sorbus intermedia (Swedish whitebeam), from north-western Europe, is up to 5.5m (18ft) high and wide. It belongs to the Aria group. White flowers in late spring in 10cm (4in) clusters, followed by large, bright red fruits.

Sorbus 'Joseph Rock' is an outstanding upright garden tree from the Aucuparia group, up to 6m (20ft) high and 3.5m (12ft) wide. The leaves are divided into narrow leaflets with red, orange, copper and purple autumn tints. Clusters of creamy fruits ripen to amber-yellow.

Sorbus sargentiana, from western China, is up to 6m (20ft) high and 4.5m (15ft) wide. It has mid green leaves up to 30cm (1ft) long, similar to *S. aucuparia*, but with fewer, larger pointed leaflets. They turn red in autumn. The sticky bright red-brown winter buds open in late spring into white flower clusters, followed later by orange-red fruits in wide, flattened bunches.

Sorbus vilmorinii, from western China, is a large shrub or small tree up to 3.5m (12ft) high and wide. It has mid green leaves similar to *S. aucuparia* but with more and smaller ferny leaflets. They turn red and purple in autumn. The loose white flower clusters, in early summer, are followed by loose bunches of rose-red fruits which turn white, tinged-pink, when ripe.

Sorbus 'Winter Cheer' is an open-branched tree with leaves similar to *S. aucuparia*. Up to 5.5m (18ft) high and wide, it bears flat bunches of long-lasting chrome-yellow fruits ripening to orange-red in early autumn.

Cultivation
Plant in any ordinary well-drained soil from mid autumn to early spring; a sunny or partially shaded position is best. Tolerant of pollution, sea sprays and winds. Trees from the Aucuparia group are unsuitable for shallow chalk.
Pruning None required.

Sorbus aucuparia, fruit

Pests and diseases

Apple canker may cause cankers and kill large shoots.

Fireblight causes flowers to blacken and shrivel; branches bear brown and withered leaves and eventually die back.

Honey fungus can kill entire trees rapidly.

Rust shows as orange horn-shaped structures borne in clusters on the leaves.

Silver leaf causes die-back of shoots which bear silvery leaves.

SOUTHERN BEECH – see *Nothofagus*
STAG'S-HORN SUMACH – see *Rhus*

Sorbus 'Joseph Rock', fruit

Stewartia

stewartia, stuartia

Stewartia pseudocamellia, autumn

- ☐ Height at 25 years 3.5-6m (12-20ft)
- ☐ Mature height up to 7.5m (25ft)
- ☐ Spread 3.5-4.5m (12-15ft)
- ☐ Well-drained acid soil
- ☐ Hardy broadleaf
- ☐ Features – flowers; autumn tints; peeling bark

Related to the genus *Camellia*, stewartias are slow-growing trees and shrubs, with lovely flowers, rich autumn tints and attractive peeling bark.

The oval leaves develop brilliant yellow, red and scarlet tints in autumn. The camellia-like flowers are white with golden centres. They are short-lived but are produced in succession throughout summer.

Popular species

Stewartia malacodendron, from Korea, is up to 3.5m (12ft) high and wide. The oval hairy leaves turn reddish purple in autumn. The white flowers, 7.5cm (3in) wide, have purple stamens and bluish anthers.
Stewartia pseudocamellia, from Japan, grows up to 6m (20ft) high and 4.5m (15ft) wide. The orange-brown bark peels away to reveal lighter orange bark beneath, and the leaves take on yellow and red autumn tints. The cup-shaped white flowers have yellow anthers.
Stewartia serrata, from Japan, is up to 6m (20ft) high and 4.5m (15ft) wide, with oval leathery

Stewartia malacodendron, flowers

leaves richly tinted in autumn. The cup-shaped white flowers are stained red and have yellow anthers. They appear earlier than other species.
Stewartia sinensis, from China, is up to 6m (20ft) high and 4.5m (15ft) wide. It has crimson autumn tints and fragrant white flowers up to 5cm (2in) wide. The bark is an attractive shade of brownish purple.

Cultivation

Plant in early to mid spring in well-drained acid soil, ideally in woodland conditions.
Pruning None required.
Pests and diseases Trouble free.

Styrax

snowbell

Styrax obassia

- ☐ Height at 25 years 6m (20ft)
- ☐ Mature height up to 10m (33ft)
- ☐ Spread 4.5-6m (15-20ft)
- ☐ Moist, well-drained, lime-free soil
- ☐ Hardy broadleaf
- ☐ Features – foliage; flowers

Japanese snowbells are handsome flowering specimen trees, slow-growing with wide-spreading branches and deep green foliage. Pendent bell-shaped white flowers with conspicuous yellow stamens appear in early summer.

Popular species

Styrax japonica, up to 6m (20ft) high and wide, has drooping branch tips and glossy oblong to oval leaves. The slightly fragrant flowers appear in long, drooping clusters.
Styrax obassia, up to 6m (20ft) high and 4.5m (15ft) wide, has rounded leaves which are velvety beneath. It bears long, loose sprays of fragrant flowers.

Cultivation

Plant snowbells in autumn or spring in moist, well-drained, lime-free soil in a site protected from cold winds. Not suitable for northern gardens.
Pruning None required.
Pests and diseases Trouble free.

SUMACH – see *Rhus*
SWAMP CYPRESS – see *Taxodium*
SWEET CHESTNUT – see *Castanea*
SWEET GUM – see *Liquidambar*
SWEET LOCUST – see *Gleditsia*
SYCAMORE – see *Acer*

Taxodium

bald or swamp cypress

Taxodium distichum, autumn

Taxodium distichum, root projections

Taxodium distichum, foliage

- ☐ Height at 25 years 7.5-11m (25-36ft)
- ☐ Mature height up to 30m (100ft)
- ☐ Spread 2.5-5m (8-16ft) or more
- ☐ Fertile moist soil
- ☐ Hardy deciduous conifer
- ☐ Features – autumn tints

Swamp cypress (*Taxodium distichum*) is a magnificent ornamental tree for large gardens with permanently moist soil and plenty of space. Its most distinctive features are the flaming autumn colours and the knee-like root projections which appear above the ground when the tree is grown by water, helping it to obtain adequate supplies of air.

This long-lived, slow-growing deciduous conifer is native to swampy parts of the southern United States, and there are many ancient specimens in the Everglades Swamp in Florida.

Swamp cypress is a columnar to broadly conical tree, up to 11m (36ft) high and 5m (16ft) wide after 25 years, and eventually reaching up to 30m (100ft). The bark is pale red-brown, rather stringy and closely ridged with smooth, shallow fissures.

The tiny, needle-like leaves are bright yellow-green above with two grey lines beneath, and develop fox-red and then russet autumn tints. They are arranged spirally on long shoots, and in opposite pairs on short shoots. The short shoots are dropped along with the leaves in autumn.

Mature trees produce male and female flowers together in winter. Male flowers are clustered in purple catkins up to 15cm (6in) long, which are held in groups of three on the tips of the shoots. The less noticeable female flowers are sometimes followed by round green cones, ripening to mid brown and measuring about 2.5cm (1in) across.

The variety 'Pendens' is a weeping form with drooping branches and branchlets.

The smaller species *T. adscendens* (pond cypress) is a conical or columnar tree up to 7.5m (25ft) high and 2.5m (8ft) wide. The awl-shaped leaves are bright green, turning rich brown in autumn.

Cultivation

Swamp cypresses thrive in fertile soil, and will also grow on poorer soil if moisture is always present around the roots. Choose a sheltered site in sun or partial shade; plant in mid spring using seedlings 60-90cm (2-3ft) high. No staking is needed. Plants less than 90cm (3ft) high require winter protection in frost-prone areas.

Pruning None required except to maintain a single leader; reduce forked specimens to a single leading shoot if forking occurs.

Pests and diseases Trouble free.

Tilia

lime, linden

Tilia petiolaris

Tilia platyphyllos, flowers

- ☐ Height at 25 years 7.5-12m (25-40ft)
- ☐ Mature height 15-21m (50-70ft)
- ☐ Spread 4.5-7.5m (15-25ft)
- ☐ Any moist, well-drained soil
- ☐ Hardy broadleaf
- ☐ Features – graceful form; scented flowers; attractive foliage

Lime trees, or lindens, unconnected with the sharp citrus fruit, are tall, graceful trees with a fine head of heart-shaped or rounded foliage. In summer deliciously fragrant creamy white flowers appear in pendent sprays towards the top of the tree, attracting swarms of bees. The flowers are followed later by rounded pea-like fruits which persist into winter.

Untrimmed, limes are too large for most gardens. However, they tolerate hard pruning and can be pollarded and pleached. They are often infested by aphids, which drop large amounts of sticky honeydew, making the ground and any objects beneath them unpleasantly sticky and stained.

Popular species

Tilia americana (American lime) is fast-growing, up to 12m (40ft) high and 7.5m (25ft) wide, with coarse-toothed leaves up to 30cm (1ft) long. 'Redmond' is dense and conical.

Tilia cordata (small-leaved lime), syn. *T. parvifolia,* is up to 9m (30ft) high and 4.5m (15ft) wide. The dark glossy green, heart-shaped leaves are up to 7.5cm (3in) long. 'Greenspire' and 'Swedish Upright' are columnar.

Tilia x *euchlora* is up to 12m (40ft) high and 6m (20ft) wide, with shiny dark green leaves on arching branches. Resists aphids.

Tilia x *europaea* (common European lime), syn. *T.* x *vulgaris,* is up to 11m (36ft) high and 6m (20ft) wide. It has mid green heart-shaped leaves and is prone to aphid infestations.

Tilea mongolica (Mongolian lime) is up to 7.5m (25ft) high and 4.5m (15ft) wide. It has red-stalked, glossy ivy-like leaves with bright yellow autumn tints.

Tilia oliveri is up to 7.5m (25ft) high and 4.5m (15ft) wide. It has finely toothed, oval to rounded leaves. Resistant to aphids.

Tilia petiolaris (weeping silver lime) is a beautiful, wide-spreading tree up to 9m (30ft) high and 5.5m (18ft) wide. The rounded, long-stalked leaves are finely toothed and mid to dark green.

Tilia platyphyllos (broad-leaved lime) is up to 12m (40ft) high and 6m (20ft) wide. It has mid green, heart-shaped leaves. Varieties include: 'Aurea' (young shoots yellow); 'Fastigiata' (broadly conical habit); and 'Rubra' (reddish young shoots).

Cultivation

Plant from mid autumn to early spring in any ordinary, moist but well-drained garden soil.

Pruning Remove sucker shoots from the base and trunk. Pleaching and pollarding should be done in late winter and early spring.

Pests and diseases The leaves may be infested by aphids, caterpillars, leaf spot and gall mites.

TULIP TREE – see *Liriodendron*
TUPELO – see *Nyssa*

Ulmus

elm

Ulmus parvifolia

☐ Height at 25 years 3.5-9m (12-30ft)
☐ Mature height up to 20m (65ft)
☐ Spread 3.5-7.5m (12-25ft)
☐ Any ordinary soil
☐ Hardy broadleaf
☐ Features – stately specimen tree

The noble elms were, until recently, a characteristic part of the British landscape. They are fast-growing trees of imposing stature, tolerant of exposure and of all types of soil, excellent as shade trees and picturesque with their golden autumn colours.

Sadly, the devastating effects of Dutch elm disease, unconnected with the Dutch elm itself, have destroyed many beautiful elms, and spores of the disease are easily transmitted to the survivors. Badly infected trees should be removed entirely and burnt, and rigorous checks should be kept on all specimens planted to perpetuate the elm population.

Asiatic species and hybrids appear to be more resistant to the disease than European and American elms.

Popular species

Ulmus glabra (wych, Scots elm), from northern Europe, grows up to 18m (60ft) high, spreading to 9m (30ft) at maturity, with a dome-shaped head. The toothed, ovate leaves are mid green, turning golden-yellow in autumn. Excellent for cold exposed sites, and one of the few elms to set seeds; these crowd the bare branches in spring. Outstanding

Tilia cordata

Tilia platyphyllos, fruits

Ulmus procera 'Louis van Houtte'

Ulmus glabra 'Camperdownii'

varieties include 'Camperdownii' (compact, with weeping branches); 'Exoniensis' ('Fastigiata', erect and columnar); and 'Lutescens' (yellow-green foliage).
Ulmus × hollandica (Dutch elm) is a natural hybrid elm, found throughout Europe. It grows rapidly to 10.5m (35ft) with a spread of 5m (16ft). The rounded to ovate leaves are glossy green and take on yellow autumn tints. Numerous varieties include disease-resistant types such as 'Bea Schwarz', 'Christine Buisman' and 'Commelin'.
Ulmus minor, syn. *U. carpinifolia*, from Europe, North Africa and Asia, grows to 9m (30ft) high and 6m (20ft) wide. It is usually a round-headed tree, the branches that often droop at the tips are set with deep green, coarsely toothed leaves, oval to round in shape and leathery in texture; they become chrome-yellow in late autumn. The tree is superseded by named varieties including 'Argenteo-variegata' (leaves striped and mottled with silver, grey and white); 'Dicksonii' (Dickson's golden elm, slow-growing, bright golden-yellow foliage); and 'Sarniensis' (Wheatley or Guernsey elm, coni-

cal habit with ascending branches, small ovate glossy green leaves).
Ulmus parvifolia (Chinese elm) is a round-headed tree 7.5m (25ft) or more high, with pendent branches spreading up to 5m (16ft). The small, glossy green leaves are leathery and persist well into winter. Very disease-resistant.
Ulmus procera, syn. *U. campestris* (English elm), from western and southern Europe, grows eventually up to 18m (60ft) high and 12m (40ft) wide. It is a noble erect tree, with young downy shoots and broadly ovate, mid to deep green leaves that turn yellow in autumn. The variety 'Louis van Houtte' has golden-yellow foliage, and 'Silver Gem' is margined with cream-white.
Ulmus pumila (Siberian or dwarf elm), from Asia, varies from a large shrub to a tree with a height of 9-12m (30-40ft) and an almost equal spread. The narrow and thin leaves are toothed and dark green, turning an attractive yellow colour in autumn.

Cultivation
Plant elms from mid autumn to

early spring in any deep and well-drained soil and in full sun. They are excellent trees for cold and exposed sites.
Pruning Cut out any diseased branches at the first sign of trouble. General pruning is not usually required, but wayward shoots can be removed in autumn to maintain shape.
Pests and diseases Caterpillars, aphids and gall mites may affect the leaves. Various fungi may cause cankers and die-back of shoots, with pink or red pustules of coral spot developing at the base of dead wood.

Dutch elm disease shows as browning of leaves which hang on dead branches. Large branches are killed but remain on the tree in the typical 'stag-headed' appearance. Eventually the entire tree dies.

Colourful hydrangea On alkaline soil, blue-flowered hortensias, such as 'Blue Wave', turn rose pink.

A-Z of deciduous shrubs

Shrubs are an important feature of the garden, furnishing it with a permanent framework around which more temporary plants can be grouped. Most deciduous shrubs are chosen for their flowers, which may be borne at any time of year, but it is worthwhile considering a potential purchase for its additional merits – foliage colours, leaf shapes, berries and the pattern and colour of its branches.

Some deciduous shrubs, such as the Japanese maples, hydrangeas and magnolias make outstanding specimen plants, others, like forsythia and lilacs, are rather uninteresting once the flowering display is over, and are better integrated in mixed borders where their green leaf colour can act as a uniform background for flowering plants. Several shrubs, such as berberis, are ideal for hedging, combining beautiful flowers, attractive leaf colours and berries with dense, sturdy growth.

There are deciduous shrubs to suit every garden site – shrubby willows and azaleas for damp soil, and brooms and spiraeas for dry shallow ground; and types that thrive in light shade and against north-facing walls, such as spindle trees and honeysuckles. There are neat-growing shrubs, like the hardy fuchsias, which are suitable for tubs and other containers, and others that billow and spread out to give quick cover, such as cotoneasters and callicarpas.

The main priority in the aftercare of any deciduous shrub is the pruning regime. Many need annual trimming to control their vigour and direct their growth, to encourage flower and berry production and coloured winter stems. The flowering habit dictates the time of pruning; generally, those shrubs which flower on shoots of the previous year should be cut back when flowering has finished, while those which bloom on shoots of the current year are pruned in early spring, as new growth begins.

VERSATILE SHRUBS

**From prostrate and ground-hugging types to
wall and tree-scrambling climbers, shrubs fulfil a
variety of useful and decorative purposes.**

By definition, shrubs are woody multi-stemmed plants, which vary from dwarf specimens through types with stiff, bushy or spreading branches to climbers whose weak stems need vertical support. Such varied growth habits make shrubs ideal for a multitude of uses.

It is important when choosing shrubs to consider not only their flowers, foliage or berries, but also their performance as long-term plants. A mixed border or shrubbery should be planned for a long flowering season so that spring-blooming, deciduous shrubs are followed by varieties whose high point comes during summer and early autumn. For continued interest, add shrubs with autumn tints and berries and those whose bare but vivid stems add colour to the winter garden.

A knowledge of their eventual shape and size is a key factor in determining the use of deciduous shrubs. Dwarf shrubs are ideal for edging borders and paths, and compact types do well in rock gardens and raised beds. Tall shrubs, either flowering types or those with interesting foliage, look perfect against a background of trees or along boundary lines; those of medium size should occupy the middle ground.

Wall shrubs can enhance any house wall but should be chosen with care – vivid-coloured flowering types can often look garish against red brick and may have little to contribute when in leaf.

True climbers are marvellous for adding finishing touches; they take up little ground space and are invaluable for hiding fences and walls with flowers and foliage. Scented climbers can clothe arbours and pergolas, and rampant types can hide eyesores.

▲ **Gamebird cover** Prostrate roses, merely a few inches high but spreading to 3m (10ft) or more, are ideal for covering large sunny banks. The Gamebird series has arching, ground-hugging stems clothed with fragrant blooms, pale pink in 'Grouse' and white in 'Partridge'.

◄ **Prostrate or upright** The familiar *Cotoneaster horizontalis* is an accommodating shrub. On level ground, its herring-bone branches spread wide but grow no more than 60cm (2ft) high. However, against a wall it can reach 2.4m (8ft). In autumn, the tiny leaves turn brilliant red, leaving in their wake ranks of bright red berries.

▲ **Low-growing shrub** Many brooms grow quite tall but *Cytisus* x *kewensis* reaches just 60cm (2ft) in height, its lax arching branches spreading to 1.2m (4ft). It is ideal tumbling over a low wall or growing on a sunny bank. Its green, almost leafless stems are smothered with cream-coloured pea-like flowers in late spring.

◀ **Cinquefoil** Strawberry-like foliage covered with silvery hairs distinguish herbaceous cinquefoils or potentillas from the shrubby types. The leaves are a brilliant foil for the sprays of rose-like flowers borne throughout summer and early autumn on 30cm (1ft) high plants.

▲ **Autumn berries** The vigorous guelder rose (*Viburnum opulus*) is covered in early summer with flat, wide flowers beautifully set off by maple-like leaves. In autumn it is loaded with clusters of translucent red berries.

▶ **Shrub companions** The diversity of deciduous shrubs is evident in the tiered-branched structure of white *Viburnum plicatum tomentosum* 'Mariesii' contrasted with a bushy weigela whose rose-purple flowers are tempered by silver-variegated cornus.

▲ **Autumn scene** A mixed border of deciduous and evergreen shrubs and conifers rises against a background of bare-branched trees whose long shadows flit across the lawn.

◀ **Foliage colours** In early autumn, deciduous foliage shrubs reach the peak of their performance. A few slender crimson trumpets still droop from the hardy *Fuchsia magellanica* 'Variegata', but they are eclipsed by the beautiful pale green foliage edged with silvery-white. The fuchsia easily holds its own against the taller *Berberis thunbergii* 'Silver Beauty' whose autumn dress changes from creamy-white and green through pink, orange or purple-red.

▶ **Happy wanderer** Using golden privet for a foothold, a slender *Clematis macropetala* parades its magnificent deep violet-blue flowers in late spring and early summer. By autumn they will have turned into fluffy, silky seed heads.

Abelia

abelia

Abelia schumannii

☐ Height 1.5-2.4m (5-8ft)
☐ Spread 1.2-2.1m (4-7ft)
☐ Flowers early summer to early autumn
☐ Ordinary garden soil
☐ Sunny position protected from cold winds

Grown for its long floral display, *Abelia schumannii* bears lightly fragrant, funnel-shaped and lilac-pink flowers from early summer to early autumn. It is a hardy, bushy shrub reaching 2.4m (8ft) high and 1.8-2.1m (6-7ft) across, with oval-shaped dark green leaves.

Cultivation

Plant in early to mid autumn or early to mid spring in ordinary garden soil in a sunny position sheltered from cold winds.

Regular pruning is unnecessary, though over-grown shoots can be thinned out after flowering to encourage new growth. Remove old wood in late winter.

Propagation Take 7.5-10cm (3-4in) long cuttings of the current season's wood in mid summer. Root in a cold frame and plant out the following spring.

Pests and diseases Trouble free.

Acer

maple

Acer japonicum 'Aureum'

☐ Height up to 6m (20ft)
☐ Spread up to 2.4-3m (8-10ft)
☐ Foliage shrub
☐ Well-drained, moist, cool soil
☐ Sunny or partially shaded site

Most maples are of tree-like proportions, but there are two species and their varieties which grow so slowly in our gardens that they are usually treated as shrubs.

Acer japonicum and *Acer palmatum* are grown for their exceptionally beautiful foliage – lobed green or coloured leaves which turn into magnificent fiery oranges, yellows and reds in autumn.

Both are hardy plants, though they are susceptible to frost and cold winds in spring and autumn – avoid planting in frost pockets.

Popular species

Acer japonicum has soft green leaves that turn crimson in autumn. Numerous varieties include the following: 'Aconitfolium' has deeply lobed and toothed green leaves and reaches 1.8m (6ft) high and 1.5m (5ft) across; 'Aureum' has yellow leaves with shallow lobes. They turn green in summer before assuming brilliant reds and oranges in autumn. The shrub reaches just 90cm (3ft) high and wide; it is liable to scorch in full sun.

Both varieties make ideal specimen shrubs in small gardens – in a raised bed, a paved area or on a lawn. 'Aureum' also looks effective grown in a tub.

Acer palmatum (Japanese maple) has large intricately cut leaves in a range of colours depending on the variety. It forms a rounded bush which becomes more wide-spreading with age. Maximum height and spread in a garden is 3.6m (12ft). Popular varieties include 'Atropurpureum' (red-purple leaves); 'Aureum' (light yellow leaves deepening in autumn); 'Bloodgood' (rich purple-red leaves); 'Dissectum' (green intricately lobed leaves turning bronze-yellow); 'Dissectum Atro-purpureum' (intricately lobed purplish-red leaves); 'Osakazuki' (finely toothed green leaves turning shades of fiery scarlet in autumn – the most brilliantly coloured of the Japanese

Acer palmatum 'Atropurpureum' and 'Dissectum'

Actinidia

actinidia

Actinidia kolomikta

☐ Height 6-9m (20-30ft)
☐ Flowers early to mid summer
☐ Well-drained rich loam
☐ Sunny or partly shaded position
☐ Hardy climber

Actinidia species are hardy climbing shrubs of twining habit, ideal for covering walls and fences. One is grown for its summer flowers, the other for its spectacular tri-coloured foliage.

Popular species
Actinidia chinensis (Chinese gooseberry) is a vigorous ornamental climber reaching some 9m (30ft) high with large, dark green heart-shaped leaves, 23cm (9in) long and 20cm (8in) wide. Clusters of small, fragrant cream-white flowers appear from mid to late summer and turn buff-yellow with age. If plants of both sexes are grown, the flowers are followed in autumn by green fruits, which, in Britain, never reach their full size, but in warmer climates are harvested as the edible kiwi fruit.
Actinidia kolomikta (Kolomikta vine) is grown for its stunning foliage – dark green heart-shaped leaves marked with pink and white at the tip. To produce the best variegation, grow in full sun. It is a slender climber and will reach 1.8-3.6m (6-12ft) high, given the right site – against a sheltered wall or fence. Insignifi-

maples); 'Rubrum' (large blood-red leaves in spring); and 'Senka-ki' (coral-red shoots and green leaves turning yellow in autumn).

Cultivation
Plant in well-drained but moist and cool soil between mid autumn and early spring. Maples tolerate sun and partial shade, but those grown for their autumn colours do best in light shade and in a site sheltered from prevailing autumn winds and from spring frosts.

Pruning is not necessary except to control growth in a restricted space. Remove entire branches rather than shoots to avoid spoiling the general appearance.
Propagation Grafting is best left to the nurseryman.
Pests and diseases Red spider mites may be troublesome.

Acer palmatum 'Dissectum', autumn

Actinidia chinensis

Aesculus parviflora in autumn

Aesculus
horse chestnut, buckeye

Aesculus parviflora

Aesculus pavia 'Atrosanguinea'

Actinidia chinensis, fruit

cant round white flowers appear in early summer.

Cultivation
Plant from early winter to early spring in a sunny sheltered site against a wall, fence or trellis. Actinidias do best in a rich well-drained but moist loam.

The male and female flowers of *A. chinensis* are on separate plants, so for fruits to form on the female, plant a male one nearby.

When *A. chinensis* is young, pinch out the growing points to encourage a spreading habit. Both species may require some initial training on wall supports. To keep the plants under control, thin out the shoots and cut others back in late winter.

Propagation Take 7.5-10cm (3-4in) cuttings of half-ripened wood in mid to late summer and root them in potting compost, preferably in a mist propagator. Pot the rooted cuttings into 10-12cm (4-5in) containers and plunge into an outdoor nursery bed until ready for planting out.

Pests and diseases Generally trouble free.

☐ Height 2.1-3m (7-10ft)
☐ Spread 1.6-2.4m (6-8ft)
☐ Flowers early to mid summer
☐ Any good soil
☐ Sunny or partially shaded site

The stately, long-lived horse chestnut trees belong in large parks and the countryside. They are not suitable as trees in the average garden, but some shrubby species have the same attributes and demand less space.

Popular species
Aesculus parviflora (bottle-brush buckeye) is a hardy upright shrub, 2.1-2.4m (7-8ft) high and across, with smooth mid green horse chestnut-like leaves that turn yellow in autumn. Tall spikes of pink-white flowers appear in mid summer.

Aesculus pavia (red buckeye) is a round-headed shrub reaching 3m (10ft) high with a spread of 1.8-2.4m (6-8ft). It bears erect spikes of red flowers in early summer. 'Atrosanguinea' has dark red flowers.

Cultivation
Plant buckeyes from mid autumn to early spring in any fertile garden soil in a sunny or partially shaded position. If necessary, thin out the shrubs from ground level in late winter.

Pests and diseases Leaf spot may affect the foliage.

Amelanchier

snowy mespilus, June berry

Amelanchier lamarckii

☐ Height 3m (10ft)
☐ Spread 3m (10ft)
☐ Flowers mid spring
☐ Good moisture-retentive soil
☐ Sunny or lightly shaded position

A springtime display of star-shaped white flowers held in loose upright clusters justifies this deciduous shrub's evocative name. The fleeting blooms, which appear just as the leaves unfold and last for only a few days, are not the only attraction of the snowy mespilus. In summer it bears red fruit, darkening to black or purple, and in autumn its mid green leaves turn bright red and gold, before falling.

Amelanchier lamarckii is a fully hardy shrub, thriving in the coldest of gardens. Under good growing conditions it will reach tree-like proportions, 3m (10ft) high and 3m (10ft) across.

'Rubescens', has pale pink flowers opening from deep pink buds.

Cultivation
Plant between late autumn and early spring in any good garden soil, well-drained but moisture-retentive, in a sunny or partially

Amelanchier lamarckii, autumn

shaded position. Pruning is rarely necessary except to cut out damaged shoots or crossing branches.
Propagation Dig up rooted suckers from mid autumn to early spring and replant.
Pests and diseases Fireblight may blacken the flowers and cause them to shrivel.

Aralia

Japanese angelica tree

Aralia elata 'Aureovariegata'

☐ Height 3m (10ft)
☐ Spread 3m (10ft)
☐ Flowers autumn
☐ Fertile, moist well-drained soil
☐ Sheltered lightly shaded site

The Japanese angelica tree is a suckering shrub that earns its place in the garden with its huge ornamental leaves and its early-autumn flowers. In spring, the terminal buds begin to unfold great rosettes of 60-120cm (2-4ft) long and wide leaves, made up of numerous toothed leaflets on spiny branches. They often take on handsome autumn tints.

Star-shaped flowers are borne in branched clusters in early to mid autumn.

Popular varieties
Two garden varieties developed from *Aralia elata* are commonly grown.
'Aureovariegata' has green leaves splashed and edged with yellow which changes to silvery-white in summer.
'Variegata' has green leaves edged with white.

Cultivation
Plant in autumn or spring in fertile, moist but well-drained soil in a sheltered lightly shaded site. Well suited to town gardens. No pruning is required, though straggly growths can be removed in mid spring.
Propagation Detach rooted suckers in early to mid spring and plant out.
Pests and diseases Trouble free.

AZALEA – see *Rhododendron*

Ballota

black horehound

Ballota pseudodictamnus

☐ Height 30-60cm (1-2ft)
☐ Spread 60cm (2ft)
☐ Flowers mid summer
☐ Ordinary well-drained soil
☐ Sunny site

Ballota pseudodictamnus is a dwarf shrub from the Mediterranean. It is chiefly grown for its silver-grey foliage – heart-shaped woolly-grey leaves – though it also produces whorls of lilac-pink flowers in mid summer. It is a low, spreading shrub, generally hardy except during severe winters.

Cultivation
Plant in mid to late spring in any ordinary, even poor, well-drained soil. The site must be in full sun. During winter protect plants in wet areas with cloches. Prune hard back in mid spring.
Propagation Take 10-15cm (4-6in) long heel cuttings of side-shoots in late summer and root in a cold frame. The following mid spring transfer to nursery rows outdoors and grow on for one year before setting in a permanent position.
Pests and diseases Generally trouble free.

BARBERRY – see *Berberis*
BEAUTY BERRY – see *Callicarpa*
BEAUTY BUSH – see *Kolkwitzia*

Berberis

berberis, barberry

Berberis x rubrostilla

☐ Height 60cm-2.1m (2-7ft)
☐ Spread 60cm-1.8m (2-6ft)
☐ Flowers spring and summer
☐ Ordinary soil
☐ Sunny or lightly shaded site

The deciduous berberis are hardy, easily grown shrubs, popular for their rich autumn colours and outstanding crops of brightly coloured berries which usually persist well into winter.

With their spiny stems, berberis make excellent barrier hedges; they also fit well into mixed borders, or they can be grown as specimen shrubs.

Popular species
Berberis aggregata, from China, grows up to 1.5m (5ft) high and wide. It is of bushy habit, with lance-shaped, pale to mid green leaves that turn brilliant red and orange in autumn. A mass of pale yellow flower clusters in high summer are followed by clusters of coral-red berries.

Good hybrids bred from this species include 'Barbarossa' (taller and more vigorous, with arching branches weighed down by a profusion of red berries), and 'Buccaneer' (erect habit, exceptionally large, brilliant red berries lasting until the end of winter).
Berberis chillanensis, from Chile, reaches a height and spread of up to 1.8m (6ft), with erect stems closely set with small, obovate, glossy green leaves. In late spring, the shrub is decked with numerous yellow and orange drooping flowers. The autumn berries are almost black.
Berberis dictyophylla, a Chinese species, grows vigorously to 2.1m (7ft) tall, with upright branches spreading to 90-120cm (3-4ft). The young shoots are covered with a waxy, white bloom, attractive against the elliptic, pale green leaves. These turn crimson in the autumn. Single pale yellow flowers are borne in the leaf axils in late spring and are followed in

Berberis thunbergii 'Atropurpurea Nana'

autumn by red berries, which also have a waxy bloom.

Berberis koreana (Korean barberry) is up to 1.8m (6ft) high and 1.2m (4ft) wide. Its drooping flower clusters in late spring are less showy than the conspicuous bunches of waxy red berries among autumn-coloured leaves.

Berberis x *ottawensis* is grown for its attractive autumn colours; it has yellow flowers in late spring followed by red berries. It is a medium-sized shrub reaching 2.1m (7ft) high and 1.8m (6ft) across. Varieties include 'Purpurea' (rich purple leaves).

Berberis x *rubrostilla* has toothed leaves that assume brilliant ruby red colours in autumn. The yellow flower clusters in late spring are followed by coral-red berries. The species reaches 1.2m (4ft) high, with a spread of 1.8-2.4m (6-8ft).

Berberis sieboldii, from Japan, is of compact but suckering habit and grows 90-120cm (3-4ft) high and wide. One of the best berberis for autumn colouring, the bright green, oblong leaves turn rich carmine red. Drooping clusters of pale yellow flowers in late spring are followed by round, shining orange-red berries.

Berberis thunbergii is a rounded and compact species grown for its attractive autumn foliage. The 1.2m (4ft) high plants spread to 1.8m (6ft) across and have yellow spring flowers and scarlet berries among brilliant red leaves. Outstanding varieties include 'Atropurpurea' (reddish purple leaves); 'Atropurpurea Nana' (60cm/2ft high, purple leaves), 'Aurea' (yellow foliage turning greenish in late summer), and 'Rose Glow' (young leaves purple and silver, turning bright rosy-red and later purple).

Berberis wilsoniae, from China, is a dwarf, almost prostrate shrub, 60-120cm (2-4ft) high with an equal spread of spiny, red brown stems. The small, lance-shaped leaves are soft green on the upper surfaces, grey-green beneath and turn brilliant red in autumn. Drooping clusters of yellow flowers in high summer are followed by coral-red berries. Excellent as ground cover on sunny banks.

Cultivation

Plant berberis between mid autumn and early spring, in a sunny site. Set hedging plants 30-60cm (1-2ft) apart. Any ordinary garden soil – including a poor or shallow one – is suitable.

Prune out old stems at ground level or back to young shoots in late winter; also train overlong shoots to maintain shape. Train hedges in late summer, though berries will be lost.

Propagation Take heel cuttings from side-shoots in late summer and root them in a cold frame. The following spring move them to a nursery bed and plant out in permanent positions two years later.

Pests and diseases Honey fungus can kill berberis.

BLACK HOREHOUND – see *Ballota*
BLACKTHORN – see *Prunus*
BLADDER SENNA – see *Colutea*
BLUEBERRY – see *Vaccinium*
BOSTON IVY – see *Parthenocissus*
BRAMBLE, ORNAMENTAL – see *Rubus*
BRIDAL WREATH – see *Spirea*
BROOM – see *Cytisus*, *Genista* and *Spartium*
BUCKEYE – see *Aesculus*
BUCKTHORN – see *Rhamnus*

Buddleia
butterfly bush

Buddleia davidii

Buddleia alternifolia

☐ Height 1.5-6m (5-20ft)
☐ Spread 1.2-3m (4-10ft)
☐ Flowers late spring to mid autumn
☐ Any good, well-drained soil
☐ Sunny site

Buddleias are excellent shrubs for instant effect. The species and varieties grow rapidly in any reasonable soil and bear a profusion of flowers in large, plume-shaped clusters.

Buddleia davidii, the butterfly bush, is a popular garden shrub and commonly found growing wild on wasteland; it is a great favourite of butterflies.

Popular species
Buddleia alternifolia is a graceful shrub with long arching branches. It grows 3.6-6m (12-20ft) high and 4.5-3m (15-10ft) across and has narrow, lance-shaped, pale green leaves. Its sweetly scented lavender-blue flowers appear in early summer and are borne in rounded clusters all along the branches of the previous year. It is often trained as a standard.

Buddleia davidii, the butterfly bush, grows rapidly to a height and spread of 2.7m (9ft). The mid green leaves are lance-shaped and toothed. From mid summer until well into autumn, the shrub bears fragrant lilac-purple flowers arranged in slightly arching plume-shaped clusters. Popular varieties include 'Black Knight' (dark violet flowers), 'Border Beauty' (deep crimson-purple), 'Empire Blue' (violet-blue with orange eyes), 'Harlequin' (reddish-purple flowers, white variegated leaves); 'Peace' (pure white, orange centres); 'Pink Delight' (bright pink flowers in long panicles); and 'White Cloud' (pure white).

Buddleia fallowiana has lavender-blue flowers similar to those of *B. davidii*, but the leaves are covered in white down and it has a more weeping habit. It reaches 1.5-3m (5-10ft) high and has a spread of 1.2-1.8m (4-6ft). It is less hardy than the other species and is best grown against a warm, sheltered wall.

Cultivation
Plant buddleias in autumn or spring in fertile soil and in full sun. Keep *B. davidii* and its varieties manageable by hard pruning in early spring, cutting all new shoots back to within 5cm (2in) of the old wood. *B. alternifolia* should be pruned after flowering, reducing the stems by about one-third of their height.
Propagation Take heel cuttings of half-ripe lateral shoots in summer or hardwood cuttings in mid autumn.
Pests and diseases Cucumber mosaic can cause the leaves to become distorted and mottled.

CALIFORNIAN LILAC – see *Ceanothus*

Callicarpa

beauty berry

Callicarpa 'Profusion'

- ☐ Height 1.5-1.8m (5-6ft)
- ☐ Spread 1.5-1.8m (5-6ft)
- ☐ Flowers mid to late summer
- ☐ Any well-drained soil
- ☐ Sunny, sheltered position

Beauty berries are hardy shrubs most suitable for southern gardens. They are grown mainly for their large clusters of inedible, violet or lilac berries.

Popular species

Callicarpa bodinieri var. *giraldii* grows 1.8m (6ft) high and wide. Insignificant lilac flowers appear in mid summer, followed by violet-purple berries in autumn. The leaves turn a distinctive purplish-pink in autumn. 'Profusion' is exceptionally free-fruiting.

Callicarpa japonica reaches 1.5m (5ft) high with an equal, compact spread. The pink flowers appear in late summer and are followed by lilac-mauve berries among golden autumn foliage.

Cultivation

Plant from mid autumn to early spring in any good garden soil in a sunny, sheltered position. For plenty of berries, plant in groups of three. In cold gardens, protect with bracken or straw in winter. In late winter cut the previous year's growth back to young wood.

Propagation Take heel cuttings of lateral shoots in summer.

Pests and diseases Trouble free.

Campsis

trumpet vine/creeper

Campsis radicans

- ☐ Height 9-12m (30-40ft)
- ☐ Flowers late summer to early autumn
- ☐ Rich, well-drained soil
- ☐ Sheltered site in full sun

Trumpet vines are vigorous, rapid-growing climbers, excellent for covering large expanses of walls, fences, pergolas or trees and clinging by means of aerial roots. The leaves are made up of numerous narrow leaflets; they resemble those of the ash and are coarsely toothed and mid or light green. From late summer onwards, these climbers bear drooping clusters of large trumpet-shaped flowers, 5-10cm (2-4in) long, from the tips of the current year's shoots. After warm summers and autumns, long seed pods may be produced which remain on the naked branches well into winter.

Popular species

Campsis grandiflora is the least hardy of the species; it needs a warm and sheltered site where it can reach a height of 6m (20ft) or more. The flowering display, in late summer and early autumn, is outstanding, each deep orange and red trumpet flower measuring up to 9cm (3½in) long.

Campsis radicans is hardier and more vigorous than *C. grandiflora*. It grows up to 12m (40ft) tall, with plenty of self-clinging roots. The scarlet and orange flowers, up to 7.5cm (3in) long, are tubular rather than trumpet-shaped, with wide-spreading lobes

Campsis 'Madame Galen'

at the mouth. The variety 'Flava' bears rich yellow flowers.

Campsis x *tagliabuana* 'Madame Galen' is a hybrid between the two species. It is hardy in most areas and climbs up to 9m (30ft) high if given support in the early stages. The salmon-red flowers resemble those of *C. radicans* in shape and size.

Cultivation

Plant between late autumn and mid spring in rich moist, but well-drained soil. The plants all need a site in full sun, preferably with shelter from winds. Apply an annual mulch over the root area in mid spring and protect the crowns with straw during winter until the plants are well established. Tie the shoots to supports until aerial roots appear.

After planting, cut all stems back to 15cm (6in) above ground in order to encourage side-branching from low down on the shrubs. Control growth of mature plants with hard pruning in late winter or early spring, before new growth begins: cut shoots of the previous year back to within about 5cm (2in) of their point of origin.

Propagation Increase the plants by layering long branches in autumn; they should have rooted after one year, when they can be severed from the parent and planted out. Alternatively, take hardwood cuttings in autumn and root in a cold frame.

Pests and diseases Infestations of aphids and scale insects may occur. Low night temperatures can cause bud drop.

Caryopteris

caryopteris

Caryopteris x clandonensis

☐ Height 60cm-1.2m (2-4ft)
☐ Spread 60cm-1.2m (2-4ft)
☐ Flowers late summer to early autumn
☐ Ordinary well-drained garden soil
☐ Sunny site

Fluffy clusters of small blue flowers and aromatic grey-green foliage are the distinguishing features of *Caryopteris* x *clandonensis*. The flowers appear in late summer and early autumn and are particularly attractive to bees.

Popular varieties
Several varieties are available. **'Arthur Simmonds'** has bright blue flowers and dull green leaves and rarely grows taller and wider than 60cm (2ft).
'Heavenly Blue' is compact, with deep blue flowers.
'Kew Blue' has particularly dark blue flowers.

Cultivation
Plant in early to mid autumn or early to mid spring in ordinary well-drained soil in a sheltered sunny position. The shrubs thrive on chalky soils.

In early spring, cut the previous year's growth back to young healthy buds, and cut weak stems back to ground level.
Propagation Take 7.5-10cm (3-4in) long cuttings of half-ripened lateral shoots in late summer or early autumn. Root them in a cold frame. The following spring, set them in an outdoor nursery bed; plant in permanent positions in autumn.
Pests and diseases Trouble free.

Ceanothus

Californian lilac, ceanothus

Ceanothus 'Gloire de Versailles'

☐ Height 0.9-2.4m (3-8ft)
☐ Spread 0.9-2.4m (3-8ft)
☐ Flowers summer to early autumn
☐ Well-drained fertile soil
☐ Sheltered sunny position

Without ceanothus Britain's gardens would have virtually no large blue-flowered shrubs. The majority of Californian lilacs are evergreens, but several deciduous shrubs also occur.

The tiny flowers, in shades of blue or pink, are borne in upright or drooping clusters or panicles from summer to early autumn.

Popular hybrids
Many deciduous ceanothus have been developed from *C.* x *delianus* and other deciduous species; they are hardy when grown against warm and sheltered walls. They include the following:
'Charles Detriche' (1.8/6ft high or more with a similar spread, rich dark blue flowers in summer); 'Gloire de Plantières' (0.9-1.5m/3-5ft high and wide, deep blue panicles); 'Gloire de Versailles' (at 1.8- 2.4m/6-8ft high and wide the most popular of the deciduous ceanothus, large fragrant powder-blue panicles, summer and autumn); 'Henri Desfosse' (resembles 'Gloire de Versailles', but with violet-blue flowers); 'Indigo' (up to 1.8m/6ft tall and wide, indigo-blue flowers in summer); and 'Topaz' (1.2-1.5m/4-5ft high and wide, with pale indigo-blue flower panicles in summer).

Cultivation
Plant in early autumn or mid spring against south- or west-facing walls, in good well-drained soil. Avoid shallow, chalky soils.

Cut the shrubs back hard in mid spring by shortening the previous year's shoots to 7.5cm (3in) of the old wood.
Propagation Take heel cuttings of side-shoots in mid summer and root in a propagating frame; overwinter in a cold frame and transplant to permanent sites in autumn.
Pests and diseases Chlorosis may occur on alkaline soils.

Celastrus

climbing bittersweet, staff vine

Celastrus orbiculatus, autumn

☐ Height 9m (30ft)
☐ Autumnal foliage and fruit
☐ Any well-drained soil
☐ Any site sheltered from north and
   east winds

This hardy and rampant climber is grown chiefly for its decorative autumn fruits. Borne in clusters and resembling small green peas, the seed pods split open to reveal scarlet-red seeds which often last well into winter. Make sure to buy hermaphrodite forms – plants bearing flowers of both sexes – otherwise the yellow-green flowers are unlikely to set fruit.

Celastrus orbiculatus, the most commonly grown species, has mid green, oblong to obovate leaves which take on clear yellow tints in autumn. It is an invaluable climber for covering walls, arbours and tall fences, for camouflaging unsightly buildings or for clambering up tall trees.

Cultivation

Plant from late autumn to early spring in well-drained soil. Dry and shallow chalky soils are unsuitable. Climbing bittersweet will grow in any site except one exposed to north or east winds. Prepare the soil well. Once established, the plants require little attention. To keep plants under control, thin out unwanted growths, and cut back the main shoots to half their length in late winter.

Propagation Layer one-year-old growths in autumn. They should have rooted a year later. Or take cuttings in mid to late autumn and root in a propagating frame.

Pests and diseases Scale insects sometimes infest the stems.

Celastrus orbiculatus, flowers

Ceratostigma

Chinese plumbago

Ceratostigma willmottianum

☐ Height 30-90cm (1-3ft)
☐ Spread 38-90cm (15-36in)
☐ Flowers mid summer to late autumn
☐ Well-drained loamy soil
☐ Sunny sheltered position

Half-hardy until established, these sub-shrubs are suitable as ground cover in sheltered borders, in rock gardens or on low walls.

New growth starts in spring when tiny coral-red buds open into narrow leaves along pink stems. Bristly flower heads appear in mid summer and continue until autumn when the mid green leaves may turn shades of red.

Popular species

Ceratostigma plumbaginoides, a shrubby perennial with a woody base and wiry stems, grows 30cm (1ft) high and 38cm (15in) across. It bears clusters of blue flowers. *Ceratostigma willmottianum*, with a height and spread of 90cm (3ft), bears diamond-shaped, hairy leaves that turn red in autumn. The blue flowers are borne in erect clusters.

Cultivation

Plant in mid to late spring in any well-drained, loamy soil and in full sun, preferably with the protection of a warm wall.

Remove frost-damaged stems in early spring, cutting them back to ground level.

Propagation Take 7.5cm (3in) long heel cuttings of half-ripe lateral shoots in mid summer and root in a propagating frame. Pot up rooted cuttings and overwinter in a cold frame or frost-free greenhouse. Plant out in permanent positions in mid spring.

Pests and diseases Trouble free.

Chaenomeles

Japanese quince, japonica

Chaenomeles speciosa 'Moerloosei'

☐ Height 90cm-1.8m (3-6ft)
☐ Spread 1.2-2.1m (4-7ft)
☐ Flowers early to late spring
☐ Ordinary moisture-retentive soil
☐ Sunny site

Japonicas are an invaluable source of colour with their saucer-shaped flowers in red, pink, salmon or white.

In autumn, japonicas often bear bright yellow-green fruits – quinces – which can be used for making jelly.

Japanese quinces are suitable for growing against sunny walls, as specimen shrubs in mixed borders, and as hedging plants.

Popular species

Chaenomeles japonica bears an abundance of orange-red bowl-shaped flowers among rounded downy green leaves. It forms a low spreading bush 90cm (3ft) high and 1.5-2.1m (5-7ft) across.

Chaenomeles speciosa grows 1.8m (6ft) high and wide. Its bowl-shaped flowers are borne in small clusters. The small leaves are dark green and glossy. Popular varieties include 'Cardinalis' (crimson-scarlet), 'Moerloosei' (pale pink and white), 'Nivalis' (white), 'Phylis Moore' (semi-double, pink), 'Rubra Grandiflora' (dwarf, spreading shrub, crimson), 'Simonii' (dwarf shrub, semi-double blood red).

Chaenomeles x *superba* is a free-flowering hybrid group; all reach 1.8m (6ft) high and include 'Coral Sea' (coral), 'Crimson and Gold' (crimson-red, yellow stamens),

Chaenomeles x *superba* 'Crimson and Gold'

Chaenomeles x *superba,* fruit

Chaenomeles speciosa

Chimonanthus
winter sweet

Chimonanthus praecox

☐ Height 3m (10ft)
☐ Spread 2.4-3m (8-10ft)
☐ Flowers early to late winter
☐ Any well-drained soil
☐ Sunny wall

The winter sweet (*Chimonanthus praecox*) is either a joy or a disappointment. It does not begin to flower until several years after planting. Even then, although fully hardy, the display may be lost in a single severe frost. In a good year the blossoms are so unusual and so exquisitely scented that they are worth the risk. Appearing around Christmas, if the weather is mild, and lasting until early spring, they are pale lime-yellow, stained with purple in the centre. The variety 'Lutea' has pure yellow flowers.

'Fire Dance' (red), 'Hever Castle' (shrimp-pink), 'Knap Hill Scarlet' (dwarf, spreading shrub, orange-scarlet), 'Pink Lady' (rose-pink), 'Rowallane' (semi-double, scarlet) and 'Vermilion' (bright red).

Cultivation
Plant between mid autumn and early spring in ordinary soil, in full sun or against a wall of any aspect. For hedging, set the plants 75-120cm (2½-4ft) apart.

Prune wall shrubs after flowering by cutting back the previous year's growth to two or three buds. Free-standing shrubs need little pruning except to thin out crowded branches.

Propagation Take 10cm (4in) long heel cuttings of lateral shoots in mid to late summer and root in a propagating frame. Alternatively, layer long shoots in early autumn – they should be ready for separating from the parent plant two years later.

Pests and diseases Birds sometimes attack the flowers. On chalky soils, chlorosis can occur.

Chaenomeles x superba 'Coral Sea'

Fireblight may shrivel the flowers and cause die-back of the branches.

CHASTE TREE – see *Vitex*
CHERRY, ORNAMENTAL – see *Prunus*
CHESTNUT – see *Aesculus*

Cultivation
Plant between mid autumn and early spring in good garden soil in a sunny site, ideally against a south-facing or west-facing wall.

On bush-grown shrubs thin out old and crowded wood after flowering. Prune wall-trained shrubs by cutting all flowered shoots back to just above the base.

Propagation Layer long shoots in early autumn and separate from the parent plant two years later.

Pests and diseases Trouble free.

CHINESE GOOSEBERRY – see *Actinidia*
CINQUEFOIL – see *Potentilla*

Clematis

clematis

Clematis macropetala

☐ Height 1.8-12m (6-40ft)
☐ Flowers late spring to mid autumn
☐ Well-drained alkaline to neutral soil
☐ Open sunny position

The most popular of all hardy climbers, clematis are largely deciduous, producing their cup-, bell- or urn-shaped flowers from late spring until autumn, in attractive shades of purple, mauve, red, pink, yellow or white, often bicoloured. Some are borne singly, others in more prominent clusters.

Popular species and varieties

The enormous range of clematis includes species and their varieties, and large-flowered hybrids. They can be divided according to flowering seasons.

EARLY-FLOWERING TYPES bloom between spring and mid summer.

Clematis alpina bears drooping cup-shaped, violet-blue flowers in mid and late spring, and has dark green leaves. It grows up to 1.8m (6ft) high. Varieties include 'Pamela Jackson' (dark blue), 'Ruby' (rose-red) and 'Siberica' (white).

Clematis chrysocoma resembles *C. montana*, but is less vigorous, usually reaching a height of 3m (10ft). It bears trifoliate leaves covered with brown-yellow down, and single pink-white, saucer-shaped flowers. They appear in great profusion in early summer, but new shoots often continue to flower into late summer and early autumn.

Clematis macropetala is a slender climber, reaching 3.6m (12ft) high. The nodding light and dark blue bell flowers have centres of paler staminodes and appear in late spring and early summer. Varieties include 'Maidwell Hall' (deep blue) and 'Markham's Pink' (lavender-pink).

Clematis montana, an easily grown, vigorous species, can reach 12m (40ft). The pure white flowers are carried in clusters in late spring among dark green leaves. Varieties include 'Elizabeth' (pale pink) and 'Tetrarose' (lilac-rose flowers and bronze foliage).

Large-flowered hybrids are less vigorous than the species, reaching 2.4-4.5 (8-15ft) high. They flower from late spring to

Clematis viticella 'Purpurea Plena Elegans'

Clematis 'Alice Fisk'

Clematis 'Perle d'Azur' and 'Ville de Lyon'

Clematis florida 'Sieboldii'

early summer, and often again in late summer to early autumn. Popular varieties include 'Alice Fisk' (wisteria-blue), 'Barbara Jackman' (violet-purple with plum stripes and white stamens), 'Bee's Jubilee' (pink with carmine stripes), 'Nelly Moser' (mauve-pink with crimson stripes), 'The President' (purple-blue with pale stripes), 'Vyvyan Pennell' (double violet-blue with carmine stripes) and 'Yellow Queen' (cream with yellow stamens).

LATE-FLOWERING TYPES bloom between mid summer and early autumn.

Clematis flammula forms a tangled mass of hairless stems clothed with bright green leaves. From late summer and into autumn, the 3m (10ft) high climber bears abundant clusters of pure white, sweetly scented flowers; they are followed by silky seed heads.

Clematis florida is sometimes evergreen, reaching 3m (10ft) high. The flowers are cream-white with a green stripe on the reverse. 'Alba Plena' bears fully double,

greenish-white flowers over a long period; 'Sieboldii' has semi-double cream flowers with a purple centre.

Clematis orientalis is a vigorous well-branched species reaching 6m (20ft) high. It has green ferny leaves and a spectacular display of nodding, scented, yellow star-like flowers. Silky, silver-grey seed heads are an added attraction.

Clematis tangutica is similar to *C. orientalis*. Reaching 4.5-6m (15-20ft) and with silver-grey foliage, it is best left to ramble freely over a support. Rich yellow, lantern-shaped flowers are followed by fluffy seed heads.

Clematis texensis, a tender species, often dies back to the ground in winter. In summer it reaches a height of 1.8-3.6m (6-12ft). The leaves are blue-green and the urn-shaped flowers are scarlet. It is the parent of many hybrid clematis.

Clematis x *violacea*, syn. *C.* x *triternata*, is a vigorous climber 3.6m (12ft) or more high, with dark green foliage. Clusters of fragrant, pale violet-mauve flowers

are freely borne in late summer and early autumn. The variety 'Rubromarginata' has pure white flowers prominently edged with violet-red.

Clematis viticella grows 3.6m (12ft) high, though growth tends to die back in winter and should be pruned to 60cm (2ft) off the ground in late winter. It has dark green divided leaves and violet or purple-red nodding, bell-shaped flowers. Named varieties include 'Purpurea Plena Elegans' (double violet-purple flowers) and 'Royal Velours' (velvet-purple).

Large-flowered hybrids have smaller blooms than the early-flowering hybrids. The climbers reach 2.4-4.5m (8-15ft) high. Popular varieties include 'Comtesse de Bouchard' (bright mauve-pink), 'Duchess of Albany' (bright pink), 'Ernest Markham' (glowing red), 'Etoile Violette' (purple), 'Gipsy Queen' (violet-purple), 'Gravetye Beauty' (crimson-red), 'Hagley Hybrid' (shell-pink), 'Jackmanii Superba' (purple), 'Mme Edouard André' (wine-red), 'Mme Julia Correvon' (small

Clematis 'Yellow Queen'

Clematis 'Mme Edouard André'

wine-red), 'Niobe' (dark ruby-red), 'Perle d'Azur' (sky-blue) and 'Ville de Lyon' (carmine edged with crimson).

DUAL-PURPOSE CLEMATIS will flower in spring, summer or autumn, depending on pruning. Light pruning produces large early flowers and late small flowers; hard pruning results in an impressive mid summer display. Favourites include 'W.E Gladstone' (lavender-blue), 'Henryi' (cream-white), 'Mrs Cholmondeley' (palest blue) and 'William Kennet' (lavender-blue with red stripes).

Cultivation

Plant between mid autumn and late spring in deep, well-drained alkaline to neutral or slightly acid soil in an open sunny site, with shade over the base of the main stem and the roots. Mulch the root area annually in spring with well-rotted manure or compost. Water well during dry spells.

Early-flowering species and large-flowered hybrids don't require regular pruning. To keep them under control, trim rampant shoots after flowering.

Late-flowering species and large-flowered hybrids should be cut back almost to ground level in late winter or early spring, leaving just one strong shoot.

Propagation Take stem cuttings in mid summer and root in a propagating unit. Or layer long shoots in spring; they should root within one year.

Pests and diseases Slugs, earwigs and aphids can be a problem. Clematis wilt causes rapid death of shoots; new shoots usually develop from the base.

Clematis 'Hagley Hybrid'

Clematis tangutica

Clerodendrum

clerodendrum

Clerodendrum trichotomum fargesii

☐ Height 1.8-4.5m (6-15ft)
☐ Spread 1.8-4.5m (6-15ft)
☐ Flowers late summer to early autumn
☐ Fertile well-drained soil
☐ Sheltered sunny site

Only two species of *Clerodendrum* are hardy in Britain. Even then they require a sheltered sunny position. Both bear heads of pink-white flowers in late summer and early autumn.

Popular species

Clerodendrum bungei is of semi-herbaceous habit, dying back to the ground in winter. It grows 1.8-2.4m (6-8ft) high and spreads by means of suckers. The heart-shaped leaves are dark green.
Clerodendrum trichotomum is slow-growing, and of bushy but open habit. The flowers are followed by turquoise-blue berries. *C. trichotomum fargesii* has lighter blue berries.

Cultivation

Plant in fertile well-drained garden soil in early autumn or mid spring. The site should be sheltered and sunny. Remove any frost-damaged tips in spring.
Propagation Increase *C. bungei* by replanting rooted suckers in early autumn or spring. This species and *C. trichotomum* can also be propagated from heel cuttings taken in late summer and rooted in a cold frame.
Pests and diseases Trouble free.

Clethra

sweet pepper bush

Clethra alnifolia 'Rosea'

☐ Height 1.8-2.4m (6-8ft)
☐ Spread 1.8-2.4m (6-8ft)
☐ Flowers late summer to mid autumn
☐ Lime-free, humus-rich, moisture-retentive soil
☐ Sunny or lightly shaded site

With the arrival of new plants from North America in the 18th century, the so-called 'American garden' became popular in Britain, and the sweet pepper bush (*Clethra alnifolia*) was one of its favourite adornments. It is a useful late-summer flowering shrub for acid soil. The sweetly scented, small urn-shaped flowers are carried in slender spikes, set among leaves which turn yellow and orange in autumn.

Popular varieties

'**Paniculata**' bears fine branched spikes of white flowers.
'**Rosea**' has spikes of red buds which open into pink flowers.

Cultivation

Plant in early to mid autumn or early to mid spring in lime-free soil with plenty of humus and moisture. Sunny or lightly shaded woodland conditions are suitable.
Propagation Take 7.5-10cm (3-4in) long heel cuttings of lateral shoots in mid to late summer and root in a propagating frame. Pot the cuttings in lime-free compost, overwinter in a frost-free cold frame and plant out the following year.
Pests and diseases Trouble free.

CLIMBING BITTERSWEET – see *Celastrus*

Colutea

bladder senna

Colutea arborescens

☐ Height 2.4m (8ft)
☐ Spread 2.4m (8ft)
☐ Flowers early summer to mid autumn
☐ Any garden soil
☐ Sunny site

Yellow pea-like flowers marked with red that begin their display in early summer and continue until mid autumn are just one of the attractions of the hardy *Colutea arborescens*. Another bonus comes with the appearance of the seed pods, which follow the flowers and give the plant its common name – bladder senna. They are 7.5cm (3in) long inflated purses, flushed with red.

Bladder senna is fast-growing and forms an open wide-spreading bush 2.4m (8ft) high, and is well worth growing for its grey-green feathery foliage alone.

Cultivation

Plant in any well-drained soil in a sunny position between autumn and early spring. The shrubs do well on poor, sandy soils. Remove spindly shoots in early spring, and prune strong branches to within a few buds of the old wood.
Propagation Take 7.5-10cm (3-4in) long heel cuttings of ripe lateral shoots in early autumn.
Pests and diseases Trouble free.

CORNELIAN CHERRY – see *Cornus*
CORKSCREW HAZEL – see *Corylus*

Cornus

dogwood

Cornus kousa

□ Height 2.4-4.5m (8-15ft)
□ Spread 1.8-6m (6-20ft)
□ Flowers late winter to early summer
□ Moist or well-drained soil
□ Sunny or partially shaded site

Some of the hardy dogwoods are grown for their coloured winter stems while others have attractive flowers or stunning autumn foliage. The flowers themselves are tiny but are surrounded by coloured bracts resembling petals. They are often followed by coloured fruits. See also page 23.

Popular species
Cornus alba is a suckering shrub up to 1.8m (6ft) high with a spread of 3m (10ft). In winter, the young stems are a glowing red. Its oval mid green leaves turn red or orange in autumn. The yellow-white flowers are carried in inconspicuous clusters from late spring to early summer, and are followed by globular white berries. The species looks particularly attractive growing beside a pool. Popular varieties include 'Elegantissima' (leaves edged and mottled with white); 'Sibirica' (shiny coral-red stems); and 'Spaethii' (golden variegated leaves).

Cornus alternifolia is grown for its attractive foliage. The red branches grow horizontally to form a large shrub about 3m (10ft) high and wide. The leaves are often brilliantly coloured in autumn. The variety 'Argentea', sometimes listed as 'Variegata', has small bright green leaves broadly edged with cream-white. They turn red in autumn, when blue-black fruits also appear.

Cornus florida is one of the finest of the flowering dogwoods. It is a well-branched shrub reaching 3-4.5m (10-15ft) high, with a spread of up to 6m (20ft). In late spring it bears tiny flowers surrounded by broad pink or white petal-like bracts. From late summer onwards globular strawberry-like fruits appear. The dark green oval leaves turn orange and scarlet in autumn. Varieties include: 'Apple Blossom' (soft pink bracts); 'Cherokee Chief' (ruby-red bracts); 'Rubra' (rose-pink bracts); and 'White Cloud' (white bracts).

Cornus alba 'Sibirica'

Cornus kousa is an early-summer flowering dogwood. Its small purple-green flower clusters are surrounded by white, large and slender pointed bracts. They are carried along the top of the horizontal tiers of branches giving a dramatic effect. The oval mid to dark green leaves have wavy edges and take on autumn tints. In early autumn strawberry-like

Cornus stolonifera 'Flaviramea'

Cornus alba 'Elegantissima'

fruits ripen, though their appearance is erratic. The shrub reaches 3m (10ft) high and has a spread of 2.4-3m (8-10ft).

Cornus kousa chinensis is a popular form with larger bracts; the leaves turn crimson in autumn.

Cornus mas, cornelian cherry, produces small golden-yellow flowers on its bare stems between late winter and mid spring. They are sometimes followed by red semi-translucent berries. A bushy, twiggy shrub, some 2.4-3.6m (8-12ft) high with a spread of 1.8-3m (6-10ft), it eventually grows into a small tree. The oval dark green leaves turn purple-red in autumn. Popular varieties include 'Aurea' (leaves suffused with yellow); 'Aurea Elegantissima' (leaves variegated yellow and tinged pink); and 'Variegata' (leaves edged white).

Cornus stolonifera is a vigorous suckering shrub reaching 2.4m (8ft) high and spreading to 2.1-3m (7-10ft). The stems are willow-like and are covered with attractive bright red bark. The flowers are

Cornus alba 'Spaethii'

Coronilla
coronilla

Cornus mas, fruits

Coronilla emerus

yellow-white and insignificant. The dark green leaves turn red in autumn. This species is extremely invasive and needs plenty of room. 'Flaviramea' has spectacular bright yellow stems throughout winter.

Cultivation
Plant species grown for their attractive bark (C. *alba*, C. *alternifolia* and C. *stolonifera*) in early to mid spring in any moist soil in a sunny or lightly shaded position. For the continued production of coloured winter stems, prune the shrubs hard back to within a few centimetres of the ground annually in mid spring.

Plant species grown for their flowers (C. *florida*, C. *kousa* and C. *mas*) between early and late autumn in good garden soil in a sunny position. These dogwoods require no pruning though, if necessary, stems can be shortened or removed after flowering.

Propagation Take 7.5-10cm (3-4in) long heel cuttings of half ripe shoots in mid to late summer and root in a propagating case. Pot up the rooted cuttings and overwinter in a cold frame. Set out in nursery rows the following late spring, and grow on for two or three years before transplanting to permanent positions.

Alternatively, layer long shoots in early autumn. C. *alba*, C. *alternifolia* and C. *stolonifera* can be severed from the parent plant the following mid autumn; the other species usually take a couple of years to root.

The suckering species can also be increased by removing and replanting rooted suckers in winter.

Pests and diseases Trouble free.

☐ Height 1.8-2.4m (6-8ft)
☐ Spread 1.2-1.5m (4-5ft)
☐ Flowers early summer
☐ Well-drained soil
☐ Sunny position

Elegant fronds of soft-green foliage – rather like rue but without that herb's strong pungent smell – clothe this hardy Mediterranean shrub. Under suitable conditions, it grows into a scandent shrub 1.8-2.4m (6-8ft) high and will scramble up walls or tumble over sunny banks. It looks particularly effective grown against a dark evergreen background.

The coronillas, or small crowns, of golden pea-like flowers resemble those of the brooms (*Cytisus*). The one deciduous species, *Coronilla emerus*, is sometimes called scorpion senna because the tips of its slender seed pods resemble a scorpion's tail. It grows up to 2.4m (8ft) high and approximately 1.5m (5ft) wide. The yellow flowers are tinged reddish-brown at the tips. They are borne in clusters in late spring or early summer.

Cultivation
Plant in early to mid autumn, or in mid spring, in ordinary well-drained garden soil in a sunny position. Coronillas tolerate lime-rich soils and thrive in seaside gardens.

Prune the plants to shape after flowering by shortening the long shoots and thinning out straggly stems.

Propagation Take semi-ripe cuttings in late summer or early autumn; root them in a cold frame. Pot on as necessary and plant out in permanent sites in autumn or the following spring.

Pests and diseases Generally trouble free.

Corylopsis

corylopsis

Corylopsis spicata

☐ Height 1.8m-3m (6-10ft)
☐ Spread 1.5-3m (5-10ft)
☐ Flowers early to mid spring
☐ Rich acid soil
☐ Sunny, sheltered site

Corylopsis is a genus of hardy shrubs and trees native to China and Japan. Like witch hazel, corylopsis flowers early in the year on leafless branches. The bell-shaped fragrant blooms are borne in pendent clusters.

Popular species

Corylopsis pauciflora reaches 1.8m (6ft) high and 1.8-3m (6-10ft) across. It is a densely branched shrub with bright green leaves and pale yellow flowers.
Corylopsis spicata grows to a height and spread of 1.5-1.8m (5-6ft). Its upright, spreading branches bear grey-green leaves and green-yellow flowers.
Corylopsis willmottiae is the tallest of the garden shrubs in this genus, reaching 3m (10ft) high and 1.5-2.4m (5-8ft) across. It has an upright open habit, bright green leaves and pale yellow, sweetly scented flowers.

Cultivation

Plant between mid autumn and early spring, ideally in moist lime-free soil. The site should be sheltered, in sun or partial shade. Pruning is rarely necessary.
Propagation Layer shoots in mid autumn and separate one or two years later.
Pests and diseases Trouble free.

Corylus

hazel

Corylus avellana 'Contorta'

☐ Height 3-6m (10-20ft)
☐ Spread 3-4.5m (10-15ft)
☐ Catkins in late winter
☐ Any well-drained soil
☐ Open sunny or lightly shaded site

Hazels and filberts, which grow in hedgerows and woodlands, also have their place in the garden. Their yellow catkins are an attractive source of colour in winter and spring and the leaves take on attractive autumn shades.

Popular species

Corylus avellana, hazel or cobnut, reaches up to 6m (20ft) high and 4.5m (15ft) wide. Ornamental garden varieties include the shorter-growing 'Aurea' (yellow leaves) and 'Contorta', corkscrew hazel or Harry Lauder's walking stick (a slow-growing shrub with twisted branches and leaves).
Corylus maxima, filbert, has a height and spread of 3m (10ft). It is similar to *C. avellana*, but is more robust and has larger leaves. 'Purpurea' has purple leaves.

Cultivation

Plant between mid autumn and early spring in well-drained soil, in a sunny or partially shaded site.

Corylus avellana 'Aurea'

In the early years, cut back the previous year's growth by half. When flowering starts after four or five years, shorten old growth after flowering in spring. Remove suckers from below ground.
Propagation Layer in autumn and separate from the parent plant after one year.
Pests and diseases Caterpillars, powdery mildew and honey fungus can cause problems.

Cotinus
smoke tree/bush

Cotinus coggygria 'Atropurpureus'

Cotinus coggygria, flower

□ Height 2.4m (8ft)
□ Spread 2.4m (8ft)
□ Flowers in mid summer
□ Ordinary well-drained soil
□ Sunny site

This hardy shrub derives its common name, smoke tree, from the summer display of fluffy flowers. Available in pink, purple or grey, they are surrounded by clouds of silky hairs which remain a feature well into autumn.

There are other reasons for finding room for a smoke tree in the garden. In autumn, its light green, oval leaves turn red or yellow before falling to the ground. Some varieties have spectacular coloured foliage in summer and are popular with flower arrangers.

Popular varieties
Cotinus coggygria, syn. *Rhus cotinus,* has given rise to several outstanding varieties.
'Atropurpureus' has purple flowers and green leaves which turn yellow in autumn.
'Foliis Purpureis' is grown for its purple leaves which turn green and then light red in autumn.

'Notcutt's Variety' has pink and purple flowers and plum-coloured leaves which turn red in autumn.
'Royal Purple' has purple flowers and deep wine-red leaves turning deeper in autumn.

Cultivation
Smoke trees are easy to grow in

ordinary well-drained garden soil in a sunny position. They thrive on poor soils; in rich soils the leaves do not colour as well in autumn.

Regular pruning is unnecessary, but straggly growth can be shortened or removed entirely in early spring.
Propagation Layer long shoots in early autumn and separate from the parent plant after a year.

Alternatively, take 10-12cm (4-5in) long heel cuttings of lateral shoots in late summer to early autumn.
Pests and diseases Powdery mildew may affect purple-leaved varieties, showing as a powdery white deposit on the leaves.

Cotinus coggygria, autumn

Cotoneaster

cotoneaster

Cotoneaster horizontalis

☐ Height 5cm-4.5m (2in-15ft)
☐ Spread 30cm-4.5m (1-15ft)
☐ Flowers early summer
☐ Ordinary garden soil
☐ Sunny position

This large genus of hardy shrubs includes deciduous and evergreen species with an enormous range of growth habits: low and spreading,, bushy, arching or hummock- forming. Commonly grown for their conspicuous berries and colourful autumn foliage, the shrubs have small pink or white flowers.

Cotoneaster frigidus 'Rothschildianus'

Popular species

Cotoneaster frigidus is a deciduous or semi-evergreen shrub, with a height and spread of 3.6-4.5m (12-15ft), bearing oblong dark green leaves. Large clusters of crimson berries persist for a long time. Popular varieties include 'Cornubia' (red berries) and 'Rothschildianus' (cream-yellow fruits).

Cotoneaster horizontalis has branches arranged in an attractive herringbone fashion. It grows 60cm (2ft) high and 1.8-2.1m (6-7ft) across, although it may reach 2.4m (8ft) high against a wall. Pink flowers in early summer are followed by red berries in autumn.

Cultivation

Plant between mid autumn and late winter in any ordinary soil and in full sun. Pruning is unnecessary except to maintain shape and should be done in spring.

Propagation Take semi-hardwood cuttings in late summer and root in a cold frame. Grow on rooted cuttings outdoors and transplant to permanent sites after a couple of years.

Pests and diseases Birds feed on the berries. Aphids make the plants sticky and sooty. Fireblight and silver leaf may occur.

Cytisus

broom

Cytisus x beanii

☐ Height 30cm-3m (1-10ft)
☐ Spread 90cm-3m (3-10ft)
☐ Flowers late spring to mid summer or later
☐ Ordinary or poor, well-drained soil
☐ Sunny position

Cytisus, otherwise known as broom, forms a large genus of hardy shrubs grown for their profusion of flowers in late spring and early summer, sometimes later. Resembling sweet peas in shape, they are yellow, cream, scarlet and purple.

The bushy brooms are ideal for growing in borders against walls, while the low-spreading types make excellent ground cover in large rockeries.

Popular species

Cytisus albus, syn. *C. multiflorus*, grows into a graceful upright shrub with a height and spread of 1.5m (5ft). It bears white flowers in mid to late spring and small grey-green leaves on its arching branches.

Cytisus battandieri, Moroccan broom, is an upright shrub 3m (10ft) high and wide. Between early and mid summer it is smothered with golden flowers which emit a delicious pineapple scent. The leaves are felted silvery-green.

Cytisus x *beanii* is a dwarf hybrid 45-60cm (1½-2ft) high with a spread of 90cm (3ft). Golden-yellow flowers are borne either singly or in small clusters in late spring. It has mid green hairy leaves and makes a good rock garden plant.

Cytisus x *kewensis* grows 30-60cm (1-2ft) high, but as the lax branches eventually spread to 1.2m (4ft) across it is ideal for growing over a sunny ledge or as ground cover. Its mass of cream-

Cytisus scoparius

Cytisus 'Allgold' and 'Burkwoodii'

coloured flowers appear in late spring and the leaves are mid green.

Cytisus nigricans differs from other brooms in bearing its bright yellow upright flower spikes from late summer into early autumn. It is an erect shrub, with a height and spread of 90cm-1.2m (3-4ft) and bears trifoliate mid green leaves.

Cytisus x *praecox*, Warminster broom, is an arching species capable of reaching a height and spread of 1.5-1.8m (5-6ft). Cascades of creamy-white flowers appear in late spring before the grey-green leaves. Unfortunately they have a slightly acrid smell. Popular varieties include 'Albus' (white flowers), 'Allgold' (deep yellow) and 'Gold Spear' (bright yellow).

Cytisus purpureus, purple broom, is a low-spreading species 30-60cm (1-2ft) high and 1.2-1.5m (4-5ft) wide. It has dark green leaves and purple flowers which appear in late spring and early summer. 'Atropurpureus' is deeper purple, and 'Albus', a dwarf variety, has white flower clusters.

Cytisus scoparius, the common broom, is native to the British Isles, growing freely on heaths and roadsides. It forms an upright bush 2.4m (8ft) high and across, and has bright green branches which give it an evergreen appearance in winter. The deep golden

Cytisus battandieri

Daphne
daphne

Daphne mezereum

□ Height 1.5m (5ft)
□ Spread 60-90cm (2-3ft)
□ Flowers late winter to mid spring
□ Fertile well-drained soil
□ Sunny or partially shaded site

The deciduous daphnes are valued for the heady fragrance of their flowers. Although hardy, the shrubs are slow-growing and sometimes difficult to establish; severe frosts may cut them to the ground, but they usually recover.

The mezereon (*Daphne mezereum*) is an upright shrub growing 1.5m (5ft) high and 60-90cm (2-3ft) wide. From late winter to mid spring, the upper parts of the leafless branches are covered with clusters of sweetly scented flowers, from purple-pink to violet-red; they are followed by poisonous scarlet berries. 'Alba' has white flowers, and 'Rosea' is rose-pink.

Cultivation
Plant in early autumn or in mid spring, in good well-drained soil and in full sun or light shade. Use container-grown plants as daphnes resent root disturbance. Pruning is rarely necessary.
Propagation Take 5-10cm (2-4in) heel cuttings from mid summer to early autumn and root in a cold frame. Plunge the potted cuttings outdoors in spring and grow on for a couple of years before transplanting to permanent sites.
Pests and diseases Aphids may infest young growth, and leaf spot can occur.

Cytisus x praecox 'Allgold'

butterfly-like flowers appear in late spring and early summer. Numerous varieties, often bicoloured, have been developed and include 'Andreanus' (yellow and chocolate-brown flowers); 'Burkwoodii' (crimson-red); 'Cornish Cream' (cream and white); 'Dragonfly' (deep yellow and crimson); 'Firefly' (yellow and bronze); 'Golden Sunlight' (rich yellow); 'Killiney Red' (rich red and dark red); and 'Zeelandia' (lilac, pink and cream).

Cultivation
It is best to plant container-grown specimens, since *Cytisus* dislike root disturbance. Plant in autumn or spring in well-drained ordinary or poor soil in full sun. Alkaline soils are tolerated, but the plants are often short-lived.

Regular pruning is not necessary, but to restrict size, prune brooms that flower on the previous year's growth – all except *C. battandieri* and *C.* x *praecox* – by removing two-thirds of all growth immediately after flowering. *C. battandieri* and *C.* x *praecox* – which flower on the current year's growth – can be pruned in spring. Take care not to cut into old wood, or die-back will occur. Old overgrown shrubs do not respond well to pruning and are best discarded.
Propagation Take 7.5-10cm (3-4in) long heel cuttings of lateral shoots in late summer to early autumn and root in a cold frame. Pot up rooted cuttings and plunge in a nursery bed outdoors. Transplant to the final positions in early to mid autumn. Species can easily be raised from seed sown in a cold frame in mid spring; pot on seedlings as necessary before planting out.
Pests and diseases Gall mites may disfigure new growth.

Deutzia

deutzia

Deutzia x *rosea*

☐ Height 90cm-3m (3-10ft)
☐ Spread 90cm-2.4m (3-8ft)
☐ Flowers late spring to mid summer
☐ Ordinary well-drained soil
☐ Sunny or lightly shaded position

Deutzias are excellent value for small gardens. All are hardy and most grow no higher or wider than 2.4m (8ft); the entire shrub is smothered with small white to pale purple-pink flowers in early summer.

Popular species

Deutzia x *elegantissima* has fragrant, star-shaped pink to pale purple-pink flowers in late spring and early summer. It is an upright shrub, 1.2-1.5m (4-5ft) high and wide, with green lance-shaped leaves. The variety 'Rosealind' has deep carmine-pink flowers.

Deutzia x *hybrida* is the collective name given to several named hybrids. All are bushy plants 1.2-1.8m (4-6ft) high with a spread of 1.2-2.4m (4-8ft). They flower in early summer. Popular varieties include 'Contraste' (rich magenta pink and purple); 'Magicien' (mauve-pink and purple edged white) and 'Mont Rose' (rose-pink with darker tints).

Deutzia x *magnifica* bears dense clusters of white, double pompon-like flowers in early summer. It is a vigorous hybrid with a height of 2.4m (8ft) and a spread of 1.8-2.4m (6-8ft).

Deutzia x *rosea* grows into a compact shrub 90cm (3ft) high and wide, bearing soft rose-pink flowers in early to mid summer. 'Campanulata' has bell-shaped white flowers with purple calyces.

Deutzia scabra is one of the most popular species. It has bushy upright growth reaching 2-3m (6-10ft) high and 1.2-1.8m (4-6ft) wide and bearing lance-shaped pale to mid green leaves. The cup-shaped flowers are white, sometimes flushed with pink, and appear in early summer. Varieties include 'Candidissima' (double, pure white flowers) and 'Plena' (double white flowers suffused with rose-purple).

Cultivation

Plant between mid autumn and late winter, in ordinary well-drained garden soil. They grow well in full sun, though varieties with bright flowers retain their colour better in light shade.

Remove old flowered stems at ground level in mid summer to encourage new growth.

Deutzia scabra 'Plena'

Propagation Take 7.5-10cm (3-4in) long cuttings of semi-ripe lateral shoots in mid to late summer and root in a cold frame. In the spring of the following year, plant the rooted cuttings in nursery rows outdoors and grow on until the following autumn when they can be planted in the permanent positions.

Alternatively, take 25-30cm (10-12in) long hardwood cuttings of lateral shoots in mid autumn.

Pests and diseases Trouble free.

DOGWOOD – see *Cornus*
DYER'S GREENWEED – see *Genista*

Elaeagnus
elaeagnus

Elaeagnus commutata

Elaeagnus umbellata var. *parvifolia*

□ Height 1.8-4.5m (6-15ft)
□ Spread 1.8-4.5m (6-15ft)
□ Foliage shrubs
□ Ordinary, even poor, well-drained soil
□ Sunny site

Elaeagnus species are grown for their elegant foliage which has an almost metallic sheen. These hardy shrubs are reliable, easily grown and tough enough to form hedges and shelterbelts in coastal gardens.

All the deciduous species flower in late spring and early summer. They are rather insignificant, but with a sweet fragrance; they are followed by clusters of berries much relished by birds in autumn.

Popular species
Elaeagnus angustifolia, commonly called oleaster, bears attractive, willow-like silvery leaves. With a height and spread of 3-4.5m (10-15ft), it reaches tree-like proportions and is suitable only for large gardens. In early summer small fragrant silvery flowers appear followed by silvery amber berries. The variety *E. angustifolia* var. *caspica* has broader leaves that are exceptionally silvery.
Elaeagnus commutata, syn. *E. argentea*, silver berry, is one of the slower-growing species. Reaching 1.8-2.4m (6-8ft) high and wide, it is of suckering habit. The red-brown stems are upright and carry deep silver-green leaves. Silver flowers appear in late spring followed by silver fruits in autumn.
Elaeagnus multiflora, syn. *E. longipes*, is sometimes called cherry elaeagnus. It grows 2.7m (9ft) high and as much across; the ovate leaves are dark green above, silvery beneath. The pale yellow flowers in late spring are followed by drooping clusters of edible, red, cherry-like berries. It is resistant to air pollution and an ideal town garden shrub.
Elaeagnus umbellata var. *parvifolia*, syn. *E. parvifolia*, is a large shrub, 3.6-4.5m (12-15ft) tall and wide, with arching branches and young silvery shoots. The lance-shaped leaves are glossy green above and silvery underneath. Small white fluffy, highly fragrant flowers appear in early summer followed by fruits that ripen from silver to orange-scarlet. Good specimen shrub for a lawn.

Cultivation
Plant between mid autumn and early winter. The shrubs will grow in ordinary, even poor soil, including shallow chalk soils and sandy soils. All do best in full sun. For hedging, set the plants 90cm-1.5m (3-5ft) apart.

Regular pruning is not necessary, though long straggling shoots can be shortened in mid to late spring. Trim established hedges in early summer and again in early autumn if necessary.
Propagation Increase from seed sown in late summer or early autumn. Seedlings should be grown on for at least two years before being planted out. Alternatively, increase by cuttings taken in late summer and rooted in a cold frame. Pot the rooted cuttings in spring and plunge them outdoors until mid autumn when they can be planted out.
Pests and diseases Leaf spot may cause brown blotches on the leaves.

ELDER – see *Sambucus*

Enkianthus

enkianthus

Enkianthus campanulatus

☐ Height 2.4m (8ft)
☐ Spread 90cm-1.5m (3-5ft)
☐ Flowers in late spring
☐ Rich lime-free soil
☐ Sunny sheltered position

A profusion of small bell-like flowers and brilliant autumn foliage makes *Enkianthus* outstanding garden shrubs. Native to Japan, these hardy shrubs have an upright habit. They make good companions for rhododendrons, requiring the same conditions – acid soil and dappled shade.

Popular species

Enkianthus campanulatus has cream-yellow flowers with red veining. They are bell-shaped and borne in drooping clusters in late spring. The shrub reaches 2.4m (8ft) high and has a spread of 90cm-1.5m (3-5ft). Clusters of dull green toothed leaves are carried at the end of smooth red shoots. They turn brilliant red in autumn.

Enkianthus cernuus var. *rubens* bears deep red flowers in late spring. A shorter shrub reaching just 1.8m (6ft) high, its broad dull green leaves turn orange in autumn.

Cultivation

Plant in mid to late autumn or early spring in acid soil enriched with peat substitute or leaf-mould. The site should be lightly shaded.

Propagation Take 7.5cm (3in) long heel cuttings of lateral shoots in late summer to early autumn and root in a cold frame. In mid to late spring move to a nursery bed outdoors and grow on for two or three years before planting out.

Pests and diseases Trouble free.

Euonymus

euonymus, spindle tree

Euonymus europaeus 'Red Cascade'

☐ Height 1.5-4.5m (5-15ft)
☐ Spread 1.2-3m (2-10ft)
☐ Foliage shrubs
☐ Ordinary garden soil
☐ Sun or partial shade

Spindle trees are among the most accommodating of shrubs; they are fully hardy, easy to grow in any kind of soil and spectacular in autumn with their colourful berries and rich foliage colours.

Popular species

Euonymus alatus is a slow-growing shrub reaching 1.8-2.4m (6-8ft) high. The small insignificant and green-yellow flowers, which appear in late spring to early summer, are followed by purple berries with scarlet seeds. But it is the leaves, which turn from brilliant crimson to rose-red in autumn, that make the species outstanding. 'Compactus' grows only 1.5m (5ft) tall.

Euonymus europaeus, the common spindle tree, is a familiar site on chalk and limestone hills. It grows 1.8-3m (6-10ft) high and 1.2-3m (4-10ft) across, and looks splendid when its rose-red capsules split open in autumn to reveal orange seeds. 'Albus' has white fruits and 'Red Cascade' has large rose-red fruits.

Euonymus hamiltonianus var. *yedoensis*, syn. *E. yedoensis*, is a strong-growing large shrub or small tree up to 4.5m (15ft) high and 3m (10ft) wide. The ovate glossy green leaves turn yellow and red in autumn. Pink orange-seeded fruit hang from the branches long after the leaves have fallen.

Euonymus latifolius is a 3m (10ft) high shrub with a spread of 1.5-2.4m (5-8ft). The mid green leaves assume brilliant red

Euonymus latifolius

autumn tints. Large clusters of drooping rose-red fruits with orange seeds appear in late summer.

Cultivation
All euonymus species and varieties thrive in ordinary garden soil. Plant between mid autumn and early spring in sun or partial shade. Pruning is rarely necessary, but shoots may be thinned out or shortened to shape in late winter.
Propagation Take heel cuttings of lateral shoots in late summer to early autumn.
Pests and diseases Aphids, scale insects and caterpillars can be a problem. Euonymus may also be affected by honey fungus, leaf spot and powdery mildew.

Exochorda
exochorda

Exochorda x macrantha 'The Bride'

☐ Height 90cm-3m (3-10ft)
☐ Spread 2.1-4.5m (7-15ft)
☐ Flowers late spring
☐ Well-drained, moisture-retentive soil
☐ Sheltered sunny or lightly shaded site

Even among the profusion of other late-spring flowering shrubs, exochordas always catch the eye. Their branches bear dense clusters of large white flowers. Although the blooms last only 7-10 days in late spring, the display is truly spectacular.

These hardy green-leaved shrubs have a bushy habit. Reaching 90cm-3m (3-10ft) high, and spreading 2.1-4.5m (7-15ft) across, they should be given plenty of room to develop.

Popular species
Exochorda giraldii is a tall, upright shrub reaching 3m (10ft) high and 4.5m (15ft) across. The pink young shoots are distinctive in spring. The form *E. g.* var. *wilsonii* bears the largest flowers, up to 5cm (2in) across.
Exochorda x *macrantha* 'The Bride' forms a compact mound of weeping branches 90cm (3ft) high and 2.1m (7ft) across. It is particularly free-flowering.
Exochorda racemosa, syn. *E. grandiflora*, is a bushy, spreading species with a height and spread of 3m (10ft). It tends to be chloritic on chalky soils.

Cultivation
Plant container-grown specimens in autumn or spring in fertile, well-drained but moisture-retentive soil; they are generally unsuitable for shallow chalky soils. Choose a sunny or lightly shaded position, sheltered from cold winds. The short floral display will last slightly longer if the shrubs are in partial shade. After flowering, remove weak shoots from the base, and tip the remainder to encourage side-shoots.
Propagation Take cuttings in summer and root under glass, or larger long shoots in autumn; they should have rooted after one year and can be severed from the parent and planted out.
Pests and diseases Trouble free.

FALSE ACACIA – see *Robinia*

Forsythia

forsythia

Forsythia x *intermedia* 'Spectabilis'

☐ Height 2.4m-3m (8-10ft)
☐ Spread 2.4-3m (8-10ft)
☐ Flowers early to mid spring
☐ Ordinary garden soil
☐ Sunny or partially shaded site

With their modest growing requirements and spectacular display of yellow flowers, it is not surprising that the hardy forsythias are among the best-loved of spring-flowering shrubs.

The yellow flowers smother the bare stems from early to mid spring, before the fresh green leaves unfurl.

Popular species

Forsythia x *intermedia* is a vigorous shrub with a height and spread of 2.4m (8ft). Its clusters of golden yellow flowers appear in abundance between early and mid spring. 'Spectabilis' is the form usually grown – it makes a good hedging shrub. Other varieties include 'Beatrix Farrand' (canary-yellow) and 'Lynwood' (broad-petalled, rich yellow).

Forsythia suspensa has drooping branches which give it a rambling appearance. It grows about 3m (10ft) high. The long streamers of pale lemon-yellow flowers open in early to mid spring. The variety 'Nymans' has bronze-purple stems, conspicuous with their primrose-yellow flowers.

Cultivation

Plant between mid autumn and mid spring in ordinary garden soil in sun or partial shade.

Forsythias flower on shoots of the previous year; after flowering, remove old or damaged shoots and prune about a third of the remainder back to 10cm (4in) off the ground.

Propagation In mid autumn, take 25-30cm (10-12in) long hardwood cuttings of strong shoots of the current season. *Forsythia suspensa* can be layered.

Pests and diseases Birds may destroy the young flower buds. Honey fungus can sometimes kill the shrubs.

Forsythia x *intermedia* 'Lynwood'

Fothergilla

fothergilla

Fothergilla major

☐ Height 60cm-2.4m (2-8ft)
☐ Spread 90cm-1.8m (3-6ft)
☐ Flowers mid to late spring
☐ Moist, rich and lime-free soil
☐ Sunny site

Fothergillas are grown as much for their brilliant autumn colours as for their flowers in mid to late spring – fragrant bottle-brush-like spikes consisting of numerous long cream-white stamens.

Popular species

Fothergilla gardenii has a slender, upright growth habit, and reaches about 60-90cm (2-3ft) high and 90cm-1.2m (3-4ft) across. Its oval mid green leaves turn red and crimson in autumn. The flowers are carried in erect spikes in mid to late spring.

Fothergilla major reaches 1.8-2.4m (6-8ft) high and 1.2-1.8m (4-6ft) across. The oval leaves, which are dark green above and grey-green below, assume brilliant orange-yellow or red autumn tints. Erect spikes of white flowers open in late spring.

Cultivation

Plant in mid to late autumn or in early spring in moist, lime-free soil with plenty of organic matter. The site should be sunny. Pruning is unnecessary.

Propagation Layer long shoots in early autumn; separate from the parent after two years when they should have rooted.

Pests and diseases Trouble free.

Fuchsia
fuchsia

Fuchsia 'Mrs Popple'

Fuchsia 'Gracilis Variegata'

☐ Height 15cm-1.8m (6in-6ft)
☐ Spread 15cm-1.2m (6in-4ft)
☐ Flowers mid summer to mid autumn
☐ Well-drained rich soil
☐ Sunny or lightly shaded site

Most of the popular fuchsias, originally from South America and New Zealand, are hybrids developed from a few species. Some of these are tender and only suitable for growing under glass, or as summer bedding plants, while others are sufficiently hardy to be planted permanently outdoors. Those described here are hardy in all but the coldest northern regions of Britain. In severe winters they are often cut to the ground, but they will usually sprout again from the base.

The pendent flowers which make fuchsias such popular ornamental shrubs, appear between mid summer and mid autumn. They vary enormously in size and come in shades of red, pink, purple, blue, white and cream – most are bicoloured. All are set off by small lance-shaped green leaves.

Fuchsias have a wide range of uses in the garden. The large shrubby types make excellent informal hedges, or they can be grown against walls. Others can be trained as standards. The low trailing fuchsias are shown off to best effect in hanging baskets, window-boxes or other containers.

Popular varieties
Fuchsia magellanica is the hardiest fuchsia, and is much used as a hedging shrub in mild coastal gardens. It is a bushy shrub with an average height of 1.2-1.8m (4-6ft) and a spread of 60cm-1.2m (2-4ft). The small flowers are carried on slender stems. They have crimson tubes, a spreading skirt of crimson sepals and purple petals. Several varieties, generally hardy in southern gardens, include the following:
'Alba' has pale pink flowers and bright green leaves.
'Gracilis' carries numerous slender red and purple flowers and has narrow leaves.
'Gracilis Variegata' has red and purple flowers and leaves edged with cream and flushed pink. Less hardy than 'Gracilis'.
'Pumila' is a miniature variety just 15cm (6in) high with tiny, narrow red and purple flowers.
'Riccartonii' is exceptionally vigorous and hardy, and has scarlet and purple flowers.
'Versicolor' carries slender red and purple flowers. It is chiefly grown for its attractive leaves variegated with grey-green, cream or yellow, and tinged pink.
GARDEN HYBRIDS, derived chiefly from *F. magellanica* and *F. fulgens*, offer an enormous range of growth habits, flower sizes and colours. When grown as free-standing shrubs they rarely exceed 60cm (2ft) high and wide. They survive most winters under a mulch.
'Alice Hoffman' has small double flowers with carmine sepals and white petals. Purple-tinted leaves.
'Brilliant' has large scarlet and rose-purple flowers.
'Chillerton Beauty' has rose-tinted white sepals and violet-purple petals.
'Corallina' is of strong spreading habit and bears red and purple flowers.
'Display' has uniform carmine and rose-pink flowers.
'Dr Foster' has red stems and scarlet and mauve flowers.
'Dunrobin Bedder' grows into a small but spreading shrub, with small red and purple flowers.
'Lena' has large semi-double white, pink and mauve flowers.
'Madame Cornelissen' has semi-double flowers with red sepals and white petals.
'Margaret' is a vigorous hybrid with semi-double, purple-veined crimson flowers.
'Mrs Popple', particularly hardy, has arching stems bearing flowers with red sepals and purple petals.

Genista

broom

Fuchsia 'Dr Foster'

'Mrs W.P. Wood' has small but profuse white flowers tinged pink. **'Prosperity'**, upright and vigorous, has large double rose and white flowers veined pink. **'Tom Thumb'**, usually less than 30cm (1ft) high and wide, has cherry-red sepals and mauve petals.

Cultivation

Plant in late spring in a sheltered position in full sun or light shade. Any well-drained garden soil is suitable, preferably enriched with organic matter. Treat the shrubs as perennials in all but the mildest areas, cutting them back to near ground level in late autumn; cover the crowns with a deep winter mulch. In spring, trim unpruned shrubs if necessary, pruning out dead and damaged twigs.

Propagation Take 7.5-10cm (3-4in) long tip cuttings in spring and root in a propagator unit. Pot on the rooted cuttings as necessary.

Pests and diseases Trouble free.

Genista tinctoria

☐ Height 7.5cm-1.2m (3in-4ft)
☐ Spread up to 90cm-2.4m (3-8ft)
☐ Flowers late spring to late summer
☐ Any well-drained soil
☐ Sunny site

There are two large genera of brooms – *Genista* and *Cytisus*. *Genista* can usually be recognized by their wiry stems, which are sometimes spiny, and small leaves. Grown for their profusion of pea-shaped yellow flowers in late spring and early summer, they are hardy and easy to cultivate, tolerating poor dry soils. Tall types make fine specimen plants while others are excellent for ground cover and rock gardens.

Popular species

Genista hispanica, Spanish gorse, is a dwarf but wide-spreading shrub, 60cm-1.2m (2-4ft) high and 2.4m (8ft) wide. The flowers, which appear in early to mid summer, are so profuse that the shrub takes on a golden-yellow hue. It is a many-branched species with dense prickles and small deep green leaves.

Genista lydia is of elegant habit, with slender, arching spine-tipped stems. It reaches 60-90cm (2-3ft) high with a spread of 1.8m (6ft). Bright yellow flowers appear in late spring and early summer – the small leaves are grey-green.

Genista sagittalis

Genista lydia

Excellent for training over walls, for covering banks or large rock gardens.

Genista sagittalis is a ground-hugging species with slender almost prostrate stems. It grows only 20cm (8in) high but spreads to 90cm (3ft). Its green leaf-like 'wings' give it an evergreen appearance. The small heads of yellow flowers appear in early summer.

Genista tinctoria, commonly called dyer's greenweed because of the yellow dye which can be obtained from it, has a varied habit. Sometimes it grows as a low, spreading shrub, and sometimes as an erect shrub. It reaches anything from 7.5cm (3in) to 90cm (3ft) high and up to 1.8m (6ft) across. The yellow flowers are carried among dark green leaves between early and late summer. 'Royal Gold' has dense sprays of golden-yellow flowers.

Cultivation
Plant container-grown shrubs between mid autumn and mid spring in ordinary well-drained soil. They thrive on poor soil, and in full sun.

Encourage bushy growth by pinching out the growing points on young plants after flowering. Thin out the crowded shoots of mature bushes after flowering.
Propagation Take heel cuttings of lateral shoots in late summer.
Pests and diseases Trouble free.

GRAPE VINE – see *Vitis*
GUELDER ROSE – see *Viburnum*

Hamamelis
witch hazel

Hamamelis mollis

☐ Height 1.8-3m (6-10ft)
☐ Spread 1.8-3m (6-10ft)
☐ Flowers mid winter to early spring
☐ Neutral or acid, moist soil
☐ Sunny sheltered site

The hardy witch hazels are invaluable shrubs for winter interest as the shrubs flower abundantly between mid winter and early spring. The spider-like flowers are carried on bare branches and range in colour from yellow through to red. Many are fragrant. In autumn the leaves turn rich shades of red and orange or yellow.

Popular species
Hamamelis x *intermedia* is a hybrid between *H. japonica* and *H. mollis*. With a height and spread of 2.4-3m (8-10ft), it can be distinguished by the flowers which have twisted and crinkly yellow or copper-tinted petals. They appear in late winter. The oval mid green leaves turn yellow in autumn. Popular varieties include 'Allgold' (deep yellow flowers with reddish centres, and yellow autumn foliage); and 'Diane' (coppery-red flowers, good autumn colour).
Hamamelis japonica grows 2.4-3m (8-10ft) high and wide.

The flowers, which open in late winter and early spring, have yellow twisted and crinkly petals which are sometimes tinged red.
Hamamelis mollis is the earliest flowering species, its blooms appearing in mid winter. They are a rich golden-yellow, flushed red at the base – and sweetly scented. Reaching 1.8-2.4m (6-8ft) high, it has green felted leaves which turn yellow in autumn. 'Pallida', a popular variety, has sulphur-yellow blooms.

Cultivation
Plant in suitable weather between mid autumn and early spring in neutral or acid moisture-retentive soil. Heavy soils should be enriched with organic matter. The site can be sunny or lightly shaded, but it should be sheltered from cold east winds.

Cut back straggly branches after flowering.
Propagation Layer long shoots in early autumn; separate from the parent plant two years later.
Pests and diseases Trouble free.

HARDY ORANGE – see *Poncirus*
HAZEL – see *Corylus*

Hibiscus

hibiscus

Hibiscus syriacus 'Woodbridge'

☐ Height 1.8-3.6m (6-12ft)
☐ Spread 1.2-1.8m (4-6ft)
☐ Flowers late summer to mid autumn
☐ Well-drained fertile soil
☐ Sunny, sheltered site

Two species in this genus of otherwise tender plants are hardy enough to grow outdoors, though they need a sunny sheltered spot. They produce a succession of funnel-shaped flowers in summer and autumn.

Popular species
Hibiscus sinosyriacus, up to 3m (10ft) high and 1.8m (6ft) wide, bears broad, lobed, sage-green leaves. The flowers appear in late summer. Popular varieties include 'Lilac Queen' (white, lilac tinted) and 'Ruby Glow' (white with a cerise-pink base).
Hibiscus syriacus is a well-branched shrub with upright stems, up to 3.6m (12ft) tall. Varieties include 'Blue Bird' (blue with a white eye); 'Hamabo' (white with a crimson eye); 'Lady Stanley' (semi-double white flowers tinted pink); and 'Woodbridge' (rose-pink).

Cultivation
Plant from mid autumn to early spring in well-drained fertile soil in a sheltered sunny border. Shorten long branches after flowering.
Propagation Take heel cuttings of half-ripe non-flowering shoots in mid summer.
Pests and diseases Aphids and mealy bugs can infest growth.

HIMALAYAN HONEYSUCKLE – see *Leycesteria*

Hippophaë

sea buckthorn

Hippophaë rhamnoides

☐ Height 2.4-3m (8-10ft)
☐ Spread 2.4-3m (8-10ft)
☐ Grown for its berries
☐ Any well-drained soil
☐ Sunny or partially shaded site

The sea buckthorn (*Hippophaë rhamnoides*) is one of Britain's most beautiful native shrubs, making great thickets in the sand dunes of the Norfolk coast. It is a remarkably tolerant and accommodating plant, growing equally well inland.

The scaly bark is covered with the sharp spines that give the plant its name, and the upright stems are clothed with elongated silver willow-like leaves that glisten in the sun. But the sea buckthorn's true glory appears in autumn, when the leaves have fallen – shining bright orange-gold berries that often remain all winter long. For female plants to produce berries, a male specimen is essential – ideally one male to every three females.

Cultivation
Plant between mid autumn and late winter in well-drained soil in a sunny or partially shaded site. Excellent on poor soils and as windbreaks for seaside gardens.
Cut back long straggly growths in mid to late summer.
Propagation This is only possible by seed and takes many years, so buy new stock from a nursery.
Pests and diseases Trouble free.

Hoheria

hoheria

Hoheria glabrata

☐ Height 3-4.5m (10-15ft)
☐ Spread 1.4-3m (8-10ft)
☐ Flowers in mid summer
☐ Good well-drained soil
☐ Sunny or partially shaded site sheltered from cold winds

Hoheria glabrata, syn. *H. lyallii*, a native of New Zealand, is not fully hardy but thrives in southern and western parts of Britain, given a warm, sheltered spot. Any gardener who succeeds with the plant will be well rewarded, since it is one of the loveliest white-flowered shrubs. The leaves are a distinctive downy-grey that turns soft yellow in autumn. In mid summer the branches are weighed down with clusters of creamy-white flowers which have a faint fragrance.

Cultivation
Plant in mid to late spring in any good well-drained soil, and preferably against a sunny and sheltered wall.
Cut out dead and damaged wood, and shorten straggly shoots in early to mid spring.
Propagation Layer long shoots in early autumn and separate from the parent plant one year later.
Pests and diseases Trouble free.

HONEYSUCKLE – see *Lonicera*
HORSE CHESTNUT – see *Aesculus*

Hydrangea

hydrangea

Hydrangea macrophylla 'Hamburg'

☐ Height 90cm-15m (3-50ft)
☐ Spread 1.2-4.5m (4-15ft)
☐ Flowers summer to early autumn
☐ Loamy, moisture-retentive soil
☐ Sun or light shade; shelter

Hydrangeas are excellent shrubs for providing interest in the late-summer garden – climbing types flower in early summer. They are fully or moderately hardy and are ideal for town and seaside gardens as they tolerate pollution and salt spray.

Popular species
Hydrangea arborescens reaches 1.2-1.8m (4-6ft) high and wide. Fully hardy, it is usually represented by 'Grandiflora' with large pure white flowers in rounded clusters. The bright green leaves are oval and pointed.
Hydrangea macrophylla is the species from which garden varieties have been developed. Hardy in the south and west, they grow to a height and spread of 90cm-

1.5m (3-5ft) or more. Blue and pink types are influenced by soil type. On alkaline soils flowers are pink-red or purple-red; on acid soils they are blue. Varieties divide into mop-heads (hortensias) and lace-caps. Both flower in summer and autumn.

Mop-head hydrangeas have 12-20cm (5-8in) wide heads of sterile flowers. They include 'Altona' (cherry-pink or mid-blue); 'Ami Pasquier' (deep red or light blue); 'Europa' (deep pink or pale blue); 'Générale Vicomtesse de Vibraye' (sky-blue or vivid red); 'Goliath' (brick-red or purple-blue); 'Hamburg' (deep rose or deep blue); 'Madame Emile Mouillère' (white tinted with pink or blue); and 'Westfalen' (crimson-red or purple-blue).

Lace-cap hydrangeas have delicate, flat heads 10-15cm (4-6in) across with tiny fertile inner flowers and sterile outer florets. Popular varieties include 'Blue Wave' (blue, mauve or pink);

Hydrangea petiolaris

'Geoffrey Chadbund' (brick-red); 'Mariesii' (rich pink or blue); 'Tricolor' (pale pink to blue, variegated foliage); and 'White Wave' (pink or blue, white sepals).
Hydrangea paniculata is a hardy 3.6-4.5m (12-15ft) high species with arching stems bearing conical clusters of white flowers which turn pink with age. They appear

103

Hydrangea 'Blue Wave', acid soil

Hydrangea 'Westfalen'

Hydrangea paniculata 'Grandiflora'

in summer. 'Grandiflora' has 45cm (1½ft) long flower spikes, the smaller-flowered 'Praecox' is 1.8m (6ft) high and across.

Hydrangea petiolaris is a vigorous hardy climber up to 15m (50ft) high – it clings by aerial roots. The cream-white lace-cap flowers appear in early summer.

Hydrangea quercifolia is distinguished by lobed, oak leaf-like foliage which assumes brilliant autumn tints. It grows 1.8m (6ft) high and wide. Upright white flower spikes appear in summer.

Hydrangea serrata, syn. *H. macrophylla serrata*, grows 90cm (3ft) high and wide. Varieties include 'Bluebird' (blue lace-cap

flowers); 'Grayswood (lace-cap pink or blue inner florets, white outer flowers, yellowish-green leaves edged bronze-red); 'Intermedia' (pink); and 'Preziosa' (salmon-pink to red, young reddish-brown leaves).

Cultivation

Plant in mid autumn or mid spring in good loamy, moisture-retentive soil. Choose a sheltered site, in sun or partial shade.

All hydrangeas benefit from an annual mulch of well-decayed manure in mid spring.

Dead-head after flowering. Remove weak or damaged shoots in late winter to early spring. Cut

the previous year's shoots on *H. arborescens* and *H. paniculata* back by half. On *H. macrophylla* thin out two or three year-old flowering shoots at ground level.

Propagation Increase shrubby hydrangeas by 10-15cm (4-6in) cuttings in late summer, and climbing species by 7.5cm (3in) cuttings.

Pests and diseases Aphids may feed on the stems and leaves.

Hypericum
St. John's wort

Hypericum 'Hidcote'

Hypericum androsaemum

- ☐ Height 30cm-1.5m (1-5ft)
- ☐ Spread 60cm-1.8m (2-6ft)
- ☐ Flowers mid summer to autumn
- ☐ Fertile well-drained soil
- ☐ Sunny site

The shrubby St. John's worts include hardy evergreen and deciduous plants, the latter often semi-evergreen in wild areas. Though hardy, they may be relatively short-lived.

St. John's worts are valued for their summer and autumn flowers. They come in shades of yellow, and are cup-shaped, often opening out flat to reveal a central boss of golden stamens. In some species and hybrids the flower display is followed by bright berries.

Easily grown and fast spreading, the shrubs are excellent for providing summer colour in shrubberies, or as ground cover in borders and on banks.

Popular species
Hypericum androsaemum, Tut-san, 60-90cm (2-3ft) high and wide, is free-flowering with clusters of small yellow flowers. Its chief attraction is its autumn berries which are red-purple at first, then turn dark crimson.

Hypericum forrestii reaches 1.5m (5ft) high and 1.8m (6ft) across, with leaves which turn orange and red in autumn. The abundant golden-yellow flowers are followed by bronze-red berries.

Hypericum 'Hidcote' is one of the most popular St. John's worts. Forming a dome 1.5m (5ft) high and across, it is covered with golden flowers throughout summer.

Hypericum x *inodorum* 'Elstead' is a semi-evergreen 1.2m (4ft) high shrub with a spread of 1.5m (5ft). From mid summer on, it bears a profusion of gold flowers followed by salmon-red berry clusters.

Hypericum x *moserianum* is a dwarf shrub, 30-75cm (1-2½ft) high, and spreading to 90cm-1.2m (3-4ft). Clusters of yellow flowers appear between mid summer and mid autumn. The variety 'Tricolor' has green and white variegated leaves with red margins.

Hypericum 'Rowallane' is half-hardy. At 1.2-1.5m (4-5ft) high and wide, it is best grown against a west-facing wall. The shallow, cup-shaped flowers appear from late spring onwards.

Cultivation
Plant between mid autumn and mid spring in any fertile well-drained soil in a sunny situation.

Trim the plants to shape in early spring and at the same time prune out at ground level some of the oldest shoots to encourage the formation of new stems.

Propagation To increase small species and hybrids, take 5cm (2in) softwood cuttings in late spring to early summer and root in a cold frame.

Propagate taller shrubs ('Elstead', *H. forrestii*, 'Hidcote' and 'Rowallane') from 10-12cm (4-5in) long heel cuttings of non-flowering lateral shoots between mid summer and early autumn.

Pests and diseases Rust shows as orange spots on the leaves.

Indigofera
indigofera

Indigofera gerardiana

☐ Height 1.5-2.4m (5-8m)
☐ Spread 1.2-2.4m (4-8ft)
☐ Flowers mid summer to mid autumn
☐ Good well-drained soil
☐ Sheltered sunny site

These flowering shrubs are not reliably hardy unless grown against sunny and sheltered walls. Hard frost can cut them to the ground, but they usually grow again from the base. Indigoferas are worth cosseting for their elegant, grey-green fern-like foliage and for their profuse clusters of pea-like flowers throughout summer and autumn.

Popular species
Indigofera gerardiana, syn. *I. heterantha,* grows up to 1.8m (6ft) high and 1.5m (5ft) wide. The attractive grey-green foliage does not appear until early summer, shortly before the rose-purple flowers.
Indigofera potaninii is the hardiest species. It reaches 2.4m (8ft) high and wide, with mid green leaves and rose-pink flowers.

Cultivation
Plant in early to mid autumn or mid spring in good well-drained soil which is not too rich.

In mid spring remove all weak and frosted shoots. If necessary, to maintain shape, shorten by half strong shoots of the previous year.
Propagation Increase by seed.
Pests and diseases Trouble free.

JAPANESE ANGELICA TREE – see *Aralia*
JAPANESE QUINCE – see *Chaenomeles*
JAPONICA – see *Chaenomeles*

Jasminum
jasmine

Jasminum nudiflorum

☐ Height 1.8-9m (6-30ft)
☐ Flowers in winter and summer
☐ Any well-drained soil
☐ Sun or shade

The hardy wall shrubs and climbers in this genus are grown for their attractive flowers – slender trumpet-shaped blooms which are white or yellow; they are often fragrant.

Jasmines are easy to grow. *Jasminum nudiflorum,* the winter-flowering jasmine, needs support for its floppy stems, but the common white jasmine will clamber over arbours and pergolas.

Popular species
Jasminum nudiflorum, winter jasmine, grows 3m (10ft) high against a wall if given support. The bright yellow flowers are produced from late autumn to mid spring on green scandent stems. It does well in shade.
Jasminum officinale, common white jasmine, is a vigorous climber reaching 9m (30ft) high. Its twining stems carry clusters of sweetly scented white flowers from early summer to mid autumn. Varieties include: 'Affine', syn. 'Grandiflorum', large flowers, pink in bud; 'Argenteovariegatum' (grey-green leaves

Jasminum officinale

edged white); and 'Aureum' (yellow-blotched leaves).

Cultivation
Plant between mid autumn and mid spring in ordinary soil in any site, including north-facing walls.

After flowering, cut the stems of *J. nudiflorum* back to within a few centimetres of the base. Thin the shoots of *J. officinale* but do not shorten them.
Propagation Layer in early to mid autumn and separate from the parent plant a year later.
Pests and diseases Trouble free.

JEW'S MALLOW – see *Kerria*
JUNE BERRY – see *Amelanchier*

Kerria
Jew's mallow

Kerria japonica 'Pleniflora'

☐ Height 1.8-3.6m (6-12ft)
☐ Spread 1.2-1.8m (4-6ft)
☐ Flowers mid to late spring
☐ Ordinary garden soil
☐ Light shade or sun

During mid to late spring, the shaggy buttercup-yellow flowers of *Kerria japonica* – Jew's mallow – are a familiar sight in gardens. Most specimens are the hardy, double-flowered form 'Pleniflora', which has long flexible stems ideal for training against a wall; the wedge-shaped, toothed leaves are bright green and turn golden-yellow in autumn. It may reach up to 3.6m (12ft) high. The species has single flowers and grows into a thicket of slender arching stems 1.8m (6ft) high.

Cultivation
Plant during suitable weather between mid autumn and early spring in ordinary garden soil in a partially shaded position or in full sun. In cold areas plant the shrubs against a wall with either a south-facing or west-facing aspect.

After flowering, cut back all flowered shoots to new strong growth. Thin out the new shoots of 'Pleniflora' to encourage vigorous young basal shoots.

Propagation Divide and replant shrubs with numerous stems during mild weather from mid autumn to early spring.

Pests and diseases Trouble free.

Kolkwitzia
beauty bush

Kolkwitzia amabilis 'Pink Cloud'

☐ Height 1.8-3.6m (6-12ft)
☐ Spread 1.2-3m (4-10ft)
☐ Flowers late spring to early summer
☐ Ordinary well-drained garden soil
☐ Sunny site

The apparently fragile-looking flowers of the beauty bush (*Kolkwitzia amabilis*) belie the hardiness of this shrub which grows into a thicket up to 3.6m (12ft) high. In late spring to early summer the branches arch over with the weight of its many clusters of pink yellow-throated flowers. The variety 'Pink Cloud' has an abundance of clear pink flowers.

The dark green leaves are oval, hairy and toothed. Another distinguishing feature is the peeling brown bark.

Cultivation
Plant in mid to late autumn or in early spring in ordinary well-drained soil in a sunny site.

After flowering, remove some of the older flowering stems at ground level.

Propagation Take 10-15cm (4-6in) long heel cuttings of lateral non-flowering shoots in mid to late summer and root in a cold frame.

Pests and diseases Trouble free.

KOLOMIKTA – see *Actinidia*

Lavatera

tree mallow

Lavatera olbia 'Rosea'

☐ Height 1.8-2.4m (6-8ft)
☐ Spread 1.5m (5ft)
☐ Flowers early summer to autumn
☐ Ordinary garden soil
☐ Sunny, sheltered position

With its hollyhock-like flowers, tree mallow (*Lavatera olbia*) has an old-fashioned cottage-garden appearance and is prized for its long flowering season.

It forms a 1.8-2.4m (6-8ft) high bush of pithy stems clothed with soft grey-green leaves. From early summer to late autumn, it bears a succession of pink flowers. The variety 'Rosea' has red-pink flowers; 'Barnsley' is pale pink with red centres.

Being only moderately hardy, the short-lived tree mallow is best grown in sheltered gardens and mild coastal areas. It thrives in any soil, even poor shallow types, and flourishes in alkaline soils.

Cultivation

Plant in early autumn or in spring in any well-drained garden soil that is not too rich. The site should be sunny and sheltered from cold winds.

In autumn, prune the shoots by half to avoid wind damage during the winter. Cut hard back in

Lavatera olbia

spring to control vigorous growth and to maintain shape.

Propagation Take semi-ripe cuttings in late summer and root in a cold frame.

Pests and diseases The plants may be affected by leaf spot, which shows as yellow-brown spots on leaves, leaf stalks and stems, or rust – orange spores which later turn brown.

Leycesteria

Himalayan honeysuckle

Leycesteria formosa

☐ Height 1.8m (6ft)
☐ Spread 1.5m (5ft)
☐ Flowers mid to late summer
☐ Any well-drained soil
☐ Full sun or light shade

Himalayan honeysuckle (*Leycesteria formosa*) is a useful plant as it will grow in almost any soil, and in full sun or shade. It is a hardy, highly distinctive shrub with arching 1.8m (6ft) high stems that bear pendent spikes of white tubular flowers in mid to late summer. Each bloom is partially concealed by a purple bract.

In autumn, the flowers are followed by shiny purple-black berries – the purple bracts remain. As the nights become colder, the leaves turn a similar colour and then fall to reveal sea-green shoots.

Cultivation

Plant between mid autumn and early spring in any well-drained soil. It is shade-tolerant, but flowers more freely in a sunny site. Himalayan honeysuckle is a good shrub for coastal gardens as it tolerates sea sprays.

In early spring, cut to the ground all the shoots which bore flowers the previous year.

Propagation Take 15cm (6in) hardwood cuttings in mid autumn and insert in a nursery bed. Grow on for a year before planting out in permanent sites in autumn.

Pests and diseases Trouble free.

LILAC – see *Syringa*

Lonicera

honeysuckle

Lonicera periclymenum 'Graham Thomas'

Lonicera periclymenum 'Serotina'

☐ Height 60cm-9m (2-30ft)
☐ Spread 1.2-1.8m (4-6ft)
☐ Flowers throughout the year
☐ Fertile well-drained soil
☐ Sunny or partially shaded site

To most people, honeysuckle is the twining woodbine which adorns summer hedgerows with its sweetly scented yellow and red flowers. The genus, however, contains a vast range of deciduous and evergreen shrubs as well as climbers, hardy or tender.

Climbing honeysuckles are ideal for growing up walls, fences, archways and pergolas. Those described here are hardy and deciduous, sometimes semi-evergreen. The blooms are often fragrant and followed by berries.

Shrubby honeysuckles can be grown in mixed borders, and several are also good as ground cover plants.

Popular species

Lonicera x *americana* is a vigorous climber, capable of reaching 9m (30ft) high against a wall. It produces a profusion of white, strongly scented flowers which turn yellow, later flushed rose.

They appear from late spring until early autumn.

Lonicera x *brownii*, scarlet trumpet honeysuckle, sometimes semi-evergreen, climbs 3-4.5m (10-15ft) high. The orange-scarlet blooms appear in early summer and late summer. The variety 'Dropmore Scarlet' has scarlet-red flowers and a longer flowering period.

Lonicera fragrantissima is a shrubby, winter-flowering honeysuckle, 1.8m (6ft) high and across; its sweetly scented, delicate ivory-white flowers appear from mid winter to early spring. They are followed by red berries in late spring.

Lonicera periclymenum, woodbine, grows wild in Britain. It can reach 4.5-6m (15-20ft) high, when grown against a wall. The sweetly fragrant, pale yellow flowers flushed with purple-red open from early to late summer. They are followed by bright red berries. Good garden varieties include: 'Belgica', early Dutch honeysuckle (a bushy climber with purple-red and yellow flowers); 'Graham Thomas' (cream and yellow flowers); and 'Serotina', late

Lonicera x *purpusii*

Magnolia
magnolia

Magnolia x *loebneri* 'Leonard Messel'

☐ Height 1.8-4.5m (6-15ft)
☐ Spread 1.5-5.5m (5-18ft)
☐ Flowers early spring to late summer
☐ Well-drained loamy soil
☐ Site sheltered from north and east winds

This genus contains some of the most spectacular flowering shrubs and trees (see also pages 36-38).

The magnificent blooms appear between early spring and late summer, depending on the species. All the shrubby magnolias are hardy and deciduous, with the early-flowering types carrying their blooms on bare branches.

Magnolias are shown off to best effect when they are grown on their own as specimen shrubs. They need shelter from strong, drying winds and early morning sun in spring, such as that afforded by a south-facing or west-facing wall.

Popular species
Magnolia liliiflora, lily magnolia, (syn. *M. purpurea*) has red-purple, chalice-shaped flowers which open from mid spring to mid summer. It has oval leaves which are mid green above and paler beneath. Average height is 1.8-2.4m (6-8ft) high, with a spread of 1.5-2.1m (5-7ft). It dislikes chalky soils. 'Nigra', a more compact variety has deep purple-red flowers.
Magnolia x *loebneri* carries a profusion of fragrant, white, star-shaped flowers in mid to late

Lonicera x *americana*

Dutch honeysuckle (purple-red and cream-yellow flowers).
Lonicera pileata is a semi-evergreen shrub (in severe winters it may lose all its leaves). Reaching 60-90cm (2-3ft) high, but with a spread of 1.2-1.8m (4-6ft), it is excellent for ground cover – even in the heavy shade of trees. In mid to late spring it bears inconspicuous yellow-green flowers, followed by semi-translucent violet berries.
Lonicera x *purpusii* is a shrubby species with a height and spread of 1.8m (6ft). Delicate cream-white flowers are borne on the bare branches in early spring.
Lonicera standishii, a shrubby species, resembles *L. fragrantissima*, though its scented, cream-white winter flowers appear more freely. It reaches 1.2-1.5m (4-5ft) high and wide.
Lonicera x *tellmanniana* is a vigorous climber ideal for shady walls where it may reach 4.5m (15ft) high. The copper-red and yellow flowers appear in summer.

Cultivation
Grow honeysuckles in any well-drained soil – enriched with humus for the climbing species. All will grow in sun or partial shade, but climbers do better in light shade. Plant between early autumn and early spring.

On established climbers, thin out crowded stems by removing from ground level about one-third of the shoots annually in early spring. Shrubby honeysuckles need little pruning.
Propagation Increase climbing species and varieties 10cm (4in) long stem cuttings in mid to late summer and root them in a cold frame.

Shrubby honeysuckles – and climbers – can be increased by layering between late summer and late autumn. Separate from the parent plant about a year later.
Pests and diseases Shrubby honeysuckles are usually trouble free. Climbers often suffer attacks by aphids. Leaf spot shows as small green or large brown spots and powdery mildew as a white powdery deposit on the leaves.

Magnolia liliiflora 'Nigra'

spring before the lance-shaped mid green leaves appear. It can grow up to 7.5m (25ft) high and wide, and tolerates limy soils. Popular varieties include 'Leonard Messel' (lilac-pink flowers) and 'Merrill' (white flowers).

Magnolia sieboldii, syn. *M. parviflora*, has pendent bowl-shaped flowers with white petals and conspicuous claret-red stamens. They appear between late spring and late summer and have a rich fragrance. The shrub grows to a height and spread of 3-4.5m (10-15ft) and bears dark green lance-shaped leaves which are downy beneath. Spectacular seed capsules open in autumn to reveal orange seeds. The species is intolerant of lime.

Magnolia stellata is a slow-growing tree, usually treated as a shrub since it only reaches 2.4-3m (8-10ft) high and 2.4-3.6m (8-12ft) wide. Its fragrant white star-shaped flowers open in early to mid spring. The lance-shaped leaves are pale to mid green. Several varieties are available: 'Rosea' (pink buds with flowers

Magnolia stellata 'Rosea'

111

Menziesia

menziesia

Menziesia ciliicalyx

☐ Height 90cm-1.8m (3-6ft)
☐ Spread 45cm (1½ft)
☐ Flowers late spring to early summer
☐ Lime-free soil
☐ Sunny or partially shaded site

The shrubs in this small genus belong to the heather family and are often grown in association with rhododendrons as they thrive in identical conditions. Alternatively they are excellent in a peat garden or large rockery. Their urn- or bell-shaped flowers resemble those of heather but the leaves are distinctly different: oval, pale green and bristly.

Menziesia ciliicalyx is slow-growing and the most commonly grown species. Its pinkish-purple flowers appear in late spring and early summer. The variety *M.c. purpurea* has larger, purple-red and slightly later blooms.

Cultivation
Plant between mid autumn and late winter in lime-free soil in sun or partial shade, preferably with shelter from strong winds. Mulch annually in spring.
Propagation Heel cuttings taken in summer and rooted in a propagating frame are slow to strike and take several years to produce plants sturdy enough to plant out.
Pests and diseases Trouble free.

MEZEREON – see *Daphne*
MILE-A-MINUTE VINE – see *Polygonum*
MOCK ORANGE – see *Philadelphus*

Magnolia x loebneri 'Merrill'

fading to white); 'Royal Star' (large white blooms); and 'Water Lily' (pale pink buds and many petalled white flowers).

Cultivation
Plant in early to mid spring in well-drained loamy soil. The site can be in full sun or dappled shade, but it must be sheltered from north or east winds – early-flowering species can have their blooms damaged by morning sun after a night frost.

Avoid disturbing the soil around the shrubs as their roots grow close to the soil surface. Every mid spring top-dress with leaf-mould, compost or shredded forest bark.

Pruning is not necessary.

Propagation Take 10cm (4in) heel cuttings of half-ripened shoots in mid summer and root in a propagating frame at a temperature of 21°C (70°F). Pot the rooted cuttings in 7.5cm (3in) pots and overwinter them in a cold frame. The following late spring plant in a nursery bed, and leave them for two or three years before planting in the permanent positions.
Pests and diseases Shoots damaged by frost may be attacked by grey mould. Honey fungus can kill the shrubs.

MALLOW, TREE – see *Lavatera*
MAPLE – see *Acer*

Paeonia

tree peony

Paeonia lutea

Paeonia suffruticosa 'Duchess of Marlborough'

- ☐ Height 1.2-1.8m (4-6ft)
- ☐ Spread 1.2-1.8m (4-6ft)
- ☐ Flowers late spring to early summer
- ☐ Well-drained rich soil
- ☐ Sunny sheltered site

Despite their name, tree peonies do not reach tree-like proportions but grow as medium-sized shrubs clothed with ornamental foliage. They are fully hardy but start into growth in early spring, when frosts can damage the buds unless the shrubs are grown in a sheltered site. The blooms on shrubby peonies are as spectacular as those on their perennial relatives. Appearing in late spring, they are single, semi-double or fully double and come in yellows, whites, pinks and reds.

When the flowers are over, the lush green, deeply divided leaves come into their own, providing an ornamental backdrop for summer-flowering plants in mixed borders.

Popular species

Paeonia delavayi is a suckering shrub with an open branching habit reaching a height and spread of 1.8m (6ft). It has doubly divided dark green leaves, and deep red cup-shaped flowers with yellow anthers in late spring. 'Black Pirate', a popular variety, has striking deep crimson-maroon flowers. These shrubs thrive on deep chalky soils.

Paeonia x lemoinei is the name given to a group of hybrids with blooms in varying shades of yellow.

They grow up to 2m (7ft) high and 1.5m (5ft) wide, flower in late spring and early summer and do well on chalk. Popular varieties include: 'Alice Harding' (double lemon-yellow); 'Chromatella' (double sulphur-yellow); and 'Souvenir de Maxime Cornu' (double, bright yellow edged with crimson-red, and fragrant).

Paeonia lutea is a 1.2-1.8m (4-6ft) high shrub with deeply divided pale green leaves. Its single yellow flowers, which have a lily-like fragrance, appear in early summer. The outstanding variety, *P. lutea ludlowii,* has larger, golden-yellow flowers.

Paeonia suffruticosa, syn. *P. arborea,* the Moutan peony, is the parent of a large number of varieties. All bear large, 15cm (6in)

Paeonia suffruticosa 'Rock's Variety'

Parrotia
parrotia

Parrotia persica

□ Height 3-5.4m (10-18ft)
□ Spread 3-4.5m (10-15ft)
□ Foliage shrub
□ Well-drained loamy soil
□ Sunny or lightly shaded site

Autumn foliage in magnificent tints of amber, crimson and gold makes *Parrotia persica* a shrub worth considering for the garden. It is a hardy, slow-growing, spreading specimen which eventually grows to tree size, 5.4m (18ft) high and 4.5m (15ft) wide.

The trunk is covered in grey bark which on mature shrubs flakes away to create attractive patterns – for this to be shown off to best advantage, remove the lower branches.

In early to mid spring clusters of tiny inconspicuous flowers appear which have red stamens but no petals. They are carried on bare twigs before the oval mid green leaves unfurl.

The variety 'Pendula' has weeping branches which give it a domed appearance. Rich autumn colours.

Cultivation
Plant in any well-drained loamy soil in sun or light shade between mid autumn and early spring. Parrotia tolerates limy soils.

Pruning is unnecessary, but lower branches may be removed in early spring.
Propagation Layer in early autumn and sever from the parent plant two years later.
Pests and diseases Trouble free.

Paeonia suffruticosa 'Jitsugetsu Nishiki'

wide bowl-shaped flowers in late spring, and pale to mid green leaves. Their height and spread is 1.5-1.8m (5-6ft). The young shoots of these shrubs are particularly susceptible to frost damage.

Popular varieties include: 'Duchess of Marlborough' (semi-double rose-pink); 'Jitsugetsu Nishiki' (semi-double scarlet); 'Montrose' (semi-double pale lilac); 'Mrs William Kelway' (semi-double pure white); and 'Rock's Variety' (single, pale pink to silvery white with maroon blotches).

Cultivation
Plant in mild weather between early autumn and early spring in any deep well-drained soil enriched with organic matter. Set the graft union 7.5cm (3in) below the soil surface. The site should be in sun or light shade, and sheltered from late spring frosts. Every spring mulch with well-rotted manure or compost.

Varieties with heavy double blooms may need staking. Dead-head as the flowers fade – regular pruning is not advisable. Water freely in dry weather.

Paeonia delavayi

Propagation Shrubby peonies are grafted; leave propagation to professional nurserymen.
Pests and diseases Trouble free.

Parthenocissus

Virginia creeper

Parthenocissus tricuspidata 'Veitchii'

Parthenocissus quinquefolia

☐ Height 7.5-21m (25-70ft)
☐ Foliage climber
☐ Fertile well-drained soil
☐ Sunny or shaded site

Virginia creeper is an excellent climber for rapidly clothing a sunny or shaded wall with fresh green leaves in summer, and magnificent fiery red leaves in autumn. Though usually grown against walls or fences, it can also be trained up an arch, pergola, trelliswork or old tree, where a height of 7.5-21m (25-70ft) may eventually be reached. All species are hardy; they are self-supporting, clinging to any surface by means of sticky pads.

Though grown mainly for their foliage, minute yellow-green flowers are produced between late spring and mid summer. Sometimes these are followed by blue-black berries.

Popular species
Parthenocissus henryana, Chinese Virginia creeper, has dark velvety green 'fingered' leaves which are veined silver-pink. This variegation is most pronounced when the plant is grown on a shady wall. In autumn the leaves turn bright red; dark blue fruits follow hot summers. It reaches 7.5-9m (25-30ft) high and needs a sunny, sheltered wall as it is not reliably hardy.

Parthenocissus quinquefolia, Virginia creeper, is a particularly vigorous species which grows up to 21m (70ft) high. The leaves consist of three or five serrated leaflets which turn crimson in autumn. It has tiny yellow-green flowers in late spring and early summer, sometimes followed by small, round, blue-black berries.

Parthenocissus tricuspidata 'Veitchii', Boston ivy, grows up to 15m

Parthenocissus henryana

(50ft) high. It clings to walls and other flat surfaces where it establishes itself rapidly. Leaves are usually three-lobed. Small yellow-green flowers appear in summer and may be followed by small black berries which are covered with a silvery bloom.

Cultivation
Plant container-grown specimens in suitable weather between late autumn and early spring. Sun or shade suit most species, though *P. henryana* needs warmth and shelter. Set in planting pockets 60cm (2ft) square and 45cm (1½ft) deep, filled with moist loamy soil and a dressing of rotted manure or compost.

Support young growth with twiggy sticks until the stems become self-clinging. Pinch out growing tips to encourage side-branching on wall-grown climbers.

Remove unwanted or over-crowded shoots during the summer. Prune to maintain or restrict growth in autumn.

Propagation Take 25-30cm (10-12in) hardwood cuttings in late autumn and root in a sheltered border outdoors.

Pests and diseases Scale insects infest the stems and make the plants sticky and sooty. Aphids affect young growth and red spider mites can cause mottling or wilting of the leaves. Honey fungus may kill plants.

Perovskia

Russian sage

Perovskia atriplicifolia 'Blue Mist'

☐ Height 90cm-1.5m (3-5ft)
☐ Spread 45cm (1½ft)
☐ Flowers late summer to early autumn
☐ Any well-drained soil
☐ Sunny site

This hardy sub-shrub, which from a distance resembles a tall leggy lavender, is excellent for growing on thin, chalky soils and in coastal gardens. Spikes of violet-blue flowers, which appear in late summer to early autumn, are its main attraction. They are set off by grey-green coarsely toothed leaves smelling of sage. Russian sage looks most effective in a mass planting.

Popular varieties
Varieties developed from *P. atriplicifolia* have flowers in varying shades of blue.
'Blue Mist' has light blue flowers from mid summer onwards.
'Blue Spire' has deep violet-blue flowers in late summer to early autumn, and daintily cut foliage.

Cultivation
Plant between late autumn and early spring, except in frosty weather, in any well-drained soil in a sunny site.

In spring, cut the stems down to 30-45cm (1-1½ft) above ground.
Propagation Take 7.5cm (3in) long heel cuttings of lateral shoots in mid summer and root in a cold frame.
Pests and diseases Trouble free.

Philadelphus

mock orange

Philadelphus 'Manteau d'Hermine'

☐ Height 90cm-3m (3-10ft)
☐ Spread 90cm-3.6m (3-12ft)
☐ Flowers early summer
☐ Ordinary well-drained soil
☐ Full sun or partial shade

The common name for *Philadelphus* is mock orange, because the scent of its flowers resembles that of orange blossom. In early to mid summer the branches of these hardy shrubs are weighed down with sprays of sweetly fragrant flowers which are white or cream, sometimes with a pale cerise blush at the base of each petal.

Mock oranges are easily grown, free-flowering shrubs with oval mid green, prominently veined leaves unless otherwise stated.

Popular species and varieties
Philadelphus 'Beauclerk' has single white flowers with flushed pink centres. It reaches 1.8-2.4m (6-8ft) high and has a spread of 1.5-1.8m (5-6ft).
Philadelphus 'Belle Etoile' has large white single flowers with purple central blotches. They are very sweetly scented. It grows 2.4-3m (8-10ft) high and 3-3.6m (10-12ft) wide.
Philadelphus 'Bouquet Blanc' bears large clusters of double white flowers. It grows 1.2-1.8m (4-6ft) high and wide.
Philadelphus coronarius is a dense bushy shrub with a height and spread of 1.8-2.7m (6-9ft). The flowers are cream-coloured and have prominent yellow stamens. 'Aureus' is a popular variety whose young foliage is bright yellow, becoming green-yellow in summer. The leaves retain their colour best if grown in shade or semi-shade.
Philadelphus delavayi is a vigorous species reaching 3m (10ft) high and 2.4m (8ft) wide. It bears dark green, grey-felted leaves and is best planted in shade. The single white, heavily scented flowers are borne in clusters.
Philadelphus 'Enchantment' has clusters of double, white sweetly scented flowers, borne on arching stems. It rarely grows more than 1.8m (6ft) high and wide.
Philadelphus 'Manteau d'Hermine' is a compact variety usually

Philadelphus 'Belle Etoile'

no more than 90cm (3ft) high and wide, with double cream-white, fragrant flowers.

Philadelphus microphyllus is the smallest mock orange. Growing 90cm (3ft) high and wide, it has small bright green leaves and masses of sweetly scented white flowers.

Philadelphus 'Minnesota Snowflake' bears double white flowers and grows 1.2-1.8m (4-6ft) high and wide.

Philadelphus 'Norma' is a shrub up to 1.5m (5ft) high and wide. Its arching branches carry white flowers which have only a slight fragrance.

Philadelphus 'Sybille' bears a profusion of single white flowers with purple markings on arching branches. It grows 1.2m (4ft) high and 90cm (3ft) wide.

Philadelphus 'Virginal' has a strong upright growth habit and reaches 3m (10ft) high and 1.5m (5ft) wide. The white double

or semi-double, richly scented flowers are carried in large clusters.

Cultivation
Plant between mid autumn and early spring in any ordinary well-drained soil, including chalk, in sun or light shade.

Thin out old wood from the base after flowering. Be particularly careful not to remove young shoots which will flower the following year.

Propagation Take 10cm (4in) cuttings of half-ripe lateral shoots from mid to late summer and root in a cold frame. Set out the rooted cuttings in a nursery bed the following spring and then transfer them to their permanent planting positions from mid autumn onwards.

Alternatively, take 30cm (1ft) hardwood cuttings in autumn and root in an outdoor nursery bed. Plant out a year later.

Philadelphus coronarius 'Aureus'

Pests and diseases Leaf spot may cause circular yellow blotches with darker edges on the foliage.

Polygonum

Russian vine, mile-a-minute vine

Polygonum baldschuanicum

Polygonum aubertii

☐ Height 12m (40ft)
☐ Flowers mid summer to early autumn
☐ Any well-drained ordinary garden soil
☐ Sunny or lightly shaded site

Russian vines (*Polygonum baldschuanicum*) are ideal plants for gardeners with little time to spare. Immensely vigorous (spreading 3-4.5m/10-15ft a year), these hardy climbers will tumble over anything in their path, making further gardening in that area unnecessary – and impossible. For this reason they should be planted where they have plenty of room to roam unhindered.

From mid summer to early autumn these lofty plants become impressive, their massed pale green foliage foaming with long, white or pale pink flower sprays on the current year's growth.

They can be encouraged to climb up wires, trellis, hedges and tall trees and are perfect for screening an unsightly shed or other garden eyesore. Remember,

however, that being deciduous, they will only form an attractive cover during the growing season, and in winter the bare stems can look ungainly.

Popular species

Polygonum aubertii, syn. *Bilderdykia aubertii,* scrambles its twining, slightly scaly stems to a height of 12m (40ft). They are clothed with small ovate, glossy bright green leaves that are pale green and red-tipped when young. From late summer onwards, the climber becomes a billowing mass of small white to greenish-white flowers.

Polygonum baldschuanicum, syn. *Bilderdykia baldschuanica,* the Russian vine, closely resembles *P. aubertii,* though the pale green leaves are heart-shaped and the stems smooth. The two species are often confused, *P. baldschuanicum* being the least common. It can be distinguished by a pink tinge to the huge panicles of late-summer flowers.

Cultivation

Plant young container-grown specimens in early to mid spring in any type of soil, including chalk, in sun or shade. Support the young growth with sticks after pinching out the growth tips to encourage branching. Pinch out young plants two or three more times during the summer.

The tangled mass of stems makes pruning virtually impossible but the shoots can be thinned out or shortened during the dormant season. In windy sites, they often break off naturally.

Propagation If necessary, take heel cuttings 7.5-10cm (3-4in) long from half-ripe wood during mid to late summer. Root them in a cold frame, then pot them up and plunge outdoors until the following spring when they can be planted out in their permanent positions.

Pests and diseases Aphids may infest and distort young growth.

POMEGRANATE – see *Punica*

Poncirus

hardy orange, Japanese bitter orange

Poncirus trifoliata

☐ Height 3m (10ft)
☐ Spread 1.2-1.5m (4-5ft)
☐ Flowers late spring
☐ Fertile well-drained soil
☐ Sunny site

As the common name – hardy orange – implies, this shrub belongs to the citrus family. It is reliably hardy only in milder areas and thrives in coastal gardens, where it is often grown as a hedge – the spiny stems making a formidable barrier to animals.

Poncirus trifoliata, syn. *Citrus trifoliata*, looks equally attractive

Poncirus trifoliata, fruits

grown as a specimen shrub or in a mixed border, where it will eventually reach 3m (10ft) high. It is of dense angular habit, with olive-green stems covered with strong, vicious spines. Clusters of sweetly scented white flowers appear in late spring just before the leaves unfurl. In late summer, aromatic fruits resembling small tangerines begin to ripen from green to yellow. Though too bitter to eat raw, they can be used for marmalade.

Cultivation
Plant in autumn or spring during mild weather. Fertile well-drained soil and a sunny site provide the best growing conditions.

Remove dead and damaged growth in spring. If growing hardy orange as a hedge, clip it into shape after flowering.

Propagation Take semi-ripe cuttings in late summer and root in a propagator.

Pests and diseases Trouble free.

Potentilla

potentilla, cinquefoil

Potentilla fruticosa 'Tangerine'

☐ Height 30cm-1.2m (1-4ft)
☐ Spread 90cm-1.5m (3-5ft)
☐ Flowers early summer to mid autumn
☐ Any well-drained soil
☐ Sun or light shade

Potentillas are among the most popular of hardy flowering shrubs, prized for their succession of brightly coloured flowers between early summer and mid autumn. The single or double blooms are saucer-shaped and borne in small terminal clusters.

Shrubby potentillas are suitable for the front of borders and for sunny banks; they have the greatest impact when planted in groups of three. Prostrate types make excellent ground cover plants.

Few species are grown, but numerous garden varieties have been developed, offering flowers in shades of yellow, orange, red, pink and white.

Popular species
Potentilla arbuscula, syn. *P. fruticosa* var. *rigida*, has small rich yellow flowers between late spring and late summer. It is a prostrate shrub with a height of 60cm (2ft) and a spread of 1.5m (5ft). The small, finely divided leaves are pale to mid green and covered with silky bronze hairs. 'Beesii', a popular variety, has silvery leaves.

Potentilla fruticosa has golden-yellow flowers which appear in

Potentilla fruticosa 'Red Ace'

Potentilla fruticosa 'Elizabeth'

Potentilla fruticosa 'Abbotswood'

succession between early summer and mid autumn. It grows into a small twiggy bush about 90cm (3ft) high and wide. The mid green leaves are deeply cut. A large number of varieties have been developed from this species and include: 'Abbotswood' (a dwarf shrub with white flowers and dark green leaves); 'Day-dawn' (small bushy shrub with peach-pink flowers suffused with cream); 'Elizabeth' (tall and spreading to 1.2m (4ft), with rich canary-yellow flowers); 'Goldfinger' (bushy with deep yellow flowers, blue-green foliage); 'Katherine Dykes' (vigorous bushy shrub with primrose-yellow flowers); 'Manchu' (prostrate shrub with white flowers and grey leaves); 'Primrose Beauty' (dense shrub with primrose-yellow flowers, deep yellow centres, and greyish-green leaves); 'Red Ace' (low, compact shrub with vermilion-red flowers, yellow undersides to the petals); 'Royal Flush' (similar to 'Red Ace', but with rose-pink flowers); 'Sunset' (small, compact shrub with deep orange to brick-red flowers, best in light shade); 'Tangerine' (a wide-spreading, dwarf shrub with orange-yellow flowers, best in light shade); and 'Vilmoriniana' (erect shrub up to 2.1m/7ft, with cream-white flowers and silver leaves).

Cultivation
Plant between mid autumn and early spring in any well-drained soil in a sunny site. Pink and red-flowered varieties tend to fade in sites with hot midday sun and do better in light shade.

Regular pruning is not necessary. Remove weak and old stems occasionally at ground level to keep the shrubs bushy. After flowering, trim off the tips of flowering shoots.

Propagation Take 7.5cm (3in) heel cuttings of half-ripe lateral shoots in early to mid autumn. Root in a cold frame. In late spring transplant to a nursery bed and grow on until mid autumn of the following year before setting the plants in their permanent positions.

Pests and diseases Trouble free.

Prunus

ornamental almond, apricot, cherry, peach and plum

Prunus tenella 'Fire Hill'

☐ Height 60cm-6m (2-20ft)
☐ Spread 60cm-6m (2-20ft)
☐ Flowers late winter to late spring
☐ Ordinary well-drained soil
☐ Sunny site

Prunus is an enormous genus containing ornamental trees and shrubs grown for their stunning spring blossom. Some also have richly coloured autumn foliage and attractive fruits.

All shrubby species and varieties described here are hardy and easy to grow, given an open sunny site. They make handsome specimen shrubs and many are also suitable for hedging. See also pages 47-49.

Popular species and varieties

Prunus x *cistena* 'Crimson Dwarf', the purple-leaved sand cherry, has small rich red oval leaves which set off the white blossom from early to mid spring. Growing 1.2-1.5m (4-5ft) high and wide, it is often grown as a hedge.

Prunus glandulosa, Chinese bush cherry, grows into a neat bushy shrub 1.2-1.5m (4-5ft) high and across, with erect shoots. It has mid green leaves and white or pink flowers in mid spring. Popular varieties include 'Alba Plena' (double white flowers in late spring) and 'Rosea Plena'/ 'Sinensis' (double bright pink flowers in mid spring).

Prunus incisa, Fuji cherry, can reach 3-4.5m (10-15ft) high and wide. The small sharply toothed leaves take on rich autumn tints. Pink buds open into white flowers in early spring before the leaves unfurl. The variety 'Praecox' flowers in late winter.

Prunus mume, Japanese apricot, grows into a round open shrub, occasionally a small tree, 4.5-6m (15-20ft) high and wide. It bears pale pink scented flowers which cluster thickly along the slender branches in late winter or early spring. The leaves are mid green. Popular varieties include: 'Albo Plena' (semi-double white flowers); 'Alphandii' (semi-double pink blooms); 'Beni-shidare' (strongly fragrant, double rose-pink blooms); and 'Pendula' (weeping habit and single or semi-double pale pink flowers).

Prunus persica, common peach, is a small tree or a vigorous shrub, which grows 4.5-7.5m (15-25ft) high and wide. It has lance-shaped mid green leaves and pale pink flowers in mid spring. Ornamental varieties include: 'Albo-plena' (double white flowers); 'Cardinal' (glowing red semi-double flowers); 'Foliis Rubris' (reddish-purple foliage becoming bronze-green, single pink flowers); 'Helen Borchers' (large semi-double rose-pink blooms), 'Iceberg' (abundant pure white semi-double flowers); 'Klara Mayer' (double peach-pink flowers); 'Prince Charming' (rose-red double flowers); 'Russell's Red' (double crimson flowers); and 'Windle Weeping' (weeping habit, semi-double pinkish-purple flowers).

Prunus spinosa, blackthorn or sloe, is a hedgerow shrub native to Britain. Masses of snow-white flowers smother the spiny branches in early spring before the dark green leaves unfurl. The small damson-like fruits (sloes) are used in cooking and wine-making. The shrub grows 3-4.5m (10-15ft) high and wide. Ornamental garden varieties include

Prunus incisa

Prunus x cistena

'Plena' (with double white flowers) and 'Purpurea' (rich purple foliage and white flowers). *Prunus tenella*, syn. *P. nana*, dwarf Russian almond, is a low-growing suckering shrub with a height and spread of 60cm-1.2m (2-4ft). It has erect willowy stems with glossy bright green leaves which are pale green underneath. Bright pink flowers cover the branches in mid spring. The variety 'Fire Hill' has rose-crimson flowers.

Prunus triloba, a species of dense twiggy habit, grows 3-4.5m (10-15ft) high and wide. The form usually grown is 'Multiplex', which bears double, rosette-like, clear pink flowers in profusion along the slender branches in mid spring. They are good for cutting and forcing into bloom indoors. The bright green leaves are coarsely toothed. An excellent shrub for training against a sunny wall.

Cultivation

All species and varieties thrive in ordinary well-drained garden soils, preferably with a trace of lime. But most soils are suitable provided they are neither dry nor waterlogged. The site should be sunny.

Plant in early autumn while the soil is still warm, though planting can continue during suitable weather until early spring.

Prunus spinosa

Punica
pomegranate

Rhamnus
buckthorn

Punica granatum

Rhamnus frangula

Prunus persica 'Klara Mayer'

Most shrubs are shallow-rooting, and should not be planted too deeply, nor should the soil around them be cultivated too often.

For hedging use 45-60cm (1½-2ft) high plants and set them 60cm (2ft) apart. After planting, cut back the upper third of all shoots to promote bushy growth.

Little pruning is needed except to remove weak, damaged or dead shoots as soon as they are noticed. On *P. glandulosa* and *P. triloba*, especially well-trained types, cut back flowered shoots to within two or three buds of the base immediately after flowering.

Clip hedges at any time, ideally after flowering.
Propagation Take 7.5-10cm (3-4in) long heel cuttings in late summer to early autumn and root them in a cold frame. Pot up the rooted cuttings, then transfer them to a nursery bed in spring and grow on for one or two years before transplanting.

P. tenella can also be increased by removing and replanting rooted suckers, and *P. glandulosa* by layering in early spring. Sever from the parent plant two years later and plant out.
Pests and diseases In winter birds sometimes eat young buds. Aphids may infest leaves and young shoots, and caterpillars sometimes feed on the leaves. Diseases which can cause problems include canker, chlorosis, honey fungus and silver leaf.

☐ Height 2.4-3m (8-10ft)
☐ Spread 1.5-2.4m (5-8ft)
☐ Flowers early summer to early autumn
☐ Ordinary well-drained soil
☐ Sunny sheltered site

Pomegranate, cultivated in hot climates for its succulent fruits, is grown in Britain for its summer display of crimson flowers. They are trumpet-shaped and borne singly or in clusters from early summer to autumn.

Pomegranate is half-hardy and suitable only for mild, frost-free regions. Even then it requires a warm sunny position against a south-facing wall. Here it will reach a height of 2.4-3m (8-10ft) and a spread of 1.5-2.4m (5-8ft). The oblong leaves are pale to mid green, and yellow in autumn.

Popular varieties
A few garden varieties have been developed from *Punica granatum*. **'Albopleno'** has double cream-white flowers.
'Flore Pleno' bears double, orange-red flowers.
'Nana' has red flowers and grows only 90cm (3ft) high and wide.

Cultivation
Plant in late spring in ordinary well-drained soil in a sunny sheltered site.
Propagation Take 7.5cm (3in) long heel cuttings of half-ripened lateral shoots in mid summer.
Pests and diseases Trouble free.

QUINCE – see *Chaenomeles*

☐ Height 4.5m (15ft)
☐ Spread 3.6m (12ft)
☐ Foliage shrub
☐ Any well-drained soil
☐ Sunny or lightly shaded site

The alder buckthorn (*Rhamnus frangula*) is a hardy shrub grown for its attractive foliage and its colourful autumn berries. The dark green glossy leaves are ovate and toothed; they turn attractive shades of yellow in autumn.

Inconspicuous white flowers in spring are followed by abundant clusters of berries that ripen slowly from green to red and finally black. Good varieties include 'Asplenifolia', with narrow, thread-like foliage, golden in autumn; and 'Columnaris', a slender upright form to 3.6m (12ft) high.

Cultivation
Plant in autumn or spring in any well-drained soil, and in full sun or light shade. Tolerant of salt sprays and town pollution.

Regular pruning is unnecessary; remove dead or damaged shoots in early spring.
Propagation Increase buckthorn by layering in spring; roots should have formed after one or two years when the new plants can be separated from the parent.
Pests and diseases Trouble free.

Rhododendron (azalea)

azalea

Rhododendron Knap Hill hybrids

☐ Height 90cm-3m (3-10ft)
☐ Spread 60cm-3m (2-10ft)
☐ Flowers mid spring to mid summer
☐ Sheltered lightly shaded site
☐ Moist rich, acid soil

Deciduous azaleas are among the most brightly coloured spring-flowering shrubs. When the spectacular blooms open, they are often so profuse that they cover the entire bush.

Though botanically classified as rhododendrons, azaleas are often regarded as a separate group. They have more delicate flowers and leaves, and tend to be smaller in size.

Azaleas are either deciduous or evergreen. Those described here are deciduous and generally hardy; they have an upright habit and bear clusters of wide trumpet- or funnel-shaped blooms with distinct petals. They come in a wide range of colours, particularly yellows, oranges and orange-reds,

and are often fragrant. In autumn the leaves take on marvellous rich red, orange and yellow hues before falling to the ground.

Azaleodendrons are hybrid crosses between evergreen rhododendrons and deciduous azaleas; they have sparse semi-evergreen foliage and large clusters of funnel-shaped flowers.

Like other rhododendrons, azaleas will grow only in acid soil and generally thrive in sheltered, lightly shaded sites. This makes them an obvious choice for woodland gardens and mixed or shrub borders in partial shade. Azaleas look most effective in a massed group, in single or mixed but harmonious colour combinations.

Popular species
Unless otherwise indicated, the following species flower in mid to late spring.
Rhododendron albrechtii, a 90cm-1.5m (3-5ft) high shrub with a

spread of 90cm (3ft), has clusters of mauve-pink, green-flecked flowers. The rounded leaves are mid green above and pale green below – they turn yellow in autumn. This species is susceptible to spring frosts.
Rhododendron arborescens grows 1.2-1.8m (4-6ft) or more high, with a spread of 1.5-1.8m (5-6ft). It has ovate, glossy bright green leaves that are grey and hairy underneath; they are tinted red in autumn. Clusters of funnel-shaped, strongly fragrant and white, sometimes pink-flushed flowers are borne in early and mid summer.
Rhododendron calendulaceum, one of the most vividly coloured azaleas, grows 1.2-3m (4-10ft) tall and 1.5m (5ft) wide. The leaves turn vivid orange and crimson in autumn. In late spring and early summer, it bears huge clusters of yellow, orange or scarlet flowers.
Rhododendron kaempferi, syn. *R.*

125

Rhododendron luteum

obtusum kaempferi, is one of the parents of the evergreen Kurume azaleas. The species itself is usually deciduous, 1.5m (5ft) high and wide, with ovate dark green leaves, downy in the younger stages of development. It flowers in late spring, with a profusion of small clusters of funnel-shaped flowers ranging from orange to salmon-pink and brick red.

Rhododendron luteum, syn. *R. flavum*, bears fragrant yellow flowers in late spring and early summer. A suckering shrub with a height of 1.8-3m (6-10ft) and a spread of 1.2-1.8m (4-6ft), it has light green leaves which turn rich orange, purple and crimson in autumn.

Rhododendron occidentale has clusters of fragrant white flowers tinged pink in early to mid summer. It reaches 3m (10ft) high and 1.2-1.8m (4-6ft) across and has shiny, lance-shaped green leaves. It is the parent of many azalea hybrids.

Rhododendron reticulatum grows 3m (10ft) or more high, spreading to 2.4m (8ft), and bears rounded to diamond-shaped, strongly veined leaves. These are purplish and hairy when young and turn orange and red in autumn. Bright purple flowers, borne singly or in pairs, appear in mid spring, before the leaves.

Rhododendron schlippenbachii has wide funnel-shaped flowers ranging from white to shades of pink speckled with dull red. It reaches 1.8-4.5m (6-15ft) high and 1.2-2.4m (4-8ft) across and bears rounded mid green leaves which assume red and orange tints in autumn. In open sites, the species is easily damaged by spring frosts.

Rhododendron vaseyi, an ultra-hardy pink-flowered species, reaches 2.4-4.5m (8-15ft) high and 1.2-1.8m (4-6ft) across. It bears lance-shaped pale green leaves which turn orange and red in autumn.

Rhododendron viscosum, a bushy shrub known as the swamp honeysuckle, reaches a height of 1.8-2.4m (6-8ft) and a spread of 1.2-1.8m (4-6ft). The leaves turn orange and red in autumn. It is a summer-flowering species, with clusters of sweetly scented, honeysuckle-like flowers that are white, tinted pink.

Azalea hybrids

These generally flower in late spring and early summer. The popular hybrids fall into five different categories.

Ghent hybrids reach 1.5-1.8m (5-6ft) high and wide and have long-tubed, usually fragrant flower clusters. The leaves often assume brilliant autumn tints. Popular varieties include: 'Coccineum Speciosum' (brilliant orange-red); Corneille' (cream tinged with rose); 'Daviesii' (cream-white blotched yellow); 'Gloria Mundi' (bright orange and yellow, frilled); 'Nancy Waterer' (golden-yellow); 'Narcissiflorum' (double, soft yellow); and 'Unique' (large, orange-yellow).

Knap Hill and Exbury hybrids all have large trusses of wide trumpet-shaped flowers in late spring to early summer. Their height ranges from 1.2-2.4m (4-8ft) and their spread up to 1.5m (5ft). The leaves are often tinted with bronze when young and are attractively coloured in autumn. Popular hybrids include: 'Avon' (pale yellow); 'Ballerina' (white with orange markings); 'Balzac' (fragrant, orange-red); 'Berry-rose' (salmon-pink blotched yellow); 'Coronation Lady' (salmon-pink blotched orange); 'Firefly' (rose-red, flushed orange); 'Gibraltar' (bright orange); 'Klondyke' (orange-gold); 'Persil' (white blotched orange); 'Pink Ruffles' (carmine-rose blotched orange); 'Silver Slipper' (white

Rhododendron 'Avon' (Knap Hill hybrid)

Rhododendron 'Glory of Littleworth' (Azaleodendron)

flushed pink with a yellow blotch) and 'Strawberry Ice' (translucent pink with yellow blotches).

Mollis hybrids flower in late spring, usually on naked branches. The funnel-shaped flowers have no scent but they come in brilliant colours. Average height and spread is 1.2-1.8m (4-6ft), though they can grow wider under ideal conditions. Narrow hairy leaves cover the shrubs and turn bright orange and scarlet in autumn. Popular named hybrids include 'Dr M. Oosthoek' (rich orange-scarlet) and 'Spek's Orange' (large, salmon-orange).

Occidentale hybrids have fragrant delicately coloured blooms in late spring and early summer. The shrubs reach 1.8-2.4m (6-8ft) high and 2.4-3m (8-10ft) or more across. Favourites include: 'Exquisitum' (cream flushed pink with a ray of orange, frilly); 'Irene Koster' (rose-pink); 'Summer Fragrance' (pale yellow, deep yellow markings); and 'Westminster' (clear pale pink).

Rustica hybrids have double fragrant flowers in late spring and early summer. They reach 1.2-1.5m (4-5ft) high and wide and include 'Freya' (pale pink tinted salmon-orange) and 'Il Tasso' (rose-red and salmon).

Azaleodendrons

These hardy hybrids between evergreen rhododendrons and deciduous azaleas are deciduous or semi-evergreen and bear large clusters of flowers in late spring and early summer. They grow 1.5-2.4m (5-8ft) high and have a spread of 1.2-1.8m (4-6ft). Named varieties include: 'Glory of Littleworth' (fragrant cream flowers blotched orange); 'Martine' (bright pink); 'Nellie' (pure white with large yellow blotches); and 'Odoratum' (fragrant, pale lilac).

Cultivation

Azaleas have the same soil requirements as other rhododendrons – moist acid soil with a rich organic content. But while evergreen species and hybrids grow best in a sheltered, partially shaded site, the deciduous types tolerate more open positions and will thrive in sun, provided their roots are kept cool and moist. It is essential to protect azaleas which flower in early spring from morning sun after night frost or their flower buds can be damaged by sudden thawing. Plant in mid autumn, or in early spring during frost-free weather. They are shallow-rooting and should be set with their root ball just below soil level.

In spring give azaleas an an-nual lime-free mulch and feed with John Innes base fertilizer.

Regular pruning is not necessary though it is important to dead-head. Use fingers to twist off the faded flower trusses taking care not to damage the immature buds beneath.

Propagation Deciduous azaleas are best increased by layering. This can be done at any time of year. Separate from the parent when rooted, after about two years, and plant out.

Pests and diseases Rhododendron bugs, weevils and caterpillars can infest azaleas. Rust, silver leaf and azalea-gall may cause problems. On neutral or alkaline soils, leaves turn yellow as a result of chlorosis.

Rhus

sumach

Rhus glabra, *autumn colour*

- [ ] Height 1.5-4.5m (5-15ft)
- [ ] Spread 1.5-4.5m (5-15ft)
- [ ] Foliage shrub
- [ ] Ordinary garden soil
- [ ] Sunny site

Sumachs are hardy suckering shrubs grown for their magnificent foliage which turns stunning shades of red and orange in autumn after a warm summer. In summer they bear felty spikes of small red or green flowers which are followed by colourful plumes of fruits.

Popular species

Rhus glabra, smooth sumach, reaches 1.5-2.7m (5-9ft) high and has a spread of 1.5-1.8m (5-6ft). Its large, deeply divided leaves are smooth and mid green with blue-green undersides; they turn brilliant red in early to mid autumn. In mid summer conical spikes of light red flowers eventually open and develop into striking clusters of deep red seeds.

Rhus typhina, stag's horn sumach, so-named because the bare winter branches have a velvety coating of brown-red hairs, is a taller shrub reaching 3-4.5m (10-15ft) high and 3.6-4.5m (12-15ft) wide. The mid green leaves are up to 45cm (1½ft) long and turn orange-red, purple and yellow from early autumn onwards. Long conical spikes of red and green flowers appear in summer, followed in autumn by clusters of crimson fruits on female plants. This species is particularly good for town gardens as it tolerates atmospheric pollution. The variety 'Dissecta' ('Laciniata'), a female shrub, has deeply cut leaflets.

Cultivation

Plant between mid autumn and mid spring in ordinary garden soil in a sunny situation. To encourage an abundance of large foliage, prune to the ground between late winter and mid spring.

Propagation Increase by removing and replanting suckers in autumn.

Pests and diseases Trouble free.

Ribes

flowering currant

Ribes sanguineum *'Album'*

- [ ] Height 1.8-3m (6-10ft)
- [ ] Spread 1.2-2.1m (4-7ft)
- [ ] Flowers early spring to early summer
- [ ] Any well-drained soil
- [ ] Sunny or lightly shaded site

The *Ribes* genus, which includes the edible currants and gooseberries, also contains several ornamental flowering shrubs. These decorative species have drooping or upright spikes of blooms in early spring to early summer. They come in white, cream, red and varying shades of pink.

They are generally hardy, easily grown and reach 1.8-3m (6-10ft) high, slightly less across.

Popular species

Ribes odoratum, syn. *R. aureum,* has bright yellow clove-scented flowers held in drooping clusters in mid spring. The shrub grows 1.8-2.4m (6-8ft) high and 1.2-1.5m (4-5ft) wide and bears pale green toothed leaves which turn yellow with an orange flush in autumn.

Ribes sanguineum grows 1.8-2.4m (6-8ft) high and 1.5-2.1m (5-7ft) wide and bears rounded mid green leaves with pale undersides. The flowers are held in long drooping clusters between early and late spring and are followed, in autumn, by round blue-black inedible berries. The shrubs have a strong pungent aroma. Popular varieties include: 'Albescens' (fine clusters of white flowers tinged

Robinia

rose acacia

Robinia hispida

☐ Height 1.8-2.4m (6-8ft)
☐ Spread 1.8-2.4m (6-8ft)
☐ Flowers late spring to early summer
☐ Ordinary well-drained soil
☐ Sheltered sunny position

This lovely pink-flowered shrub, a relative of the handsome ornamental tree, false acacia (*Robinia pseudoacacia* 'Frisia'), makes an unusual and attractive choice for training against a sunny sheltered wall. Its delicate, deep green leaves are divided into several pairs of leaflets. They provide a perfect foil for the deep rose-pink pea-like flowers which open in late spring and early summer. The sparse branches of rose acacia (*Robinia hispida*), covered with red bristly hairs, fan out to a height and spread of 1.8-2.4m (6-8ft). The variety 'Macrophylla' has larger flowers and less bristly stems.

Cultivation

Plant between mid autumn and early spring in ordinary well-drained soil in a sheltered position. As a wall shrub, tie in the vigorous shoots to a wire or trellis support in summer. Remove frost-damaged shoots and unwanted suckers from ground level.

Propagation Remove suckers from below ground between mid autumn and early spring and root in a nursery bed. Plant out in the permanent position one or two years later.

Pests and diseases Scale insects may infest the stems.

Ribes sanguineum 'Pulborough Scarlet'

pink); 'Album' (white flowers); 'Brocklebankii' (smaller slow-growing variety with deep rose-red flowers and golden foliage); 'King Edward VII' (small deep crimson flowers); 'Pulborough Scarlet' (rich red blooms); and 'Tydeman's White' (exceptionally large, pure white flower clusters). *Ribes speciosum* is the most showy of the ornamental currants. Unfortunately, it is only half-hardy, and needs the shelter of a warm wall in all but the mildest gardens. It carries profuse clusters of three to four bright red flowers in mid spring to early summer. The prickly stems are clothed with deeply lobed mid green leaves. It grows 1.8-3m (6-10ft) high, with a spread of 1.2-1.5m (4-5ft).

Cultivation

Plant during mild spells between autumn and spring in any well-drained garden soil in sun or light shade.

Prune annually, after flowering, by removing old and congested stems at ground level, in order to maintain shape and control growth.

Propagation Take hardwood cuttings 25-30cm (10-12in) long in mid to late autumn and insert in a nursery bed. Plant out in the permanent flowering positions one year later.

Pests and diseases Leaf spot causes small brown blotches on the foliage, which drops off.

Ribes speciosum

Romneya
tree poppy

Romneya coulteri

☐ Height 1.2-1.8m (4-6ft)
☐ Spread 1.2-1.8m (4-6ft)
☐ Flowers mid summer to early autumn
☐ Rich, well-drained soil
☐ Sheltered sunny position

The handsome tree poppy (*Romneya coulteri*) is a herbaceous sub-shrub suitable for mixed or shrub borders where it commands attention with its large white poppy-like flowers. They have crinkled petals and gold stamens in a prominent central boss, and appear in mid summer to early autumn.

Tree poppies can be grown successfully only in southern gardens, where they can become invasive underground runners.

Cultivation
Tree poppies dislike root disturbance so plant young container-grown specimens in mid to late spring in a sheltered sunny spot. Well-drained soil with plenty of organic matter produces the best results.

In mid autumn cut all the stems down to a few centimetres above ground level. Protect against frost by covering the base of the plants with bracken or straw.
Propagation Dig up and replant rooted suckers appearing well away from the crown in mid to late spring.
Pests and diseases Poor growing conditions may result in yellowing leaves and wilting shoots.

ROSE ACACIA – see *Robinia*

Rubus
ornamental bramble

Rubus odoratus

☐ Height 30cm-3m (1-10ft)
☐ Spread 30cm-3m (1-10ft)
☐ Flowers late spring to late summer
☐ Ordinary well-drained soil
☐ Sunny or partially shaded site

Most species in the large *Rubus* genus are grown for their edible fruits, such as the raspberry, blackberry and loganberry. Several other hardy species, most of which have thorny stems, have ornamental value and are grown in the flower garden for their foliage, flowers, fruits or handsome winter stems.

Popular species
Rubus cockburnianus, syn *R. giraldianus*, is a useful choice for a winter garden, its ghostly upright white stems gleaming in sunshine after the slender pointed mid green, fern-like leaves have fallen. Reaching 2.1-2.7m (7-9ft) high and 1.5-1.8m (5-6ft) wide, it bears small, purple star-shaped flowers in early summer.
Rubus illecebrosus, strawberry-raspberry, is a dwarf creeping species 30-45cm (1-1½ft) high and wide, grown for its fruits. They resemble strawberries, borne on upright stems, and are large and red, but fairly tasteless.
Rubus odoratus grows 1.8-2.4m (6-8ft) high and spreads to 1.2-1.5m (4-5ft). It is grown for its bright green vine-like leaves on thornless stems and its fragrant bowl-shaped, purple-rose blooms which open in summer.
Rubus phoenicolasius, Japanese wineberry, has long flexible stems and is best trained against a wall as a climber. Reaching 1.8-2.4m (6-8ft) high and 2.4-3m (8-10ft) across, it carries small pink flowers in mid summer and mid green leaves. The stems are covered in brilliant red hairs. In early autumn the orange-red, sweet and edible berries ripen.
Rubus x *tridel* 'Benenden' is a fast-growing hybrid reaching 1.8-2.4m (6-8ft) high and spreading to 2.4-3m (8-10ft). In late spring, glistening white saucer-shaped flowers with masses of yellow stamens are borne on the thornless arching stems. The broad mid green oval leaves are three-lobed.
Rubus ulmifolius is a semi-evergreen species which grows into an arching mound of tangled and prickly growths up to 1.2m (4ft) high and 1.8m (6ft) wide. The form in cultivation is 'Bellidiflorus', with typical bramble leaves, deep green above and grey-green underneath. In mid to late

Salix

willow

Rubus cockburnianus

Rubus x *tridel* 'Benenden'

summer it bears clusters of double pompon-like rose-pink flowers.

Cultivation
Plant between mid autumn and early spring in ordinary well-drained soil in sun or partial shade. After flowering, remove a proportion of old shoots from ground level.

Propagation Take semi-hardwood cuttings 7.5-10cm (3-4in) long in late summer.

Pests and diseases Generally trouble free.

RUSSIAN SAGE – see *Perovskia*
RUSSIAN VINE – see *Polygonum*

Salix hastata 'Wehrhahnii'

☐ Height 30cm-4.5m (1-15ft)
☐ Spread 30cm-3.6m (1-12ft)
☐ Catkins from late winter to mid spring
☐ Moist loamy soil
☐ Sunny site

The name *Salix* or willow is usually associated with the magnificent weeping willows (see page 55) that grow beside water. There are, however, numerous hardy shrubby species and varieties suitable for ornamental use because of their coloured stems, attractive foliage and their outstanding catkins. Male and female catkins are borne on separate trees, in late winter and spring before the leaves unfold; the male catkins are the more conspicuous.

The taller species and varieties are an invaluable source of interest in winter and early spring while the neat and low dwarf willows make ideal plants for ground

cover or as specimens in rock gardens, raised beds and containers.

Popular species
Salix acutifolia is an elegant species 3m (10ft) high and 1.8m (6ft) wide. Its slender damson-purple shoots, silvered with a white bloom in winter, are clothed with narrow, long-tapered mid green leaves. In late winter, the bare branches are studded with male yellow catkins.

Salix aegyptiaca has striking yellow male catkins from late winter to early spring before the mid green downy leaves unfurl. It grows 3-3.6m (10-12ft) high and 2.4m (8ft) wide.

Salix apoda, an alpine species, grows up to 30cm (12in) high and spreads to 60cm (24in), hugging its gnarled branches close to the ground. They bear glossy green, ovate leaves, but before these appear, erect, silver-grey and

Salix elaeagnos

furry male catkins line the branches. As they mature they become covered with bright yellow anthers.

Salix x boydii, a natural, slow-growing hybrid first discovered in Scotland, is of dwarf stature being only 30cm (12in) high and wide, and ideal for a rock or trough garden. It is female and only rarely produces small, dark grey catkins; its attraction lies in the leaves, which are ovate to rounded in shape, silvery-grey and prominently veined and corrugated.

Salix caprea, the pussy willow or goat willow native to Britain, is a bushy 4.5m (15ft) high shrub with a spread of 3.6m (12ft). It has grey-green leaves which are woolly below. Male specimens have yellow catkins in early spring. 'Kilmarnock' ('Pendula'), the variety most commonly grown, has attractive weeping branches. It is often grafted as a standard.

Salix lanata

Salix caprea 'Kilmarnock'

Salix elaeagnos, hoary willow, has long slender branches covered with narrow grey-green leaves. Yellow male catkins appear in mid spring. It grows 3m (10ft) high and spreads to 2.4m (8ft).

Salix gracilistyla 'Melanostachys', a Japanese hybrid, is startling in winter when its naked branches are lined with velvety male catkins so dark crimson as to appear black. Later they become studded with red stamens and, later still, these explode into golden pollen. The shrub, clothed during the season with long, narrowly ovate, glossy deep green leaves, grows 2.4m (8ft) high and wide.

Salix hastata 'Wehrhahnii' has striking dark purple-brown bark and, in mid spring, silvery male catkins which mature to yellow. The oval leaves are mid to grey-green. The shrub grows 1.2-1.5m (4-5ft) high and spreads 1.5-1.8m (5-6ft) wide.

Salix lanata, woolly willow, is a slow-growing shrub suitable for a rock garden. It grows 60cm-1.2m (2-4ft) high and 30cm-1.2m (1-4ft) wide and has rounded mid green leaves covered with a grey-white felt. Stout upright yellow catkins appear in early to mid spring.

Salix purpurea, purple osier, is named after its purplish young stems which yellow with age. It has dark green glossy leaves and grey male catkins which turn reddish-purple. 'Nana' or 'Gracilis' is 1.2m (4ft) high and wide; and

Salix purpurea

'Pendula', a weeping shrub often grafted on to an upright willow stem, forms a small weeping tree about 1.8m (6ft) high.

Salix repens, creeping willow, is a dwarf shrub suitable for large ground cover or creeping over drystone walls. It grows 90cm-1.8m (3-6ft) high and 1.5-2.4m (5-8ft) wide and bears oval grey-green leaves covered in silky silver hairs. These turn dark green in summer. Silver-grey male catkins appear in mid to late spring on bare branches.

Cultivation

Plant between mid autumn and late winter in moist soil in a sunny position.

Dwarf species need no pruning, but cut back willows grown for their coloured stems in late winter to just above ground level every two or three years in early spring.

Propagation Take hardwood cuttings 23-38cm (9-15in) long between mid autumn and mid spring and root in moist soil in a nursery bed. Plant out the rooted cuttings a year later.

Pests and diseases Caterpillars and various beetle larvae eat the leaves, gall mites distort young shoots and sawfly larvae produce galls on the leaves. Aphids and scale insects may colonize the stems and young shoots making them black and sticky. Willows are sometimes prone to die-back, canker, honey fungus and rust.

Sambucus

elder

Sambucus racemosa 'Plumosa Aurea'

☐ Height 3-4.5m (10-15ft)
☐ Spread 2.4-4.5m (8-15ft)
☐ Flowers late spring to summer
☐ Any good soil
☐ Sunny or partially shaded site

Elder, a hardy fast-growing shrub, has been grown in Britain since the 18th century. It is an excellent foliage shrub, with sprays of deeply cut leaves in a range of attractive colours. Heads of small, white star-shaped flowers in spring and summer are followed by shiny black or scarlet berries.

Popular species

Sambucus canadensis, American elder, reaches 3-3.6m (10-12ft) high and has a spread of 2.4-3m (8-10ft). 'Maxima', a popular variety, has large mid green leaves and large flattened heads of white flowers in summer, followed by purple-black fruits.
Sambucus nigra grows 3.6-4.5m (12-15ft) high and wide. Cream-white flowers appear in early summer, followed by black berries. 'Aurea', with yellow-green young foliage , is particularly outstanding.
Sambucus racemosa is usually represented in gardens by the variety 'Plumosa Aurea'. Reaching 2.4-3m (8-10ft) high and wide, it has finely cut golden leaves, upright spikes of cream flowers in late spring and scarlet berries which ripen in summer.

Cultivation

Plant in any good garden soil between mid autumn and early spring in sun or partial shade. The golden-leaved varieties colour earlier in sunny situations, but retain their yellow-green hue longer in cool moist shade.

For more brilliant colour and larger leaves from young shoots, cut the stems back to within a few centimetres of their base, or to near ground level in early spring.
Propagation Take hardwood cuttings in autumn and root in an outdoor nursery bed. Grow on for a year before planting out in the permanent positions.
Pests and diseases Mosaic virus may show on the leaves as yellow bands along the veins and dense colonies of aphids sometimes infest stems and leaves.

SEA BUCKTHORN – see *Hippophaë*
SILVER BERRY – see *Elaeagnus*
SLOE, ORNAMENTAL – see *Prunus*
SMOKE TREE – see *Cotinus*
SNOWBERRY – see *Symphoricarpos*
SNOWY MESPILUS – see *Amelanchier*

Sorbaria

sorbaria, false spiraea

Sorbaria aitchisonii

☐ Height 1.8-2.7m (6-9ft)
☐ Spread 2.4-2.7m (8-9ft)
☐ Flowers late summer to early autumn
☐ Ordinary well-drained soil
☐ Open sunny or lightly shaded position

These hardy easily-grown shrubs resemble enormous clumps of meadowsweet. The species commonly grown – *S. aitchisonii* – grows into a 1.8-2.7m (6-9ft) high bush with a fountain of red-tinged shoots. In late summer to early autumn the light ferny leaves set off the great white fuzzy flowers.

The shrub, which spreads rapidly by underground suckers, is ideally suited to the wild garden.

Cultivation

Plant between mid autumn and early spring in ordinary well-drained soil. The site should be open, in sun or partial shade.

Prune all stems back almost to ground level in early spring.
Propagation Remove rooted suckers at any time between mid autumn and early spring and grow on in a nursery bed for one year before planting out.
Pests and diseases Trouble free.

SPANISH BROOM – see *Spartium*
SPANISH GORSE – see *Genista*

Spartium

Spanish broom

Spartium junceum

☐ Height 2.4-3m (8-10ft)
☐ Spread 1.8-2.4m (6-8ft)
☐ Flowers early to late summer
☐ Ordinary well-drained soil
☐ Open sunny position

One of the best of all summer-flowering shrubs, Spanish broom (*Spartium junceum*) has been grown in British gardens for at least 400 years. An excellent shrub for coastal gardens, it thrives on sandy or alkaline soils and is effective in preventing soil erosion.

The shrub is almost leafless, the bright green stems losing their small, narrow leaves early on. Throughout the summer, it puts on a marvellous display of clear golden pea-like flowers with a strong fragrance. Reaching a height of 2.4-3m (8-10ft), and slightly less wide, it is easy to grow but can be damaged by severe winter weather.

Cultivation

Plant young pot-grown plants in mid autumn or mid spring in an open sunny position in any well-drained soil. Prune to shape in early spring, but avoid cutting into old wood or the shrubs will die back.
Propagation Spanish broom is best increased by seed.
Pests and diseases Trouble free.

SPINDLE TREE – see *Euonymus*

Spiraea

spiraea

Spiraea japonica 'Anthony Waterer'

☐ Height 45cm-2.4m (1½-8ft)
☐ Spread 75cm-2.4m (2½-8ft)
☐ Flowers early spring to late summer
☐ Deep fertile soil
☐ Open sunny position

Spiraeas are hardy, easily grown shrubs popular for their wealth of tiny, star-shaped flowers borne in wide heads or sprays from early spring to late summer. Many also have handsome autumn foliage. Most of the shrubs are of hybrid origin and display a range of growth habits, sizes and colours that will fit into any garden scheme.

All spiraeas revel in sunny open sites, in mixed borders and rock gardens, or as specimen shrubs. Arching varieties look splendid trailing over low walls, while suckering types need plenty of room to accommodate their thickets of shoots. Compact bushy types are suitable for informal hedges.

Popular species and hybrids

Spiraea x *arguta*, foam of May, bridal wreath, bears a profusion of white flower clusters on its slender arching stems between mid and late spring. Often likened to a 'fountain of flowers', it grows 1.8-2.4m (6-8ft) high and wide. The narrow, lance-shaped leaves are mid green.

Spiraea thunbergii

Spiraea nipponica 'Snowmound'

Spiraea prunifolia 'Plena'

Spiraea cantoniensis, syn. *S. reevesiana*, is a graceful wide-spreading shrub with arching shoots 1.2-1.8m (4-6ft) high. The deeply toothed, three-lobed dark green leaves take on red autumn tints. Rounded clusters of double white flowers line the branches in early summer.

Spiraea japonica is a twiggy mound-forming shrub, 90cm-1.5m (3-5ft) high and wide, clothed with sharply toothed, lance-shaped leaves that are mid green above, and pale to blue green underneath. It flowers in late summer, with wide flat heads of pink to rose-red flowers. Numerous hybrids have been bred, including 'Albiflora', syn. 'Alba' (60cm/2ft high, neat and compact, dense white flower heads); 'Anthony Waterer' (60cm/2ft tall, bright crimson);

'Bullata' (slow-growing to 30cm/1ft high and wide, dark crinkled leaves, crimson flowers); 'Bumalda' (similar to 'Anthony Waterer', but with pink and cream variegated shoots and leaves); 'Goldflame' (75cm/2½ft high, with leaves that emerge orange-red, change to yellow then green; rose-red flowers); 'Little Princess' (dwarf, compact, crimson flowers); and 'Nana', syn. 'Alpina' (45-60cm/1½-2ft high and spreading to 1.5m/5ft, lilac-pink flowers).

Spiraea nipponica 'Snowmound' bears a profusion of white flowers in early summer. It is a dense, bushy shrub reaching 2.1m (7ft) high and 2.4m (8ft) wide.

Spiraea prunifolia 'Plena' has profuse clusters of double white blooms covering the arching branches in late spring. Another

attraction is the fiery orange and red leaves in autumn. The shrub grows 1.8m (6ft) high and 2.4m (8ft) wide.

Spiraea thunbergii bears wide clusters of white flowers in early to mid spring before the pale green lance-shaped leaves unfurl. It is a 1.5-1.8m (5-6ft) high shrub with a spread of 1.8-2.4m (6-8ft).

Spiraea trichocarpa has fresh green leaves, the white flower clusters appearing in early summer. It grows 1.8m (6ft) high and wide.

Cultivation

Plant between mid autumn and early spring in deep fertile soil in an open sunny position. For hedging, set the plants 38-60cm (15-24in) apart and cut them back to 15cm (6in) off ground level.

Some spiraeas flower on shoots of the current season, others on those of the previous year. This has a bearing on pruning. *S. japonica* and its varieties all flower on shoots of the current year and should be cut back in early spring to 10cm (4in) above ground level; the largest flower heads are borne on hard-pruned plants. Dead-head after flowering.

Prune the remaining species and varieties immediately after flowering, thinning out old wood as necessary. Trim hedges after flowering.

Propagation Take 20cm (8in) hardwood cuttings in mid autumn and insert in a nursery bed. They should have rooted and be ready for planting out in permanent positions the following autumn.

Pests and diseases Sawfly larvae may eat the leaves.

Spiraea japonica 'Goldflame'

Stachyurus

stachyurus

Stachyurus chinensis

- ☐ Height 2.4-3m (8-10ft)
- ☐ Spread 2.4-3m (8-10ft)
- ☐ Flowers early to mid spring
- ☐ Ordinary well-drained soil
- ☐ Sheltered sunny or partially shaded position

Stachyurus is grown for its unusual early blooms. These first make their presence known in mid autumn when – closed – they appear in pendent clusters like long slender catkins. But it is not until spring that they open to reveal their bell-like shapes. The shrub has an open branching habit and mid green, ovate and slender-pointed leaves.

Popular species
Stachyurus chinensis bears translucent yellow bell-shaped flowers in 10cm (4in) long racemes in early and mid spring. *Stachyurus praecox* has pale yellow flowers with dull red calyces. These appear as early as late winter and continue until mid spring.

Cultivation
Plant in any well-drained soil, enriched with organic matter, between mid autumn and early spring. A sunny or partially shaded site sheltered from cold winds is suitable.
Propagation Take heel cuttings in mid summer.
Pests and diseases Trouble free.

STAFF VINE – see *Celastrus*
STAG'S HORN SUMACH – see *Rhus*

Stephanandra

stephanandra

Stephanandra incisa

- ☐ Height 1.5-2.1m (5-7ft)
- ☐ Spread 1.2-1.8m (4-6ft)
- ☐ Flowers early to mid summer
- ☐ Ordinary well-drained soil
- ☐ Sunny or partially shaded site

Some shrubs depend for their charm not on their flowers, leaves or fruits but simply on their growth habit. The hardy *Stephanandra incisa*, from mountain slopes in Japan, is such an attractive plant. It is a graceful shrub with rich brown, arching branches. At the tip of each shoot, an open cluster of tiny yellow and white flowers appears in early to mid summer. The shrub is 1.5-2.1m (5-7ft) high and 1.2-1.8m (4-6ft) wide.

The green, deeply cut lobed leaves, which resemble those of currant bushes, turn bronze and clear yellow in autumn.

Cultivation
Plant from mid autumn to early spring in any well-drained soil, in sun or partial shade.

Thin out old and decayed shoots in late winter to early spring.
Propagation Remove rooted suckers between mid autumn and early spring. Plant directly in the permanent positions or, if they are small, grow on for a year in a nursery bed before planting out in permanent sites.
Pests and diseases Trouble free.

SUMACH – see *Rhus*
SWEET PEPPER BUSH – see *Clethra*

Symphoricarpos

snowberry

Symphoricarpos 'White Hedge'

- ☐ Height 1.8m (6ft)
- ☐ Spread 1.8m (6ft)
- ☐ Grown for its berries
- ☐ Ordinary well-drained soil
- ☐ Shady or sunny site

The crowning glory of snowberry (*Symphoricarpos* x *doorenbosii*) is its white or pale pink berries that weigh down each branch from mid autumn to late winter.

The hardy shrub forms a dense bush of smooth blue-green leaves from spring to autumn, with small pink bell-shaped flowers appearing in clusters throughout summer.

Popular varieties
'**Magic Berry**' is a compact, spreading shrub with abundant rose-pink berries.
'**Mother of Pearl**' has white, rose-flushed marble-like berries.
'**White Hedge**' has white berries held in upright clusters. It makes a fine informal hedge.

Cultivation
Plant between mid autumn and early spring in any well-drained soil in sun or shade. For hedging, set plants 38-45cm (15-18in) apart and cut them back to 30cm (12in). Thin out overgrown specimens and remove unwanted suckers in mid autumn to late winter. Trim hedges into shape during summer.
Propagation Remove and replant rooted suckers between mid autumn and late winter.
Pests and diseases Leaf spot can occur on the foliage.

Syringa
lilac

Syringa microphylla 'Superba'

☐ Height 1.5-3.6m (5-12ft)
☐ Spread 1.5-2.1m (5-7ft)
☐ Flowers late spring and early summer
☐ Fertile garden soil
☐ Sunny or lightly shaded site

Lilacs are among the most popular of all spring-flowering shrubs and small trees. They are fully hardy and easily grown, and while the foliage is fairly uninteresting, the flowering display is glorious. The large upright or arching flower panicles are often heavily scented and come in pure white, cream, yellow, pink and several shades of blue and purple.

Lilacs make handsome specimen shrubs, and look equally effective in shrub borders. The bushier species and varieties are sometimes used for informal hedges or screens. Lilacs are useful shrubs for town gardens as they tolerate pollution.

Popular hybrids and species
Syringa x *chinensis* grows into a dense bushy shrub 2.4-3m (8-10ft) high and 1.8m (6ft) wide. Its fragrant purple flowers are carried in loose upright spikes in late spring.
Syringa meyeri 'Palibin' is a slow-growing variety with a height and spread of 1.8m (6ft). The dome-shaped shrub is covered with sprays of scented lilac blooms in late spring and early summer.
Syringa microphylla is one of the smaller lilacs, reaching only 1.2-1.5m (4-5ft) high and wide. It has

Syringa x *chinensis*

a delicate growth habit – when the panicles of fragrant rose-lilac flowers appear in early summer, and sometimes again in early autumn, the slender twigs bend over with their weight. 'Superba' has rose-pink flowers from late spring to mid autumn and grows 1.8-2.4m (6-8ft) high.
Syringa x *persica*, Persian lilac, is a bushy rounded shrub 1.8-2.4m (6-8ft) high and 1.8-2.1m (6-7ft) wide. Its upright clusters of fragrant lilac flowers open in late spring. The variety 'Alba' has white flowers.
Syringa x *prestoniae* is a group of Canadian hybrids noted for their hardiness and large, erect or drooping flower panicles in late spring. They grow 3m (10ft) high and wide. Popular varieties include 'Elinor' (purple-red buds opening to pale lavender flowers);

Syringa x *persica*

Tamarix

tamarisk

Tamarix parviflora

☐ Height 3-4.5m (10-15ft)
☐ Spread 3-4.5m (10-15ft)
☐ Flowers late spring and late summer
☐ Ordinary well-drained soil
☐ Sunny open position

There are some plants which not only do best in a certain habitat but seem to epitomize it. Such plants are the hardy tamarisks, which thrive when exposed to harsh salt winds, dry regions and windy situations. They are particularly suited to maritime gardens.

Popular species
Tamarix parviflora carries an abundance of feathery, bright pink flowers in late spring. Growing 3-4.5m (10-15ft) high and wide, it has scale-like green leaves. *Tamarix pentandra* bears long feathery spikes of tiny rose-pink flowers on slender branches in late summer. It grows 3.6-4.5m (12-15ft) high and wide and has narrow pale green leaves. 'Rubra' has deep rose-red flowers.

Cultivation
Plant in well-drained soil in an open sunny position between mid autumn and early spring. Prune *T. parviflora* after flowering and *T. pentandra* in early spring.
Propagation Take 23-30cm (9-12in) hardwood cuttings in mid autumn.
Pests and diseases Trouble free.

TRUMPET CREEPER – see *Campsis*

Syringa vulgaris 'Vulcan'

'Isabella' (pale purple flowers); and 'Royalty' (violet-purple flowers).
Syringa vulgaris, common lilac, is the parent of numerous popular hybrids. They have heart-shaped leaves and pyramidal panicles of fragrant, single or double flowers in late spring. Generally the shrubs grow 2.4-3.6m (8-12ft) high and 1.5-3m (5-10ft) wide. Readily available named varieties include: 'Charles Joly' (double deep purple-red); 'Esther Staley' (red buds, single pure pink flowers); 'Firmament' (single pinkish-mauve); 'Katherine Havemeyer' (double purple-lavender); 'Madame Lemoine' (double cream-white); 'Maréchal Foch' (single carmine-rose); 'Maud Notcutt' (single white); 'Mrs Edward Harding' (semi-double pink and red); 'Président Poincare' (double claret-mauve); 'Primrose' (single cream-yellow); 'Souvenir de Louis Späth' (single wine-red); 'Vestale' (single pure white); and 'Vulcan' (single reddish-mauve).

Cultivation
Plant between mid and late autumn in full sun or very light shade. Lilacs thrive in any good well-drained soil, including chalk. For hedges and screens, set plants 60-120cm (2-4ft) apart.
Remove faded flowers and, from mid autumn onwards, thin out crossing and weak branches. Overgrown bushes can be rejuvenated by cutting them down in winter to 60-90cm (2-3ft) above ground level. Flowers should appear on new growths after two or three years.
Remove all suckers as close as possible to the roots.
Propagation Take 7.5-10cm (3-4in) long heel cuttings of half-ripe shoots in mid to late summer and root in a propagating frame.
Pests and diseases Leaf miner caterpillars may eat the foliage, and frost can kill the flower buds and cause die-back. Honey fungus may kill the shrubs and lilac blight can also be a problem.

Vaccinium

blueberry

Vaccinium corymbosum

☐ Height 1.2-3m (4-10ft)
☐ Spread 1.8-3m (6-10ft)
☐ Flowers late spring to early summer
☐ Moist acid soil
☐ Sunny or partially shaded site

Blueberries are usually grown for their edible fruits, but many species are also suitable for the shrub border. They bear small clusters of bell-shaped flowers in spring and summer, but their true beauty lies in the handsome foliage which colours richly in autumn, and in the shiny berries.

Popular species

Vaccinium arctostaphylos, Caucasian whortleberry, bears long, finely toothed lance-shaped leaves. They turn reddish purple in autumn. It is slow-growing but eventually reaches a height and spread of 1.8-3m (6-10ft). It bears white flowers flushed purple in summer followed by shiny black edible berries.
Vaccinium corymbosum is a suckering shrub 1.2-1.8m (4-6ft) high and 1.8-2.4m (6-8ft) wide. White flowers in late spring – tinted pink – are followed by blue berries. The glossy dark green leaves turn brilliant orange and scarlet in autumn.

Cultivation

Plant between mid autumn and early spring in moist acid-rich soil in sun or partial shade. Trim established shrubs in mid spring.
Propagation Layer long shoots in early autumn.
Pests and diseases Trouble free.

Viburnum

viburnum

Viburnum lantana

☐ Height 90cm-4.5m (3-15ft)
☐ Spread 1.2-4.5m (4-15ft)
☐ Flowers winter, spring and summer
☐ Any moist, well-drained soil
☐ Sunny or lightly shaded site

The *Viburnum* genus contains a large number of species and varieties of enormous diversity. These hardy and invaluable shrubs can provide colour and interest in the garden throughout the year – some produce their flowers on bare branches during the coldest winter months, others bloom in spring and yet others in summer and autumn. The flowers, which are often scented, are borne in dense, round clusters or in flat wide heads, and in several species are followed by heavy crops of berries as striking as the flowers.

The leaves, which are generally broadly ovate, often assume attractive autumn colours.

Viburnums include evergreen and deciduous types; those described here are all deciduous.

Popular species and hybrids

Viburnum betulifolium is 2.4-3.6m (8-12ft) high and wide. It bears clusters of white flowers in late spring and early summer which are followed by a profusion of red berries on mature plants.
Viburnum x *bodnantense* bears clusters of white scented flowers flushed pink on the bare branches between early and late winter. It has a stiff upright habit reaching 2.7-3.6m (9-12ft) high and wide. The young leaves are often tinged with bronze. Outstanding varieties include 'Dawn' (rose-red buds and scented white flowers flushed pink) and 'Deben' (shell-pink buds and fragrant white flowers flushed shell-pink).
Viburnum x *carlcephalum* grows 2.4m (8ft) high and 1.8-2.1m (6-7ft) wide. It bears broad rounded heads of fragrant white flowers in mid to late spring. The foliage is light green, coloured in autumn.
Viburnum carlesii is a small species, 1.2-1.5m (4-5ft) high and

139

Viburnum plicatum tomentosum 'Mariesii'

wide. The clusters of deeply fragrant waxy white flowers appear
in mid to late spring among dull
green leaves that turn red in
autumn. 'Aurora' has red buds
and pink flowers.

Viburnum farreri, syn. *V. fra-
grans*, is a winter-flowering
species 2.7-3.6m (9-12ft) high and
wide. The richly scented white,
pink-tinged flowers are carried in
drooping clusters any time
between late autumn and early
spring. The leaves are bright
green, but bronze when young.

Viburnum lantana, wayfaring
tree, is a native species, grown for
its red berries which mature to
black, and for its dark red autumn
leaves. White flowers appear in
early summer. It grows 3m (10ft)
high and 2.4m (8ft) wide.

Viburnum opulus, guelder rose, is
grown for its flat heads of heavily
scented white flowers which
appear in late spring and early
summer. They are followed by
translucent red berries. It is a
bushy species, 3.6-4.5m (12-15ft)
high and wide, with dark green
maple-like leaves that are richly
coloured in autumn. Popular varieties include: 'Aureum' (golden
foliage); 'Compactum' (90cm/3ft

Viburnum x bodnantense

Vitex

chaste tree

Vitex agnus-castus

☐ Height 3-3.6m (10-12ft)
☐ Spread 3-3.6m (10-12ft)
☐ Flowers late summer to early autumn
☐ Fertile well-drained soil
☐ Sunny sheltered site

Viburnum x carlcephalum

high and wide); 'Roseum' (the snowball bush, with creamy-white globular flower heads); and 'Xanthocarpum' (yellow fruits).

Viburnum plicatum var. *tomentosum* is distinguished by its horizontal branches bearing dull green leaves which turn wine-red in autumn. It grows 2.4-3m (8-10ft) high and 3-4.5m (10-15ft) wide and bears white lace-cap flowers in late spring. 'Mariesii' (small profuse flowers) and 'Pink Beauty' (pink flowers) are popular.

Viburnum sieboldii grows 1.8-3m (6-10ft) high and spreads to 2.4m (8ft). It is clothed with toothed,

yellow-green leaves which take on bronze-red colours in autumn. Clusters of cream-white flowers in early summer are followed by striking berries that ripen from green to pink, red, blue and finally black.

Cultivation

Viburnums thrive in any good moist, but well-drained soil, and in full sun; they tolerate light shade. Give the early-flowering shrubs a site sheltered from cold north and east winds, and where early morning sun after night frost cannot damage the flowers. Plant between mid autumn and early spring; for good berry production, it is advisable to plant two or three shrubs together.

Little pruning is necessary, except to remove dead wood and to thin out overgrown shrubs after flowering.

Propagation Take semi-ripe heel cuttings in late summer and root in a cold frame.

Pests and diseases Aphids can be troublesome. Grey mould, leaf spot and honey fungus may also occur.

VIRGINIA CREEPER – see
Parthenocissus

The only species in this genus which tolerates the British climate, *Vitex agnus-castus*, though only moderately hardy, will generally succeed in southern gardens if grown against a south-facing wall. It is valuable for its slender spikes of small fragrant violet-blue flowers which appear between late summer and early autumn. The variety 'Alba' has white flowers, while 'Latifolia' is a hardier, more vigorous form.

The chaste tree grows into a bushy shrub, 3-3.6m (10-12ft) high and wide. Its aromatic, narrow lance-shaped leaflets are arranged like the fingers of a hand along grey downy shoots.

Cultivation

Plant in mid spring in any good well-drained soil in a sunny, sheltered site against a south-facing wall.

In early spring, remove dead, frosted or weak growth, cutting back the previous year's shoots to 7.5-10cm (3-4in).

Propagation Take semi-ripe cuttings in mid summer and root in a propagating frame.

Pests and diseases Trouble free.

Viburnum opulus 'Compactum'

Vitis

vine

Weigela

weigela

Vitis coignetiae, autumn colour

Weigela florida 'Variegata'

☐ Height 6-25m (20-80ft)
☐ Foliage climber
☐ Rich, well-drained but moisture-retentive soil
☐ Sunny or lightly shaded site

☐ Height 1.5-1.8m (5-6ft)
☐ Spread 1.5-2.4m (5-8ft)
☐ Flowers late spring to early summer
☐ Good well-drained soil
☐ Sunny or partially shaded site

Ornamental vines are hardy vigorous climbers ideal for growing up walls, pergolas, fences and tall trees where they support themselves by twining tendrils. Their large handsome, lobed leaves are especially attractive when dressed in rich autumn colours.

Popular species

Vitis coignetiae, Japanese crimson glory vine, is the most vigorous species – it easily grows 25m (80ft) high. The large, thick and heart-shaped mid green leaves take on yellow, orange-red and purple-crimson tints in autumn. Clusters of green flowers appear in late spring, followed by inedible black berries.

Vitis vinifera, the commercial grape vine, has given rise to several ornamental and fruiting varieties. They grow about 6m

(20ft) high and include 'Apiifolia', parsley vine (deeply cut dark green leaves); 'Brant' (to 9m/30ft, deep green leaves turn crimson, pink and orange in autumn, black fruits); and 'Purpurea' (young red leaves turning purple).

Cultivation

Plant between autumn and spring in humus-rich soil which is well-drained but moisture retentive. If the soil is acid, add lime. Any aspect is suitable, though a sunny site is preferable for fruiting vines. Thin out old shoots and shorten young ones in late summer.

Propagation Layer one-year-old shoots of *V. coignetiae* in autumn. They should have rooted a year later. *V. vinifera* can be increased by 10-12cm (4-5in) heel cuttings taken from half-ripened growth in summer.

Pests and diseases Scale insects and aphids may infest the plants and weevils and caterpillars sometimes feed on the leaves.

Weigelas are among the most popular of flowering shrubs, their small but abundant clusters of funnel-shaped blooms clothing the arching branches in late spring and early summer. They are fully hardy, easy to grow and thrive in most soils and sites.

Popular hybrids

The species have largely been superseded by named garden varieties.

Weigela florida bears clusters of rose-pink flowers with paler insides. It grows 1.8m (6ft) high and wide and is of arching habit. The oval, prominently veined and wrinkled leaves are light green. Varieties include 'Foliis Purpureis', a dense slow-growing shrub up to 1.2m (4ft) high and wide with dark purple foliage and rose-pink flowers; and 'Variegata' with green cream-edged leaves.

Weigela x hybrida is the name for a group of showy free-flowering shrubs. They grow 1.5-1.8m (5-6ft) high, 1.5-2.4m (5-8ft) wide and bear oval, wrinkled mid green leaves. Readily available hybrids include: 'Abel Carrière' (carmine-rose flowers); 'Avalanche' (white flowers); 'Bristol Ruby' (dark buds and ruby-red flowers); 'Looymansii Aurea' (pink flowers, young golden leaves); 'Mont

Weigela 'Bristol Ruby'

Blanc' (white fragrant flowers); and 'Styriaca' (red buds and carmine-pink flowers).

Cultivation
Plant between mid autumn and early spring in any good well-drained soil that does not dry out in summer. The site can be sunny or partially shaded. Every year after flowering, remove one or two of the old stems, cutting them back to ground level.
Propagation In mid autumn, take 25-30cm (10-12in) long heel cuttings and root in a cold frame.
Pests and diseases Trouble free.

WILLOW – see *Salix*
WINTERSWEET – see
Chimonanthus

Weigela florida

143

Wisteria

wisteria

Wisteria floribunda 'Alba'

Wisteria sinensis, standard

☐ Height 9-21m (30-70ft)
☐ Flowers late spring to early summer
☐ Any deep, fertile soil
☐ Sunny site

There is no sight more breath-taking than a mature wisteria in full bloom. This vigorous hardy climber is capable of reaching a height of 9-21m (30-70ft). It is unsuitable for small gardens unless it is trained as a small weeping standard. Wisteria is usually grown on a firm support against a sunny wall, pergola or up through an old tree.

The flowers that appear in late spring and early summer are one of the joys of the gardener's year. As the elegant, pale green leaf sprays unfold, long streamers of pale mauve, white or pink blooms cascade from every twig, although not on younger specimens.

Popular species

Wisteria floribunda grows up to 9m (30ft) high and has light to mid green leaflets. The scented violet-blue flowers are borne in 30cm (1ft) long racemes. Varieties include: 'Alba' (white); 'Rosea' (pale rose-pink and purple); 'Violacea' (violet-blue); and 'Violacea Plena' (double violet-blue).

Wisteria sinensis is the most vigorous (21m/70ft high) and popular species. It bears dark to mid green leaves, with fewer leaflets than *W. floribunda*, and 20-30cm (8-12in) long drooping racemes of fragrant mauve flowers. Popular varieties include: 'Alba' (white); 'Black Dragon' (double purple-blue); and 'Plena' (double lilac-mauve).

Wisteria venusta reaches 9m (30ft) high and has dark green leaves covered with down. The white, lightly fragrant flowers are borne in shorter, but denser racemes than those of the other species.

Cultivation

Plant out young pot-grown specimens from mid autumn to early spring. Wisterias will grow in any soil except a poor, thin one, though a moist, rich loamy soil provides the best conditions. In all but the mildest parts, the protection of a south- or west-facing wall is advisable, as the flower buds are susceptible to frost damage. Provide support and tie in the shoots until the twining stems have gained a firm hold. Wisterias rarely flower until they are seven years old.

In late winter, cut back all new shoots to within two or three buds of the base of the previous year's growth. Where climbers need to be restricted, cut the season's young growths back to five or six buds in summer.

Propagation Most wisterias are grafted by nurserymen, but *W. sinensis* can be increased by layering in late spring. The layers should root within a year.

Pests and diseases Aphids may infest young growths and thrips can damage the foliage. Chlorosis may occur on shallow chalky soils.

WITCH HAZEL – see *Hamamelis*
WOODBINE – see *Lonicera*

Wisteria sinensis

Floribunda rose The clear yellow, fragrant 'Mountbatten' is an outstanding modern bush rose.

A-Z of roses

The origin of the rose is long forgotten, but for
thousands of years it has been a symbol of purity
and perfection, and it remains the supreme joy of most
gardeners. The rose is so diverse in habit, bloom, foliage
and performance that it fits into every garden and
almost every garden position. The shrubby roses, native
to the Northern Hemisphere, vary from miniatures only
a few inches high to ramblers as much as 18m (60ft)
tall. The blooms, whatever their size and shape, are
perfect in form and may be single, semi-double or fully
double; they range from the delicate, five-petalled
flowers of some species roses, through the full-blown
cabbage roses and quartered Gallicas to the elegant,
high-pointed hybrid teas.

Only a single, short flowering season was expected
from virtually all types of roses until the beginning of
the last century. This is still to be expected of most old,
early-flowering roses, but such is the beauty and scent
of the Musks and Albas, the Centifolias and Damasks
that it would be unreasonable to demand any more.
Modern roses, however, are the result of hybridization
and flower from early summer until the first frosts of
autumn, either continuously or in repeat flushes.

The choice of roses is so vast that they are organized
into groups according to origin, flower type and habit.
The roses described here are arranged into the following
groups: climbing roses; floribunda roses (cluster-
flowered bush roses); hybrid tea roses (large-flowered
bush roses); miniature and patio roses; modern shrub
roses; old garden roses; polyantha and ground cover
roses; rambler roses; and species roses.

Climbing roses

'Mme Grégoire Staechelin'

'Altissimo'

☐ Height 1.8-9m (6-30ft)
☐ Flower early summer to early autumn
☐ Rich, well-drained soil
☐ Full sun or partial shade

Climbing roses are derived either from true climbing species or they are 'sports' of modern bush roses – mainly hybrid tea and floribunda types. All climbers have relatively large flowers carried in small trusses. The blooms are single or double, often fragrant, and come in a range of colours that include scarlet, pink, orange, yellow and white. Most modern climbing roses are repeat-flowering – blooming at intervals from early summer to early autumn.

Climbing roses are scrambling shrubs rather than true climbers as they have no means of attaching themselves to their supports, and need tying in. Vigorous, tall-growing varieties are suitable for training on large house walls or for scrambling up trees. Less vigorous types are suitable for more restricted areas – pillars, pergolas, fences, arbours and screens.

Popular varieties
'Aloha' has double, rose-pink flowers of the hybrid tea-type. They are sweetly scented, repeat-flowering and rain-resistant. It is a slow grower, reaching only 2.4m (8ft), and is best trained up a pillar or a low wall.
'Altissimo' has large, single blooms with blood-red petals and golden stamens. It is repeat-flowering. Growing 3.6m (12ft) high, it is suitable for boundary walls, fences and pillars.
'Bantry Bay' has bright pink semi-double blooms with conspicuous yellow stamens. It is repeat-flowering and lightly scented. Not over-vigorous, reaching only 3m (10ft) high, it is best trained up a wall, fence or pillar.
'Casino' bears double, yellow blooms fading to soft yellow as they age. It is repeat-flowering with a sweet scent and grows

3m (10ft) high. Semi-hardy and best grown along a warm sheltered wall.
'Cécile Brunner' is a climbing sport of the polyantha rose, with small double, fragrant shell-pink flowers. It flowers in summer, and again in autumn with a smaller display. It is extremely vigorous, up to 6m (20ft), and an excellent choice for training up an old tree.
'Compassion' has a profusion of large, double, apricot-pink blooms among handsome, dark glossy green foliage. It is repeat-flowering and strongly scented. New growth comes freely from the base but it is not sufficiently tall enough to cover a house wall. Pillars, pergolas and arches make more suitable supports.
'Copenhagen' bears large double scarlet-red flowers with an attractive fragrance. It is repeat-flowering and grows up to 3m (10ft) high. The bronze-tinted leaves tend to fall from the lower branches as the plant ages, giving it a leggy appearance.
'Crimson Glory' has double, deep velvet-crimson strongly fragrant flowers of the hybrid tea-type from mid summer to early autumn. It reaches 2.7-3m (9-10ft) high – ideal for growing over arches or along a fence.
'Danse du Feu' has spectacular double, scarlet-orange blooms but no fragrance. It is repeat-flowering and reaches 3.6m (12ft) high. It looks effective covering a screen and grows well on a north-facing wall.
'Dortmund' has large single flowers with crimson-red petals, a white eye and golden stamens. It

'Dublin Bay'

'Aloha'

is a repeat-flowering pillar rose, reaching 2.4-3m (8-10ft) high.

'Dublin Bay' bears large, double, deep red flowers that are slightly fragrant. It is repeat-flowering and moderately vigorous, reaching 2.4m (8ft) high.

'Ena Harkness' has double crimson, sweetly scented, hybrid tea type flowers. Though repeat-flowering, the early blooms tend to be more spectacular than the autumn ones. At 3m (10ft) high, it is suitable for house walls.

'Étoile de Hollande' has double, deep red, loosely formed flowers. These are of the hybrid tea-type and are highly fragrant. It is a repeat-flowering variety which reaches 3-3.6m (10-12ft) high.

'Galway Bay' has large, double, cerise-pink blooms, borne in great profusion. It is repeat-flowering. Plenty of shoots grow from the base and it reaches 2.4m (8ft) high, making a good pillar rose. It is resistant to most rose diseases.

'Gloire de Dijon' has double, buff-yellow blooms that are sweetly scented. It is a repeat-flowering variety – one of the earliest to bloom when grown against

'Compassion'

a warm wall. It reaches 3-4.5m (10-15ft) high. Despite its susceptibility to mildew, it remains extremely popular.

'Golden Showers' bears large bright golden-yellow flowers. These are fragrant and resistant to rain. It reaches 2.4m (8ft) high and makes a good pillar rose; it is almost thornless.

'Grand Hotel' is a reliable repeat-flowering climber bearing double hybrid tea-type blooms among dark green, leathery foliage. They are bright red and scarlet and keep their colour well. It grows 3.6m (12ft) high.

'Guinée' has dark velvet-red, double, sweetly scented flowers. A

strong, repeat-flowering climber, it reaches 2.4-3m (8-10ft) high and looks most effective trained against a wall or stout rustic screen.

'Handel' has double, cream-white flowers heavily flushed and tipped with carmine that are moderately scented. Though resistant to rain, mildew and black spot can be a problem. A repeat-flowering variety, it reaches 3-3.6m (10-12ft) high. Train up a wall or pergola.

'Iceberg', a climbing sport of the floribunda rose, bears double and slightly fragrant white blooms. It is repeat-flowering. It grows up to 3m (10ft) high and looks most effective against a wall. Mildew can be a problem.

'Joseph's Coat' is of moderate vigour; it is sometimes grown as a large shrub but is also ideal as a pillar or arbour rose. It is a well-branching variety, about 1.8m (6ft) high, with recurrent flowers that are yellow-orange and red.

'Kathleen Harrop' is a sport of 'Zéphirine Drouhin' but less vigorous, up to 2.1m (7ft) high. It is repeat-flowering, with strongly scented, double blush-pink blooms.

'Kiftsgate', a variety of the species rose *R. filipes*, is slow to become established, but then bears large clusters of single, cream-white blooms in mid summer, which are followed by bright red hips. Growing 10-20m (30-60ft) high, it is suitable only for large gardens where it looks spectacular scrambling up an old tree. It is not suitable as a wall climber.

'Leverkusen' bears large sprays of semi-double, pale yellow blooms. It is repeat-flowering and slightly fragrant. It is vigorous and grows 3-3.6m (10-12ft) high.

'Golden Showers'

'Handel'   'Iceberg'   'Meg'

'Mermaid'

This is a useful variety as it tolerates cold, exposed conditions.

'Maigold' has semi-double, golden-yellow fragrant flowers. It normally flowers just once a year, in early summer, though dead-heading may encourage another smaller flush. It reaches 3.3m (11ft) high and is suitable for growing against a wall.

'Masquerade', the climbing sport of the floribunda rose of the same name, bears large trusses of slightly fragrant blooms which open yellow, then turn pink and red. It is repeat-flowering, although a later flush only appears if early flowers are dead-headed. It reaches 2.4m (8ft) high and can be grown as a shrub or trained along a fence.

'Meg' has trusses of large apricot-pink, single, sweetly scented flowers. It is rarely repeat-flowering, though occasionally there may be a few late blooms. The average height is 3m (10ft) – grow it up a pergola or a pillar, or along a fence.

'Mermaid' bears single, scented, cream-yellow flowers. It is a repeat-flowering climber – one of the tallest, reaching 7.5-9m (25-30ft) high. Train it up a south-facing or west-facing house wall where it is less likely to be affected by frost.

'Mme Alfred Carrière' has white pink-flushed blooms of the old-fashioned noisette type. They are strongly scented and borne in great profusion. It is a repeat-flowering climber that reaches 4.5-6m (15-20ft) high.

'Mme Grégoire Staechelin' has large, double, pink blooms with ruffled petals and a particularly heady fragrance. The magnificence of the blooms makes up for the fact that it only flowers for a few weeks in early summer. It is a vigorous climber, 4.5-6m (15-20ft) high – suitable for training

'New Dawn'

against the north-facing wall of a house. Prone to mildew.

'New Dawn' bears a profusion of small, semi-double shell-pink blooms. It is repeat-flowering and fragrant. Reaching 2.7m (9ft) high, it has a bushy habit which makes it suitable as a pillar rose or for growing through a hedge.

'Parkdirektor Riggers' has large clusters of semi-double, blood-red flowers. A vigorous repeat-flowering climber, it reaches 3.6-4.5m (12-15ft) high. Mildew and black spot can be troublesome.

'Pink Perpétue' has deep two-toned pink flowers appearing in early and mid summer, and again in early autumn. The blooms are double and slightly fragrant. Though it only reaches 1.8-2.4m (6-8ft) high, it spreads well, making it a good variety for a low wall or fence.

'Schoolgirl' has large double apricot-orange blooms shaded pink. It is repeat-flowering, fragrant and reaches 3-3.6m (10-12ft) high. Suitable for training against a wall though it tends to grow leggy and bare at the base.

'Shot silk' bears salmon-pink blooms flushed yellow. They are of hybrid tea-type, double and heavily fragrant. They are rain resistant. It is a repeat-flowering variety, reaching 3-3.6m (10-12ft) high.

'Souvenir de Claudius Denoyel' is a long-established and vigorous variety, up to 3.6m (12ft) high and suitable for growing against a wall. It is repeat-flowering, with large double blooms of the hybrid tea-type, strongly scented and deep crimson to scarlet.

'Summer Wine' bears large, single, soft coral pink blooms with prominent red stamens. It is repeat-flowering and strongly fragrant, with dark green foliage. It grows up to 3m (10ft) high.

'Swan Lake' has large, double, white blooms tinged pink in the centre. They are slightly fragrant and resistant to rain. It is repeat-flowering and reaches 2.1-2.4m

'Pink Perpétue'

'Gloire de Dijon'

'Zéphirine Drouhin'

(7-8ft) high – ideal for training up an arch, pillar or pergola. Black spot and mildew can be troublesome.

'Sympathie' has double, bright red velvety blooms of the hybrid tea-type. It is repeat-flowering, fragrant and resistant to disease. Height 3m (10ft).

'White Cockade' has double, white, hybrid tea-type blooms. It is a repeat-flowering variety, with a profusion of flowers continuing well into autumn. Reaching 1.8-2.4m (6-8ft) high, it is suitable for training along a fence or up a pillar; it can also be grown as a shrub.

'Zéphirine Drouhin' is a climbing bourbon rose with semi-double, carmine-pink, and richly fragrant blooms. It is a repeat-flowering variety, often with an autumn display even more spectacular than the summer display. It grows 2.7m (9ft) high. Mildew is a common problem.

Cultivation

Plant bare-rooted roses between late autumn and mid spring, during warm, dry spells; container-grown roses can be planted at any time of year. Like all roses, climbers need rich, well-drained soil. Most varieties thrive in full sun, though one or two will tolerate partial shade, and even north-facing walls. Prepare a planting area of at least 1.2 x 1.2m (4 x 4ft) for each climber and dig in plenty of organic matter. After planting keep the ground free of weeds.

In mid to late spring, mulch both recently planted and established roses; feed them from late spring onwards once a month.

As the plants grow, train them up supports. Climbers grown against walls and fences should be trained into a fan shape: tie in the main shoots as horizontally as possible to encourage flower-bearing side-shoots to grow. Wind the stems of roses trained up pillars and pergolas around the support in an upward spiral. No climbers are self-supporting and they need to be tied with wire.

Pruning methods are the same for all climbers. Little pruning is needed in the early years, except to remove damaged and crossing stems. Thereafter, cut back lateral shoots to three or four buds in the autumn, and remove the tips of unripened growths. Remove old or unwanted growth at the same time and dig in plenty of organic matter. Dead-head all varieties if you can reach them.

Propagation Most modern roses are grafted or budded on to various rootstocks; it is a process best left to professional rose growers.

Pests and diseases Black spot, the most common rose disease, may develop on the leaves, eventually causing them to drop off. Mildew sometimes affects leaves, stems and flower buds. Rust appears as bright orange pustules in spring, which then develops into yellow patches on the leaves in summer, gradually turning black in autumn. The leaves eventually drop. Spray against greenfly in summer – these are usually found in large numbers on the tips of growing shoots.

Floribunda roses

(cluster-flowered bush roses)

'Matangi'

'Amber Queen'

- ☐ Height 45cm-2.1m (1½-7ft)
- ☐ Spread 60-75cm (2-2½ft)
- ☐ Flower early summer to mid autumn
- ☐ Rich well-drained soil
- ☐ Full sun

Floribunda roses are crosses between polyantha and hybrid tea roses. They are hardy bushy shrubs, varying widely in height but all bear a profusion of double flowers which are borne in clusters – hence the other name for floribundas – cluster-flowered roses. The flowering season extends from early summer to mid autumn.

Grow floribundas in beds of their own, in mixed borders or as hedges. Tall varieties make good specimen shrubs, and dwarf types are suitable for edging and ground cover.

Popular varieties

An enormous number of floribunda varieties exists and new ones are constantly being introduced.

'**Amber Queen**' has well-formed, fragrant amber-yellow flowers. A fine bedding rose, 60-75cm (2-2½ft) high.

'**Anne Cocker**' bears vivid vermilion, long-stalked flowers. Good for cutting, exhibiting and bedding. It grows 90cm (3ft) high and is susceptible to mildew.

'**Arthur Bell**' has large golden-yellow flowers fading to cream. They are fragrant and rain-resistant. It grows 1.05m (3½ft) high.

'**Bonfire Night**' has well-formed bright orange-red blooms, splashed yellow and scarlet. Vigorous and upright, to 75cm (2½ft).

'**Chinatown**' has large, strongly fragrant yellow flowers flushed pink. It is vigorous, 1.2-1.5m (4-5ft) high, and a good specimen shrub.

'**City of Leeds**' bears slightly fragrant rich salmon flowers. It grows 75-90cm (2½-3ft) tall.

'**Dearest**' has salmon-pink blooms, camellia-like in shape, with a spicy fragrance. A good bedding rose, 75cm (2½ft) high, but susceptible to disease.

'**Elizabeth of Glamis**' has large, fragrant, well-formed, salmon-pink flowers which fade slightly with age. Vigorous and upright, it reaches 75cm (2½ft) high.

'**Evelyn Fison**', an old bedding favourite, bears semi-double, scarlet flowers that are large, prolific and rain-resistant. Bushy habit, up to 75cm (2½ft) high.

'**Eyepaint**' bears an abundance of small, single, scarlet flowers with white centres and gold stamens. Up to 1.2m (4ft) high, it is good as a hedge or in a border.

'**Fragrant Delight**' has shapely, copper-coloured blooms, strongly fragrant. Good bedding rose, 75cm (2½ft) high.

'Korresia'

'Arthur Bell'

'Bonfire Night'

'**Frensham**' is an old, popular rose, excellent for hedging. It bears deep crimson flowers and grows vigorously to 90cm (3ft). It is prone to mildew.

'**Hannah Gordon**' bears hybrid tea-shaped flowers, white shaded deep pink. Good bedding rose, up to 75cm (2½ft) high.

'**Iceberg**' has small, pure white early blooms, flushed with pale pink in autumn. A free-flowering rose 1.5m (5ft) high with a vigorous, branching habit, it needs space – a hedge, at the back of a bed, or as a specimen shrub.

'**Korresia**' is a fine yellow-flowered rose, with large fragrant blooms that keep their colour. Bushy, up to 75cm (2½ft) high.

'**Lilli Marlene**' has scarlet-red, slightly fragrant flowers, resistant to rain, though mildew can be a problem. A vigorous, bedding rose, 75cm (2½ft) high.

'**Margaret Merril**' has beautifully formed white scented flowers. Prone to black spot and rain damage. Height 1.2m (4ft).

'**Masquerade**' bears flowers that open yellow, turn pink, and then red. Vigorous, up to 1.2m (4ft) high, it is suitable for a hedge.

'**Matangi**' has orange-red blooms with petals shaded silvery white towards the centre, and gold stamens. It is disease- and rain-resistant; a good bedding rose, up to 75-90cm (2½ft-3ft) high.

'**Memento**' bears a profusion of flat salmon-vermilion blooms which are rain-resistant. Vigorous and upright, 75cm (2½ft) high. Good as a bedding rose.

'**Mountbatten**' bears large clusters of rich golden-yellow blooms with a pleasant fragrance. It is a vigorous rose, up to 1.2m (4ft).

'**Orange Sensation**' has bright vermilion-orange flowers. They are fragrant and borne in numerous clusters. Of bushy, spreading

'Eyepaint'

'Elizabeth of Glamis'

'Orange Sensation'

habit and 75cm (2½ft) high. Resistant to rain; black spot and mildew can be troublesome.

'Pink Parfait' has salmon-pink and ivory flowers, opening flat to reveal golden stamens. It is prolific and vigorous, growing 90cm (3ft) high.

'Queen Elizabeth', one of the most popular floribundas, has well-shaped clear pink blooms with a slight fragrance. It has a very vigorous, upright growth habit and can reach 1.8-2.1m (6-7ft) high, at the back of a large border, as a hedge, or as a specimen shrub. It is rain-resistant, but black spot can be a problem.

'Rob Roy' has large trusses of slightly fragrant, bright scarlet-crimson blooms. It is an upright, vigorous grower, best planted as a hedge or in a large border. Maximum height is 105cm (3½ft). It is rain- and disease-resistant.

'Rosemary Rose' bears bright carmine blooms, similar in form to those of old-fashioned shrub roses. Of vigorous, branching growth, up to 75cm (2½ft) high.

'Queen Elizabeth'

Good as a bedding rose, but susceptible to mildew.

'Southampton' has apricot-orange blooms flushed scarlet with a slight fragrance. Upright and vigorous, up to 105cm (3½ft) high. Suitable for a rose bed, border, or as a hedge.

'The Times Rose' bears clusters of crimson-red flowers. It is free-flowering, bushy and 75cm (2½ft) high. It is exceptionally resistant to disease.

'Trumpeter' bears a profusion of slightly fragrant, bright orange-scarlet flowers. Reaching 50cm (20in) high, this low-growing compact rose is suitable for the front of a border. Disease-resistant.

'Warrior' has bright red flowers which rarely fade. It is a dwarf rose, 45cm (1½ft) high, and ideal at the front of a border.

'Wishing' bears large, well-formed peach-pink blooms. It is short and bushy, reaching 60cm (2ft) high; a good bedding rose.

Cultivation

Plant bare-rooted floribundas between late autumn and mid spring. Set the shrubs 60-75cm (2-2½ft) apart in rich well-drained soil. All varieties require a sunny position.

Prune in early spring. Cut newly planted roses back to 15cm (6in) above ground. On established bushes remove all dead, crossing and diseased shoots and reduce the remaining stems by up to half.

Mulch in mid to late spring, and feed two or three times from late spring onwards.

After flowering, remove the entire truss of dead flowers, cutting it back to the first true leaf.

Propagation Floribunda roses do not grow on their own roots but are budded or grafted professionally; cuttings are rarely successful.

Pests and diseases Floribundas are susceptible to most common rose problems, including greenflies, mildew, black spot and rust.

'Margaret Merril'

Hybrid tea roses

(large-flowered bush roses)

'Alec's Red'

'Whisky Mac'

☐ Height 60cm-1.5m (2-5ft)
☐ Spread 60-75cm (2-2½ft)
☐ Flower early summer to late autumn
☐ Rich, well-drained soil
☐ Open site in sun or light shade

To most gardeners, hybrid teas represent the ultimate in roses. Originally a cross between the old-fashioned hybrid perpetuals and tea roses, they produce the largest and most perfectly formed flowers, in a colour range that includes all but true blue and black. Yellow-flowered types tend to fade in full sun.

The blooms are usually double, though a few single-flowered varieties are also available. Each flower starts off as a well-shaped conical bud and opens into a bowl-shaped bloom with velvety petals arranged around a high central cone. Most have a fragrance; some a particularly strong one. The flowers are not produced in such profusion as those on floribunda roses – there's usually only one per stem. They appear in flushes rather than continuously, at intervals from early summer until the end of autumn. They are excellent for cutting.

Hybrid tea bushes have a vigorous, upright habit, ideal for growing in rose beds or mixed borders. Varieties with a more spreading habit are often budded on to tall stems and grown as standards, while roses with perfectly shaped blooms are popular for exhibiting.

Popular varieties

Numerous varieties are available, and new ones are regularly being introduced.

'Alec's Red' is one of the most popular red-flowered hybrid teas. The flowers have a rich fragrance and are suitable for garden decoration, cutting and exhibiting. They are fairly resistant to rain damage. The growth is vigorous and upright, reaching 90cm (3ft) high.

'Alexander' has brilliant orange-vermilion blooms with a slight fragrance. It is resistant to both rain and disease. Growing 1.5m (5ft) high, it is suitable for a large bed or as a hedge.

'Alpine Sunset' bears peach-pink flowers flushed with yellow. They are strongly fragrant. Suitable for growing in rose beds, for cut flowers and for exhibition. Growth is upright and vigorous, reaching 75cm (2½ft) high.

'Blessings' has profuse coral-pink flowers from early summer until mid autumn. The fragrant flowers are resistant to rain damage and disease. It makes a good bedding rose, with vigorous upright growth, and a height of 90cm (3ft).

'Congratulations' bears exquisitely formed, soft pink flowers that are slightly fragrant. Free-flowering on strong upright stems. Height 1.2m (4ft).

'Double Delight' has unusual flowers – ivory edged with cherry-red. Their fragrance is strong and, although they have only moderate disease and rain resistance, they are shapely enough to be used in exhibitions. Growth is vigorous and upright, with a height of 75cm (2½ft).

'Dutch Gold' has large well-shaped yellow blooms which keep their colour as they age. They are strongly fragrant, freely produced and make excellent exhibition roses. This is a vigorous, upright bush, reaching 90cm (3ft) high.

'Blessings'

'Fragrant Cloud'

'Elina', formerly known as 'Peaudouce', has large, pale primrose blooms. They are well formed with a pleasant fragrance. It is suitable as a bedding rose, for cutting and for exhibiting. The growth is vigorous and bushy, up to 90cm (3ft) high.

'Elizabeth Harkness' has large, fragrant, cream-white flowers tinged with pink. They appear early in the season, and are good for cutting. Rain damage can be a problem. This rose has an upright, bushy habit, growing 90cm (3ft) high.

'Ernest H. Morse' bears rich red, well-shaped, fragrant flowers which appear in great numbers and stand up well to rain. An ideal bedding rose, useful also for cutting and exhibiting. The growth is vigorous and upright, with a height of 90cm (3ft).

'Evening Star' has well-shaped white blooms, borne in great profusion. They have a pleasant scent and are resistant to rain. Reaching 1.05m (3½ft) high, growth is vigorous and upright.

'Fragrant Cloud' bears large shapely flowers which are red in bud, open to coral-salmon and then fade with age. They have a particularly strong fragrance, and appear in profusion early in the summer. Mildew and black spot can be troublesome. The vigorous upright bushes grow 90cm (3ft) high.

'Grandpa Dickson' has large pale yellow well-formed blooms that become pink-edged with age. They are abundant and resistant to rain. Good bedding rose. The vigorous, upright growth reaches 75cm (2½ft) high.

'Josephine Bruce' carries strongly fragrant, deep crimson-velvet flowers which are susceptible to mildew. It grows 75cm (2½ft) high, but the vigorous and spreading, somewhat floppy stems look most effective when grown as a standard rose.

'Just Joey' has attractive coppery-veined red buds, followed by flowers which fade to copper-orange. The slightly ruffled petals make it an excellent rose for cutting. Free-flowering and rain-resistant, it is also a good bedding variety. It grows 75cm (2½ft) high.

'Lover's Meeting' has soft tangerine-orange blooms with a slight fragrance. Grown as a bedding rose, this variety is also good for cutting. Growth is upright and vigorous, up to 75cm (2½ft) high.

'Mme Louis Laperrière' produces well-formed deep crimson flowers with a strong fragrance. It is free-flowering with a floral display that begins in early summer and continues into late autumn. Rain-resistant. A low-growing, spreading shrub, up to 60cm (2ft).

'Mischief' has well-shaped coral-salmon, fragrant blooms which are freely produced. It is rain-resistant and prone to rust, but makes an excellent bedding rose. Height 90cm (3ft).

'National Trust' has a profusion of perfectly shaped dark crimson flowers. Good bedding rose of vigorous upright habit, up to 75cm (2½ft) high. Rain-resistant.

'Ophelia' is an old favourite, with pale pink flowers which are yellow at the base. They are fragrant and good for cutting. It grows upright, with slightly spindly stems up to 75cm (2½ft) high.

'Pascali' produces a mass of faintly scented white flowers. They are carried on long upright

'Grandpa Dickson'

'Just Joey'

stems and are ideal for cutting. The growth is upright and vigorous, and 90cm (3ft) high.

'Paul Shirville' has elegant blooms with light salmon-pink petals shaded yellow at the base. Their fragrance is strong and sweet. Of strong upright habit, the shrub grows 90cm (3ft) high. Good as a bedding rose and for cutting.

'Peace' – often regarded as the world's favourite rose – bears pale yellow blooms edged with cerise pink. They are large, but only slightly fragrant. Being vigorous and bushy, and reaching 1.35m (4½ft) high, it should be given plenty of space.

'Peer Gynt' produces large slightly fragrant rich yellow flowers which fade to peach in full sun and as they age. Good bedding rose with a vigorous, bushy habit, and height of 90cm (3ft). Prone to diseases.

'Piccadilly' has scarlet flowers with a yellow reverse to the petals. They appear early, and in great profusion, making the shrub an excellent bedding variety. The slightly fragrant flowers fade in full sun but have good disease resistance. Growth is vigorous and upright, 75cm (2½ft) high.

'Pink Favourite' bears large well-formed blooms in shades of rose-pink. Renowned for its excellent resistance to disease, it is usually grown as a bedding plant, and it is also suitable for cutting and exhibition. Growth is upright and vigorous, up to 90cm (3ft) high.

'Precious Platinum' produces handsome, glowing, rich red flowers with a sweet fragrance. They are borne in an abundance of small clusters. Usually grown as a bedding rose, with good disease resistance; vigorous branching habit, 90cm (3ft) high.

'Prima Ballerina' bears richly scented, deep rose-pink flowers,

up to 12.5cm (5in) across. Bushy growth, up to 90cm (3ft) high. Sometimes susceptible to mildew.

'Rose Gaujard' has pink flowers with carmine veins and a silvery reverse. It is free-flowering, resistant to disease and tolerant of poor growing conditions. With a branching habit, it makes a good bedding rose. Height 90cm (3ft).

'Royal William' has velvety, deep crimson flowers of classic shape, strongly scented. Upright growth up to 90cm (3ft).

'Silver Jubilee' bears an abundance of fragrant, coral-pink blooms. They are perfectly formed and keep their colour well. Good bedding rose and resistant to disease. Vigorous, bushy growth, 75cm (2½ft) high.

'Super Star' is an upright and erect variety, with lightly fragrant, brilliant light vermilion perfect blooms. Free-flowering, the autumn flush often borne in clusters. Up to 1.2m (4ft) high.

'Sutter's Gold' has well-shaped fragrant yellow flowers shaded

'National Trust'

158

'Peace'

'Pascali'

red and orange, and good for cutting. The growth is upright, but spindly, up to 90cm (3ft) high.

'Troika' bears orange-bronze blooms shaded red on the outside. They are large, fragrant and maintain their colour in full sun; rain-resistant. Good as a bedding rose, for cutting and exhibiting. The growth is upright and vigorous, up to 90cm (3ft) high.

'Whisky Mac' has attractive amber-yellow blooms with a strong fragrance. Despite its susceptibility to disease and its tendency to die back, it is one of the most popular hybrid teas. Growth is vigorous and it reaches 75cm (2½ft) high.

Cultivation
Plant bare-rooted hybrid teas

between late autumn and mid spring, and container-grown bushes at any time of year, during mild dry weather. Set the shrubs 60cm (2ft) apart in well-drained soil enriched with well-rotted manure or compost, and bone meal. Choose a sunny or lightly shaded site, sheltered from prevailing winds but away from high trees or walls.

In spring, prune newly planted

bushes, cutting back the stems to 10cm (4in) off the ground above outward-facing buds. On established roses, remove all dead, diseased and crossing stems. Prune the remainder by removing about one-third of the stems. Roses grown for exhibition should be pruned harder, leaving only a few stems cut back to four buds.

Disbudding is important if exhibition shrubs are to produce large, perfect flowers. Remove any buds clustering below the main terminal bud.

Mulch all roses in mid to late spring, to retain moisture in the soil around them, and feed with a liquid rose fertilizer every four weeks from late spring onwards.

To encourage a long flowering season, dead-head regularly.

Propagation Like floribunda roses, hybrid teas are budded, a propagation method best left to the professionals.

Pests and diseases Hybrid teas suffer from the same troubles as other roses. Look out for black spot and mildew; rust can also be a problem. In summer, greenfly often infest bushes.

'Silver Jubilee'

Miniature and patio roses

'Baby Masquerade'

'Pretty Polly'

☐ Height 15-45cm (6-18in)
☐ Spread 15-25cm (6-10in)
☐ Flower summer and autumn
☐ Rich, well-drained soil
☐ Full sun

True to their name, miniature roses reach only 15-45cm (6-18in) high and resemble tiny floribundas or hybrid teas, with their miniature leaves and flowers. They are the most recently developed group – a cross between a tiny China rose and either polyantha or floribunda roses.

There is little difference between miniature and the so-called patio roses, though the latter are generally at the taller end of the range and of more bushy habit, with luxuriant foliage.

Miniature roses show a wide range of colours from scarlet through pink to orange, yellow or white. Most have double or semi-double blooms. They are borne in clusters, and some are fragrant. The flowering season is from early to mid summer, with a second display in autumn.

In the garden, miniatures can be grown as edging or in a small rose bed of their own; they are also suitable for pockets in a rock garden and for raised beds. They can look charming in window-boxes and other decorative containers. Several of the smallest miniatures can also be grown as house plants.

Popular varieties
'Angela Rippon' has well-shaped, fragrant, double, salmon-pink blooms appearing in profusion on compact healthy bushes 45cm (18in) high.
'Baby Masquerade' has fragrant double blooms that open yellow, turn pink, and finally rose-red. They appear in great profusion over a long flowering season. A bushy miniature, this rose reaches 38cm (15in) high.
'Bright Smile' bears clusters of well-shaped, bright yellow flowers of the floribunda type. Neat compact habit, up to 30cm (1ft) high.
'City Lights', a recent introduction, has a profusion of small deep

yellow, classic-shaped blooms, deliciously scented. Well-proportioned variety, with lush foliage, on 30cm (1ft) tall shrubs.
'Colibri' has double, orange-yellow blooms edged with red. Their fragrance is only slight but they appear in profusion. Growth is bushy, reaching 25cm (10in) high.
'Darling Flame' has rich orange-vermilion flowers with a yellow reverse. They are double, and have a fruity fragrance. Growth is vigorous, reaching 38cm (15in).
'Lavender Jewel' bears small dainty, soft lavender blooms, produced freely on a vigorous bush reaching 38cm (15in) high.
'Perla de Alcanada' has a profusion of attractive buds that open into semi-double, deep crimson flowers with white markings. It grows 30cm (1ft) high.
'Perla de Monserrat' bears clusters of small rose-pink flowers. They are of hybrid tea-shape and appear in abundance. Compact in habit, it grows only 23cm (9in) high.
'Pour Toi', an old favourite, has cream-white flowers of the hybrid tea-type. It is bushy and dainty, growing 25cm (10in) high.
'Pretty Polly' is of neat habit, with fresh, glossy green foliage. It is smothered with clusters of soft, china-pink blooms on a 30cm (1ft) high shrub.
'Queen Mother' is repeat-flowering, blooming throughout summer and early autumn, on a spreading plant about 45cm (1½ft) high, set with dark green, glossy foliage. The semi-double, soft pink flowers have wavy edges to the petals.

'Bright Smile'

'Royal Salute'

'Royal Salute' bears trusses of double, rose-red flowers with a slight fragrance. It has a vigorous, compact habit and reaches 38cm (15in) high.

'Starina' bears well-formed bi-coloured scarlet and golden blooms that appear in great numbers from early summer onwards. A vigorous grower, it reaches 25-30cm (10-12in) high.

'Sweet Fairy' has delicate lilac-pink blooms which are double and have a sweet fragrance. It grows only 20cm (8in) high.

'The Valois Rose' has an unusal colouring to its clusters of double blooms – they are creamy-yellow suffused with deep carmine-rose. The bushy plant is of neat habit, about 38cm (15in) high.

Cultivation

Miniature and patio roses are usually offered as container-grown specimens since many have been raised from cuttings. They can be planted at any time of year, provided the soil is not frozen or waterlogged, and the weather is relatively mild. Set them 15-25cm (6-10in) apart in fertile well-drained soil in a sunny site. They usually look best grown in groups on their own.

Miniature roses for containers should be planted in 10-12cm (4-5in) pots filled with potting compost. Repot annually, in late winter or early spring. In winter, plunge the pots in a deep soil bed and top-dress with a mulch to protect the roots from frost and to keep them moist. They can be returned to their flowering sites in early and mid spring.

Prune in spring, cutting old stems back to a few centimetres above ground and lightly pruning the newer shoots, removing up to one-third. All recently planted bushes should be hard pruned.

Mulch in mid to late spring, then feed every four weeks from late spring onwards. Water frequently during dry weather and dead-head regularly.

Propagation Take 5-10cm (2-4in) heel cuttings in late summer and early autumn and root in a cold frame. Nurserymen also offer mixed seed selections.

Pests and diseases Miniature roses are prone to mildew, black spot, die-back and greenfly.

'Lavender Jewel'

161

Modern shrub roses

(including New English shrub roses, hybrid musks and rugosas)

Rosa rugosa 'Alba'

□ Height 90cm-2.4m (3-8ft)
□ Spread 90cm-1.8m (3-6ft)
□ Flowers late spring to late autumn
□ Rich well-drained soil
□ Full sun

Modern shrub roses have been developed from species and old roses. They are fully hardy, of informal habit and usually have handsome foliage. They include the New English shrub roses, a hybrid race of modern shrub roses crossed with old roses that combines the beautiful form and heady scent of the old roses with the repeat-flowering performance of modern types.

Also in this group are the hybrid musk roses, prized for their delicious fragrance, and the rugosa roses, which have spectacular hips following their scented floral displays.

Unless otherwise stated, the modern shrub roses described here are repeat-flowering, with flushes of blooms appearing between early summer and late autumn. They have single, semi-double or double blooms in a wide range of colours, and many are deliciously fragrant.

Modern shrub roses are ideal for growing in shrubberies and in mixed borders; many are also spectacular as specimen shrubs.

Popular varieties

'**Angelina**', a modern shrub rose, has dainty, single, rich pink blooms with white centres and gold stamens. The slightly fragrant flowers appear in great profusion on shrubs with a bushy height and spread of 1.2m (4ft).

'**Ballerina**', a modern shrub rose, bears an abundance of tiny apple-blossom pink flowers in early summer, and again in early autumn. They are carried in clusters on shrubs that grow to a height of 1.2m (4ft) and spread of 90cm (3ft).

'**Blanc Double de Coubert**' is a rugosa shrub rose with large, semi-double, pure white blooms. It has a strong, sweet fragrance and good disease resistance, though the blooms are prone to rain damage. It grows 1.8m (6ft) high and 1.5m (5ft) wide.

'**Buff Beauty**' produces clusters of large, double, pale orange-apricot blooms that fade to ivory with age. This sweetly scented hybrid musk has a spectacular autumn flush. Mildew can be a problem. The loose growth reaches 1.2m (4ft) in height and spread.

'Buff Beauty'

'**Constance Spry**', a modern shrub rose, bears sprays of double, fragrant and clear rose-pink flowers. The arching stems, spreading 1.8m (6ft) across and reaching 2.1m (7ft) high, are best trained up a wall.

'**Cornelia**', a hybrid musk rose, bears a profusion of double apricot-pink flowers with a pleasant fragrance and good resistance to rain. The best blooms appear in autumn. It grows 1.5m (5ft) high and 2.1m (7ft) across.

'**Evelyn**' has large, deeply fragrant rosette-type flowers. They are densely packed with apricot petals. It is one of the New English shrub roses and grows 90cm (3ft) high and wide.

'**Fru Dagmar Hastrup**' bears single shell-pink flowers with a strong fragrance. As a rugosa shrub, it produces a striking display of large red hips in autumn.

'Constance Spry'

'Marguerite Hilling'

'Fru Dagmar Hastrup'

'Roseraie de l'Hay'

It is of compact habit, 90cm (3ft) high and wide, and a good hedging shrub. Disease-resistant.

'Fred Loads', a modern shrub rose, has large trusses of single orange-vermilion flowers. They keep their colour and have a sweet fragrance. Of vigorous upright habit, it grows 1.8m (6ft) high and spreads to 1.2m (4ft). It is suitable for the back of a border.

'Gertrude Jekyll', a New English shrub rose, is of strong upright habit, up to 1.2m (4ft) tall and 90cm (3ft) wide. It bears large, strongly scented cerise-pink flowers.

'Golden Wings' has large, single, pale yellow blooms which fade with age; they are sweet-scented and resistant to rain. It is a modern shrub rose, 1.8m (6ft) high and 1.5m (5ft) wide.

'Graham Thomas' grows 90cm-1.5m (3-5ft) high and 90cm (3ft) wide. It has full-cupped, heavily scented, rich yellow flowers. It is a

vigorous shrub, one of the first introductions to the range of New English shrub roses.

'Heritage' has large and perfect quartered blooms of clear shell-pink. This strong-growing, free-flowering New English rose grows 90cm (3ft) high and wide.

'Marguerite Hilling', a modern shrub rose, is a sport of 'Nevada'. Its pale pink flowers, flushed darker pink, are semi-double and slightly fragrant; they appear in

abundance in early summer and again in early autumn. It has an arching habit and a height and spread of 2.1m (7ft). Black spot can be a problem.

'Mary Rose' is a bushy, wide-branching shrub, usually 90cm (3ft) high and wide. A New English rose, the large pink flower clusters are of typical damask-rose shape, full petalled and richly scented.

'Moonlight' has pale cream-white flowers with golden stamens. They are semi-double, strongly fragrant and borne in large trusses.

'Golden Wings'

'Scabrosa'

'Mary Rose'

'Evelyn'

It is a hybrid musk rose with an open habit reaching up to 1.8m (6ft) high, and with a spread of 1.5m (5ft).

'Nevada', a modern shrub rose, has cream buds opening into large, semi-double white flowers with gold stamens. During early and mid summer flowers are abundant; for the rest of the season it is less prolific. Of graceful, arching habit, it grows 2.1-2.4m (7-8ft) high and wide and needs plenty of space. It is prone to black spot.

'Penelope' is a hybrid musk rose with semi-double, apricot-pink flowers. These have a pleasant fragrance and are borne in large clusters in early summer, and again in early autumn. Good hedging shrub, with a height and spread of 1.8m (6ft).

'Prosperity', a hybrid musk, bears an abundance of semi-double, ivory-coloured blooms that fade to white. They are highly fragrant and carried in clusters. Excellent for hedging, growing 1.8m (6ft) high and 1.5m (5ft) wide.

'Heritage'

'Roseraie de l'Hay', a rugosa shrub, bears large, double and fragrant crimson-purple blooms. It has no autumn hips. Height and spread of 2.1m (7ft). Disease-resistant.

Rugosa 'Alba', a hybrid of the species rose *R. rugosa*, has large, single, pure white flowers with golden centres and a sweet fragrance. Large, round, orange-red hips in autumn. Good hedging or specimen rose, 1.5m (5ft) high and wide.

'Scabrosa', a rugosa shrub, has large, single magenta-pink flowers, with some fragrance. Red hips in autumn. It has a spreading habit, excellent as a hedging or specimen

'Gertrude Jekyll'

rose. It grows 1.5m (5ft) high and spreads to 1.8m (6ft).

Cultivation
Modern shrub roses are easy to grow. Plant bare-rooted specimens between late autumn and mid spring, and container-grown ones at any time of year. Like most roses, they require rich well-drained soil and a sunny position.

In spring, lightly prune the shrubs to shape and remove old weak stems from the base. Prune back side-shoots that bore flowers the previous year to 10cm (4in) of the main stems. Newly planted shrub roses do not need pruning, except for the removal of damaged shoots.

Mulch in mid to late spring, and feed with a rose fertilizer every four weeks from late spring.

During summer, dead-head to encourage later flushes. Leave the dead flowers of most rugosa varieties to produce attractive hips.

Propagation Take heel cuttings, about 30cm (12in) long, in early autumn and root in an outdoor nursery bed. Rooted cuttings should be ready for planting out the following autumn.

Pests and diseases Black spot, mildew, rust and greenfly are common problems.

Old garden roses

(Alba, Bourbon, Centifolia, China, Damask, Gallica, Hybrid perpetual, Moss and Tea roses)

'Fantin Latour'

'Céleste'

□ Height 45cm-4.5m (1½-15ft)
□ Summer or repeat-flowering
□ Ordinary well-drained garden soil
□ Full sun

Old garden roses make handsome specimen shrubs, with their open, loose habit and overwhelming displays of summer blooms in delicate and dusky colours. They are in stark contrast to the perfectly formed flowers and rigid formality of hybrid tea bush roses.

Widely grown by the Victorians, before hybrid teas and floribundas were introduced, all old garden roses are hardy hybrids or sports of true rose species. For simplicity, they are usually catalogued in smaller groups determined by their parentage; varieties developed from *Rosa* x *alba*, for example, belong to the Alba group.

The flowers of old garden roses are usually double or semi-double. They come in subtle shades of white, cream, pink, and dusky reds, purples and mauves. Some are quartered, the flattened centre of each flower consisting of densely crowded petals, loosely arranged in four groups.

Most old garden roses have only one flowering season, in early and mid summer, but the beauty of the individual blooms and their rich fragrance, as well as the handsome foliage, are ample compensation.

They are some of the best roses for growing in mixed shrub borders, and they make equally effective specimen roses. Train those with a climbing habit up walls, arbours or pillars.

Popular varieties
Old garden roses are divided into nine groups: Alba; Bourbon; Centifolia; China; Damask; Gallica; Hybrid Perpetuals; Moss; and Tea roses.

ALBA ROSES have sweetly scented flowers up to 7.5cm (3in) across. They are borne in profusion in early and mid summer. The shrubs are extremely hardy and vigorous with an upright habit, thriving in all kinds of conditions. The grey-green soft leaves are composed of five to seven finely toothed leaflets. Alba roses can be trained as espaliers on a wall or up trelliswork.

'Céleste' 'Celestial' bears large and fragrant, soft pink semi-double blooms. It grows eventually 1.8m (6ft) high and has a spread of 1.2m (4ft).

'Félicité Parmentier' has pale yellow buds that open into double, blush-pink blooms. It grows 1.2m (4ft) high and has a spread of 90cm (3ft).

'Königin von Dänemark' bears tightly packed, quartered blooms

'Boule de Neige'

'Mme Pierre Oger'

'Fantin Latour'

in a shade of pink which deepens towards the centre of the flower. They are strongly fragrant. The shrub grows 1.5m (5ft) high and 1.2m (4ft) wide.

'Maiden's Blush' has double blush-pink, sweetly scented flowers, with pale pink edges. It reaches 1.5m (5ft) high and 1.2m (4ft) wide.

'Maxima' has double cream-white flowers with a hint of pink. It is a large, vigorous shrub growing 2.4m (8ft) high, with a spread of 1.5m (5ft).

BOURBON ROSES have densely petalled blooms which are cup-shaped or globular, and up to 10cm (4in) across. They are deeply scented and repeat-flowering, starting in early summer and continuing until the first autumn frosts. All are hardy, vigorous shrubs with an open habit and glossy dark green leaves.

'Boule de Neige' has crimson buds that open to form double, white flowers. It grows 1.8m (6ft) high and 1.2m (4ft) wide.

'Louise Odier' bears well-formed rich pink flowers softly shaded lilac. Of vigorous habit, it grows 1.2m (4ft) high and wide.

'Mme Isaac Pereire' has large quartered deep pink blooms with tightly packed petals. It is one of the most fragrant of all roses. Grown and pruned as a bush it reaches 1.8m (6ft) high and spreads to 1.5m (5ft); trained up a wall or pillar it may reach 4.5m (15ft).

'Mme Pierre Oger' has large clusters of pale silver-pink cup-shaped flowers. It has a height and spread of 1.2m (4ft).

'Souvenir de la Malmaison' is

'Centifolia'

'Mme Hardy'

'Old Blush'

a long-established variety with large flowers that open out flat to flesh-pink quartered blooms. It grows 1.2m (4ft) high and spreads to 90cm (3ft). Susceptible to rain damage.

CENTIFOLIA ROSES, also known as Provence or Cabbage roses, have fragrant, double flowers up to 10cm (4in) across. They are borne in clusters in early and mid summer. The floppy, thorny stems, bearing pale to mid green leaves, usually need support.

'Centifolia' has clear pink globular flowers. The shrub reaches 1.5m (5ft) high and has a spread of 1.2m (4ft).

'Fantin Latour' bears well-formed blush-pink flowers deepening to shell-pink in the centre. It grows 1.8m (6ft) high and 1.5m (5ft) wide.

'Petite de Hollande' has pale pink flowers which deepen in colour towards the edge. It is compact, with a height of 1.2m (4ft) and a spread of 90cm (3ft).

'Robert le Diable' bears multi-shaded blooms of purple, slate grey, cerise and scarlet. It is a vigorous shrub reaching 1.2m (4ft) high with a spread of 90cm (3ft).

'Rose de Meaux' is a small, neat shrub of erect and dense habit. It grows 45-90cm (1½-3ft) high and 45cm (1½ft) wide and bears a profusion of small pale pink, very fragrant flowers.

CHINA ROSES, as their name suggests, came to the Western world from China in the 18th century. Their strong point is a long flowering season, sometimes until Christmas, and their neat, compact habit. They rarely reach more than 1.2m (4ft) high, with slender hairy stems, mid green hairy foliage, and clusters of pompon-shaped flowers.

'Comtesse du Cayla' has semi-double flowers that open copper-pink and turn salmon-pink. They appear in abundance in early summer and are scented. The slender stems need support; they grow 1.5m (5ft) high with a spread of 90cm (3ft).

'Mutabilis' has single flowers which are flame-coloured when they open, changing to coppery yellow and then coppery crimson. It grows 90cm-1.2m (3-4ft) high and 90cm (3ft) wide.

'Old Blush' bears slightly fragrant, silvery pink flowers with a crimson flush. It reaches 1.5m (5ft) high and has a spread of 1.2m (4ft).

DAMASK ROSES have short-lived fragrant flowers borne in loose clusters during early and mid summer. The shrubs have a loose, open habit, with thorny and bristly stems bearing rounded, grey-green leaves. In late summer the shrubs produce long hairy hips.

'Rosa Mundi'

'Ferdinand Pichard'

'Comte du Chambord' has pinkish lilac, double, flat flowers with a strong fragrance. They are borne continuously during summer on a small shrub 90cm (3ft) high and wide. It is sometimes classified as a Portland rose or as a Perpetual Damask.

'Gloire de Guilan' bears clear pink flowers that are double, flat, quartered and strongly scented. The sprawling shrub has a height and a spread of 1.2m (4ft).

'Ispahan' bears semi-double, bright pink flowers that keep their colour well and last considerably longer than most damask roses. The shrub grows 1.2m (4ft) high and 90cm (3ft) wide.

'La Ville de Bruxelles' has double, pure pink blooms that are quartered and scented. They are borne on a strong upright plant with a height of 1.5m (5ft) and a spread of 90cm (3ft).

'Mme Hardy' has clusters of pure white flowers with small green centres. They are tinted pink in bud and heavily scented. The shrub grows 1.5m (5ft) high and wide.

GALLICA ROSES form one of the larger groups of old shrub roses. They flower profusely from early to mid summer, with solitary flowers in colours varying from pink to crimson and mauve.

They are double, 5-7.5cm (2-3in) across and richly scented. These roses thrive in poor soil. The shrubs are compact and erect, with dark green leaves.

'Belle de Crécy' grows 1.2m (4ft) high and 90cm (3ft) across, with lax stems that usually need supporting. It bears large flowers of purple-red maturing to violet.

'Camaieux' has deep crimson-purple flowers splashed and striped with white. The arching branches reach 90cm (3ft) high and 60cm (2ft) across.

'Cardinal de Richelieu' has deep violet-purple blooms. With a height and spread of 1.2m (4ft), it makes a good hedging rose.

'Charles de Mills' bears rich maroon flowers with a hint of purple. The petals are closely packed and have a glorious fragrance. A good hedging rose, it has a height and spread of 1.2m (4ft).

'Rosa Mundi' has crimson flowers striped white. It is a long-established, showy rose, and makes a good low hedge with a height and spread of 1.2m (4ft).

'Tuscany Superb' has double purple blooms that open flat to reveal golden stamens. It reaches 1.2m (4ft) high and has a spread of 60cm (2ft).

HYBRID PERPETUALS were extremely popular in Victorian

times. They preceded the modern hybrid tea roses; though taller they make superb shrub roses for the mixed border and for training against walls. The rounded, double, cabbage-like flowers, 7.5-10cm (3-4in) across, open out flat. Borne singly or in clusters, they appear between early summer and mid autumn. The shrubs are vigorous and upright and bear dark green leaves.

'Ferdinand Pichard' has globular pink flowers striped with crimson and purple. Bushy in habit, it reaches 1.2m (4ft) high, with a spread of 90cm (3ft).

'Mrs John Laing' has double, fragrant soft pink blooms borne on stiff stems. It is an upright grower with a height of 1.5m (5ft) and a spread of 90cm (3ft).

'Paul Neyron' bears huge rich pink, scented flowers which keep their colour with age. It has an upright growth habit, reaching 1.5m (5ft) high, with a spread of 90cm (3ft).

'Roger Lambelin' has double, rich crimson-purple flowers with white margins to the petals. It reaches 1.2m (4ft) high and has a spread of 90cm (3ft).

MOSS ROSES all have moss-like growths on the bristly stems and around the buds. The deeply fragrant flowers are double or semi-double and are borne singly or in small clusters in early and mid summer. The shrubs vary from dwarf varieties to tall pillar roses.

'Common Moss' has large rose-pink blooms that open flat when mature. The shrub grows 1.2m (4ft) high and wide and is suitable for hedging.

'Nuits de Young'

'William Lobb'

'Général Kléber' bears large soft mauve-pink blooms that open flat and are quartered. Generally considered the most beautiful moss rose, it has a height and spread of 1.2m (4ft).

'Henri Martin' has semi-double vivid crimson flowers with sparse moss. A graceful shrub, it reaches 1.5m (5ft) high, with a spread of 1.2m (4ft).

'Nuits de Young' has double, deep maroon-purple blooms with prominent golden stamens. It is a wiry bush, reaching 1.5m (5ft) high, with a spread of 90cm (3ft).

'William Lobb' produces large clusters of double, purple-magenta flowers, which fade to lavender. With a height and spread of 1.8m (6ft), it makes a good pillar rose.

TEA ROSES are the roses (*Rosa odorata*) from which modern hybrid teas were developed. The few which are hardy should be given a sheltered position at the foot of a wall. The shapely flowers are borne continuously from early summer onwards on rather spindly plants.

'Lady Hillingdon' bears apricot-yellow flowers continuously through the summer. The shrub is 90cm (3ft) high with a spread of 60cm (2ft). A climbing form is also available.

Cultivation

Old garden roses are hardy plants, requiring less attention than the modern bush varieties. They grow in most ordinary well-drained garden soil, even tolerating chalk. Plant bare-rooted shrubs between late autumn and mid spring, and container-grown ones at any time of year.

Maintain the vigour and healthy growth of these long-lived shrubs with an annual mulch of organic matter in spring. Feed with rose fertilizer every four weeks from late spring onwards.

Dead-head only if the blooms are particularly untidy, perhaps after heavy rain. It is preferable to leave the petals to drop so the autumn hips can develop.

Old roses flower on shoots of the previous year; when light pruning is necessary, it should be done immediately after flowering, cutting away any old dead wood from the base. Lightly tip the branches that carried flowers to encourage side-branching.

Propagation Take 25-30cm (10-12in) long heel cuttings in early autumn and root in an outdoor trench in a nursery bed.

Pests and diseases Old garden roses are less prone to disease and pest attack than modern roses, though black spot, mildew, rust, and greenfly occasionally affect them. Usually the shrubs are strong enough to recover without chemical treatment.

Polyantha and ground cover roses

'Partridge'

- ☐ Height 15cm-1.2m (6in-4ft)
- ☐ Spread 30cm-3m (1-10ft)
- ☐ Flower early summer to early autumn
- ☐ Well-drained ordinary soil
- ☐ Sunny site

Polyanthas are a small group of turn-of-the-century roses which have recently returned to popularity. They bear a profusion of small pompon-shaped flowers in large closely packed clusters in summer, and again in early autumn.

Compact polyantha roses are ideal in beds of their own or for edging borders. Ground cover roses, often developed in part from polyanthas, are generally prostrate or they hug the ground with arching stems; they are excellent for sunny banks.

Popular varieties
'Baby Faurax' has an abundance of small lavender-purple flowers. The compact shrub is 30cm (1ft) high and wide.
'Cécile Brunner' has pale pink flowers shaded cream, the colour becoming darker in the centre. They are borne in small clusters. Height and spread 60cm (2ft).

'Partridge', a prostrate ground cover rose, spreads as much as 3m (10ft), with handsome, glossy mid green foliage. It flowers in mid and late summer with clusters of single, white and fragrant blooms. Similar varieties include 'Grouse', pale pink; and 'Pheasant', deep rose-pink on 60cm (2ft) high, spreading plants.
'Perle d'Or' bears dense clusters of small creamy yellow blooms. A vigorous rose, it grows 1.2m (4ft) high, with a spread of 90cm (3ft).
'Snow Carpet' grows only 15cm (6in) high and spreads to 90cm (3ft). It is repeat-flowering, in bloom from early summer until autumn, with a profusion of small, pure white double flowers.
'The Fairy' has double globular pink flowers, appearing later than most polyanthas, in late summer and early autumn. It has a height and spread of 75cm (2½ft).

Cultivation
Polyantha and ground cover roses grow in ordinary well-drained soils, and in full sun. Plant bare-rooted shrubs from late autumn to mid spring and container-grown ones any time of year.

'The Fairy'

Mulch in late spring and feed once a month during the growing season. Dead-head regularly.

When the autumn flush is over, lightly prune the shrubs and cut away dead wood from the base.
Propagation Take heel cuttings in autumn and root in a cold frame.
Pests and diseases Mildew and black spot can be troublesome. Greenfly is the most serious pest.

Rambler roses

'Paul's Scarlet Climber'

'American Pillar'

'Emily Gray'

☐ Height 2.7-20m (9-60ft)
☐ Flower early to mid summer
☐ Rich well-drained soil
☐ Sunny site

Ramblers, like climbers, are ideal roses for training up pillars, pergolas, arches and old trees. They are less suitable for growing up walls – the lack of air circulation encourages mildew, a disease to which many varieties are prone. Vigorous ramblers are ideal for smothering the most unsightly garden features, while those of extreme vigour look spectacular scrambling up old trees. Several ramblers are also available as weeping standards.

The main disadvantage of rambler roses is the short flowering season, in early to mid summer unless otherwise stated.

Popular varieties
'Albéric Barbier' has yellow buds opening to large clusters of fragrant, double, cream-white blooms. The vigorous stems grow 7.5m (25ft) high and can be trained up arches, pillars, trees or trellis-work.
'Albertine' bears a mass of double, glowing copper-pink blooms with a rich scent. The vigorous growth reaches 4.5m (15ft) high, ideal for arches or pergolas.
'American Pillar' has a great profusion of deep pink flowers with white eyes borne in clusters. The vigorous growth reaches 6m (20ft) high.
'Bobbie James' has semi-double, musk-scented ivory-white flowers. These appear in large trusses on vigorous stems up to 7.5m (25ft) high; ideal for training up a tree.

'Albertine'

'Dorothy Perkins'

'Crimson Shower' bears profuse trusses of semi-double, crimson flowers from mid summer onwards. Of moderate vigour, 2.7-3m (9-10ft) high, it is suitable for growing up arches or for training as a weeping standard.

'Dorothy Perkins', an old favourite though prone to mildew, bears masses of double deep pink flowers, borne in large trusses. It grows 3m (10ft) high up an arch or along a trellis screen. Also available as a weeping standard.

'Emily Gray' has small, semi-double buff-yellow flowers with a rich fragrance, appearing in early to late summer. The dark green glossy foliage, bronze-tinted when young, is almost evergreen. It

scrambles to a height of 4.5m (15ft).

'Félicité et Perpétue' is an old favourite, with slightly fragrant, double ivory flowers faintly flecked with red. They are borne in large clusters and stand up well to rain. Suitable for growing up a wall, it can reach 4.5m (15ft) high.

'François Juranville' has double pale pink blooms with a sweet fragrance that form a dense mass in mid summer. A vigorous grower, it reaches 6m (20ft) high and is ideal for covering a trellis screen or pergola.

'Paul's Scarlet Climber' bears abundant clusters of double, bright scarlet flowers whose colour dulls with age. Train this

3-4.5m (10-15ft) high rambler up a pillar, pergola or arch. It also does well on a north-facing wall.

'The Garland' bears large clusters of small, semi-double blush-pink fragrant flowers that fade to white. It is an old-established, vigorous rose, ideal for scrambling up an old tree or tall wall. It reaches 4.5m (15ft) high.

Cultivation
Plant bare-rooted ramblers between autumn and mid spring; plant container-grown ones at any time of year. They need rich soil and full sun.

Plant ramblers near their support, setting them 2.1m (7ft) apart and tying in stems as they grow. Plant weeping standards at least 90cm (3ft) apart.

In mid to late spring, mulch the roses to keep the soil around them moist; feed them once a month through the summer.

When flowering is over, cut the stems that carried blooms down to ground level and tie in young growths as replacement shoots. On weeping standards, cut out flowered stems.

Propagation Increase stock by taking heel cuttings in early autumn and rooting them in an outdoor trench.

Pests and diseases Mildew is the main problem; black spot and greenfly can also be troublesome.

Species roses

Rosa californica 'Plena'

Rosa moyesii

☐ Height 60cm-4.5m (2-15ft)
☐ Flower late spring to mid summer
☐ Ordinary well-drained soil
☐ Sunny site

These are the wild roses, the true species from which all modern roses have been bred. They are fully hardy, easy to grow, and shrug off the effects of pests and diseases with little trouble.

Their flowers have a simple beauty which makes them stand out from other garden plants. Usually single, they come in traditional pinks, reds, whites and yellows. Even though species roses cannot compete with the continuous blooming of floribundas and hybrid teas – they flower only once a year, between late spring and mid summer – many species have particularly handsome foliage and a spectacular display of hips in autumn. Do not dead-head such roses.

Species roses look most effective grown in an informal or wild part of the garden or in a large sunny, open border. They are also spectacular as specimen plants, singly or in small groups of one

Rosa moyesii, hips

particular species, so that their full beauty becomes apparent.

Popular species

Rosa californica 'Plena' has clusters of semi-double, deep pink, fragrant flowers in early summer, followed by globular red hips in autumn. It is a graceful shrub, with a spread of 1.8m (6ft) and a height of 2.4m (8ft).

Rosa **'Canary Bird'** has small, bright yellow flowers clothing its stems in late spring and early summer. The dainty foliage is fresh green and deeply cut. It grows 1.8m (6ft) high and wide and is probably a naturally occurring variety between *Rosa xanthina* and *R. hugonis*.

Rosa x *dupontii* has large, single, cream-white fragrant flowers, borne in clusters in early summer. It is a vigorous but lax shrub or climber with a height and spread of 2.1m (7ft).

Rosa foetida bicolor, Austrian copper, has single, copper-orange flowers with a golden-yellow petal reverse. They appear in early summer on arching branches which grow 1.8m (6ft) high with a similar spread. It is prone to black spot.

Rosa glauca, syn. *R. rubrifolia,* has single red-purple flowers borne in small clusters in early

summer, but it is grown as much for its handsome grey-purple foliage and decorative dark red hips as for the flowers. It is excellent as a background plant in a border. The arching branches reach 2.1m (7ft) high and spread over 1.5m (5ft).

Rosa x *harisonii* bears clear yellow, semi-double flowers in late spring. It grows 1.8m (6ft) high and 1.5m (5ft) across.

Rosa x *highdownensis* is related to and closely resembles *R. moyesii*. It bears a profusion of single, soft crimson flowers with conspicuous yellow stamens in early summer. They are followed by magnificent, flask-shaped and glossy red hips. It grows up to 3m (10ft) high and wide.

Rosa hugonis has pale yellow flowers borne freely in late spring. The hips in late summer are round and dark red. The arching branches, 2.7m (9ft) high and 2.1m (7ft) wide, are clothed with dainty fern-like leaves.

Rosa moyesii bears single, vivid blood-red blooms in early summer, followed by flask-shaped red hips. It makes a handsome specimen shrub, with a spread of 2.4m (8ft) and a height of 3.6m (12ft). 'Geranium' has a more compact habit, suitable for smaller gardens.

Rosa x *paulii* is thorny and bears

Rosa glauca

Rosa 'Canary Bird'

Cultivation

Plant bare-rooted shrubs between late autumn and mid spring, and container-grown ones at any time of year. They thrive and flourish in fertile, well-drained soil. The planting site should be open and sunny.

Mulch the shrubs in late spring with organic material and then feed them once a month during the growing season.

Don't dead-head, since this will do away with any display of hips. Remove dead wood as and when it occurs, cutting back to live wood.

Propagation Species roses can be increased from seed and from heel cuttings taken in late summer and rooted in an outdoor trench.

Pests and diseases They are resistant to most common rose pests and diseases.

clusters of fragrant white flowers with crinkly petals in early summer. It is an arching, thicket-forming shrub 1.2m (4ft) high with an impressive spread of 4.5m (15ft) and excellent as ground cover on banks; it can also be trained up a wall.

Rosa pomifera, syn. *R. villosa*, resembles the wild dog rose (*R. canina*). It grows up to 2.1m (7ft) tall and wide, with stems clothed with downy, grey-green and aromatic foliage. The solitary flowers, bright pink and semi-double, appear in early summer; they are followed by large round, dark red hips covered with bristly hairs.

Rosa primula has pale yellow flowers borne singly in late spring. On warm evenings the leaves have a heady fragrance. An upright shrub, it grows 2.4m (8ft) high and wide.

Rosa rubiginosa, syn. *R. eglanteria*, known as sweetbriar, has clusters of bright pink, single flowers in early summer, followed by orange-scarlet hips. The leaves are covered in glands which give off a sweet, pungent fragrance. With a height and spread of 2.4m (8ft), it makes a particularly good hedge.

Rosa virginiana bears single pink flowers throughout summer, and showy red hips accompanied by scarlet foliage in the autumn. It grows 2.1m (7ft) wide and 1.5m (5ft) high. A fine specimen shrub. *Rosa willmottiae* bears solitary, fragrant, rose-purple flowers in late spring and early summer. It is an elegantly arching, purple-stemmed shrub with a height and spread of 2.4m (8ft).

Rosa foetida bicolor

ACKNOWLEDGEMENTS

Photographer's Credits
A-Z Botanical Collection Ltd 24(tr), 46(tr), 139;
Richard Balfour 157(r), 158(l), 159(b), 161(br),
166(t), 172(tr), 173(r); Peter Beales 149(c);
Gillian Beckett 94(tr), 106(tl), 118(l); Biofotos
28(tl), 28(b), 110(r), 151(tl), 169(r);
Pat Brindley 149(tl), 151(b); Brian Carter 71(b),
152(tr), 154(bl); Eric Crichton 15(l), 18(l), 20(b),
21(l), 21(c), 22(l), 23(r), 25(tl), 27(tl), 29(tr),
29(b), 32(tr), 32(bc), 34(c), 35, 36(tl), 36(b),
38(r), 39(tl), 39(b), 40, 41(tr), 41(cr), 43, 45(t),
48(t), 48(cr), 52(t), 53(cr), 54(t), 59(tr), 60(cr),
64, 69(t), 71(t), 72(t), 72(cl), 73(tl), 74, 76, 78(tl),
79(tr), 83(tr), 84(t), 84(c), 85(l), 85(r), 86(t),
88(r), 89(tr)), 90(b), 92(tl), 92(b), 93, 96(r),
98(tr), 98(b), 99, 100(b), 101, 103(b), 104(r),
105(r), 106(b), 107, 108(c), 109(tl), 110(l), 111,
112(r), 119(tr), 121(b), 123(tl), 123(b), 126,
129(tl), 129(b), 130, 131(tl), 132(b), 133(l), 138,
143(t), 145, 159(tl), 160(l), 165(br); Arnaud
Descat 144(r), 53(tr), 150(bl), 172(tl); Philip Fer-
ret 166(b), 167(tl), 168(r), 175(b); Garden Picture Library (John Ainsworth) 97(tl), (David
Askam) 152(tl), (Brian Carter) 30(l), 36(tr),
67(b), 113(tl), 114, 127(l), (John Glover) 6-7,
37(b), 165(tr), (Rowan Isaac) front cover(tc),
165(bl), (Jerry Pavia) 22(r), 165(tl), (David Russell) 24(b), 113(b), 118(tr), (Brigitte Thomas)
front cover(tl), (Didier Willery) 66(b), 139(r);
Michael Gibson 150(br), 175(tl), 171(b); John
Glover front cover(cr), 1, 10(bl), 13(b), 26(l),
27(b), 72(cr), 72(b), 73(c), 80(tl), 86(b), 87(t),
90(tl), 91(b), 112(l), 117(t), 128(tr), 129(tr),
160(tr), back cover; Derek Gould 77(tl), 96(l);
Jerry Harpur 148(tl); Neil Holmes 115(tl);
Michèle Lamontagne 17(r), 18(r), 19(tr), 50,
55(tl), 57(r), 60(t), 63(l), 70(r), 75(t), 85(c), 163,
164(bl), 168(l), 169(l), 174(r), 175(tr).

Typesetting SX COMPOSING, ESSEX; Printing & Binding PRINTER INDUSTRIA, GRÁFICA S.A. BARCELONA
Separations COLOURSCAN OVERSEAS CO PTE LTD, SINGAPORE; Paper PERIGORD-CONDAT, FRANCE
53-011-1